MANUALIA DIDACTICA 15
UNISA 1991

TSWANA
for beginners

J W Snyman
J C le Roux
M le Roux

University of South Africa
Pretoria

© 1991 University of South Africa
First edition, first impression

ISBN 0 86981 699 3

Set by Pretoria Setters

Printed by Sigma Press, Pretoria
Published by the University of South Africa,
PO Box 392, 0001 Pretoria

Preface

In the areas where Tswana is spoken there is a growing need to acquire Tswana communicative skills. This need has been manifested in fields as diverse as education, the civil service and the private sector. The recent publication of *Practical Tswana Vocabulary and Phrases*, as well as the trilingual Tswana–English–Afrikaans dictionary, both published by Via Afrika, is part of an ongoing attempt to make the learning of Tswana more accessible in a wider southern Africa.

Tswana for Beginners was compiled to serve as a progression from phrase books and is integrated with the data contained in the trilingual dictionary, *Dikišinare ya* **Setswana–English–Afrikaans** *Dictionary/ Woordeboek*. This grammar for beginners can therefore serve as an introduction to a more comprehensive knowledge of the Tswana language and culture.

When writing a grammar of this nature one invariably needs to confirm one's data. To this end we are particularly indebted to Prof. D. T. Cole's seminal work *An Introduction to Tswana Grammar*. We would also like to acknowledge the advice and information supplied by our colleagues Messrs J. S. S. Shole and M. K. Mothoagae.

THE AUTHORS
University of South Africa

Contents

CHAPTER 1

Nouns

OBJECTIVES

On completion of this chapter you should:
1. be able to explain the meaning of the term "noun";
2. be able to describe the structure of nouns;
3. be able to identify the different kinds of nouns in a paragraph;
4. be able to identify the sound changes that foreign words undergo when adopted;
5. be able to explain the structural adaptation of foreign words;
6. know the reasons why certain words were adopted.

---

1. The meaning of the term *noun*

The noun is a word that denotes or names the concrete and the abstract things that occur around us, e.g.

(a) the proper names of persons, places, animals and products, e.g.
Motabogi
Phokeng
Swartland
Sunlight

(b) the things or people that we see around us, e.g.

molemo – me**lemo** p. 85 .... [1]

mokwadi – ba**kwadi** p. 79 ....

lekgarebe – ma**kgarebe** p. 62 ....

sesepa – di**sepa** p. 151 ....

(c) the things that we experience by our sense of:

---

[1] These lineated spaces are provided for you to write the meanings of these words. The page numbers refer to where these words can be looked up in your dictionary. When looking up words you are reminded that in Tswana a word is entered either under its **first** or under its **third** letter. It can be assumed that words that do not appear under their first or third letter have not been included in the dictionary. You are, however, advised to read the section **Looking up Words** in the **Preface** of your dictionary to grasp the finer details on how to look up words.

(i) touching or feeling, e.g.

bo**thitho** p. 169 ....

ma**kgwakgwa** p. 69 ....

bo**ngola** p. 105 ....

bo**kete** p. 58 ....

(ii) hearing, tasting or smelling, e.g.

mo**sumo** p. 157 ....

bo**tlhoko** p. 183 ....

se**bodu** p. 12 ....

(d) emotions, feelings or thoughts in other words things that cannot be touched, e.g.

nako p. 100 ....

bo**ipelo** p. 47 ....

lo**rato** p. 138 ....

bo**tshelo** p. 194 ....

Exercise 1.1

By using the English–Tswana section of the dictionary you should now find useful examples of nouns representative of those appearing above.

2. The noun classes

Nouns have a singular or a plural form and some nouns have singular and plural forms denoted by singular and plural prefixes, e.g.

SINGULAR	PLURAL
Mo**tswana** ....[2]	Ba**tswana** ....
mo**tse**	me**tse** ....
mmangwane	bô**mmangwane** ....
le**rato**	—
—	ma**kgakga** ....

2) *By now you should be able to look up words on your own without being assisted to find the relevant pages.*

Because of their divergent singular and plural prefixes nouns are divided into different noun classes. Some of these noun classes function as pairs.

2.1 The *mo- ba-* classes

These noun classes contain nouns that only denote people, e.g.

mo**rweetsana**	ba**rweetsana** ....
mo**sadi**	ba**sadi** ....
mo**gwe**	ba**gwe** ....
Mo**sotho**	Ba**sotho** ....

*By using the Tswana–English[3] section of the dictionary and by looking up words entered together with the abbreviation **n** (noun) you should be able to find your own examples of nouns in the **mo- ba-** classes. Your selection of nouns should be aimed at your particular communicative needs, e.g. p. 153 mo**simane** — boy.*

Besides the original noun classes the **mo- ba-** classes also contain a number of deverbatives (i.e. nouns derived from verb stems), e.g.

mo**thusi**	–	ba**thusi**	<	*thusa*
mo**tsadi**	–	ba**tsadi**	<	*tsala*[4]
mo**disa**	–	ba**disa**	<	*disa*
mo**agi**	–	ba**agi**	<	*aga*
mo**kwadi**	–	ba**kwadi**	<	*kwala*
More**boloki**	–	Bare**boloki**	<	*boloka*

Exercise 1.2

*By looking up words entered together with the abbreviation **dev** (deverbative) you should be able to find your own useful examples of deverbative nouns in the **mo- ba-** classes, e.g. p. 3 mo**anedi** — narrator.*

---

3) Nouns of the **mo- ba-** classes, i.e. nouns denoting persons, can be looked up in the English–Tswana section as well.

4) Note that **l** > **d** when followed by **-i**.

The **mo- ba-** classes also contain a number of nouns with irregular structures, e.g.

mmadi	– babadi	....	< **bala**[5]
mmusi	– babusi	....	< **busa**
mmetli	– babetli	....	< **betla**
ngwetsi	– betsi	....	
ngwale	– baale	....	
ngwana	– bana	....	
mong	– beng	....	
Mosarwa/Lesarwa	– Masarwa	....	

The – bô- classes

These noun classes are called the sub-classes of the **mo- ba-** classes and they contain:

(a) personal names, e.g.

Kabelo	– Bôkabelo
Motsei	– Bômotsei

(b) kinship terms, e.g.

mme	– bô**mme**	....
nnake	– bô**nnake**	....

(c) animal names as well as personified animal names, e.g.

matsipane	– bô**matsipane**	....
Kgosi Tau	– Bo**kgosi Tau**	....

2.2 The mo- me- classes

These noun classes contain names for parts of the body, tools, animals and most plants, e.g.

mo**lato**	– me**lato**	....
mo**gatla**	– me**gatla**	....
mo**goma**	– me**goma**	....
mo**rubisi**	– me**rubisi**	....

5) *Note that* **mo- + -b > mm-.**

4

You should be able to find your own useful examples of the **mo- me-** classes by looking up entries accompanied by the abbreviation **n** (nouns).

The **mo- me-** classes also contain a number of nouns with irregular structures, e.g.

mmala	– me**bala** ....
mmele	– me**bele** ....
mhama	– me**hama** ....
mmutla	– me**butla** ....
ngwaga	– me**ngwaga** ....
mmu	– me**bu** ....
mômô	– me**mômô** ....
mhago/mo**fago**	– me**fago** ....
mhama/mo**fama** –	me**fama** ....

2.3 The *le- ma-* classes

These noun classes accommodate divergent groups of nouns denoting parts of the body, animals, plants, natural phenomena, personal nouns, e.g.

le**ina**	– ma**ina** ....
le**ngole**	– ma**ngole** ....
le**tlametlo**	– ma**tlametlo** ....
le**katane**	– ma**katane** ....
le**sedi**	– ma**sedi** ....
le**tsholo**	– ma**tsholo** ....
Le**jeremane** –	Ma**jeremane** ....

Exercise 1.4

You should now be able to find useful examples of the nouns in the **le- ma-** classes.

2.4 The *se- di-* classes

These noun classes contain nouns denoting parts of the body, tools, animals, languages, personal nouns, e.g.

se**diba** – di**diba** ....

se**rope** – di**rope** ....

se**gokgo** – di**gokgo** ....

se**fala** – di**fala** ....

Se**rolong** – — ....

se**bini** – di**bini** ....

Exercise 1.5

You should now look up additional examples of the **se- di-** *noun classes to suit your particular communicative needs.*

2.5 The *N- diN-* classes

These noun classes contain nouns denoting animals, parts of the body, natural phenomena, tools and personal nouns, e.g.

tlhase – di**tlhase** ....

thutlwa – di**thutlwa** ....

tsebe – di**tsebe** ....

talama – di**talama** ....

phefo – di**phefo** ....

kgosi – di**kgosi** ....

Exercise 1.6

You should now find additional useful examples of nouns belonging to the **n- diN-** *classes.*

2.6 The *lo- diN-* classes

These noun classes contain nouns denoting parts of the body, natural phenomena, tools, e.g.

lo**tlhokwa** – di**tlhokwa** ....

lo**naka** – di**naka** ....

lo**gadima** – di**kgadima** ....

lo**gare** – di**kgare** ....

Exercise 1.7

You should now extend your vocabulary by finding additional examples of nouns belonging to the **lo- diN-** *classes.*

2.7 The *bo- ma-* classes

These noun classes are mostly used to denote abstract nouns. Because of the predominance of abstract nouns not all the singular forms have plural forms. Plural forms usually have specialised meanings, e.g.

bo**thitho** ....   ma**jalwa** ....

bo**ngaka** ....   ma**gwera** ....

bo**nna** ....   ma**boa** ....

bo**bedi** ....   ma**tshelo** ....

bo**tshelo** ....

Exercise 1.8

You should now find additional examples of nouns in the **bo- ma-** *classes.*

2.8 The *go-* class

This class only contains the infinitive forms of verbs, e.g.

go **bona** ....

go di **dira** ....

go se **rate** ....

Exercise 1.9

You should now be able to compile a list of useful examples of nouns belonging to this class.

2.9 The locative classes with prefixes *fa-, go-* and *mo-*

The locative nouns consist of:

(a) original locative nouns with the prefixes *fa-, go-* and *mo-*, e.g.

fatshe ....

godimo ....

morago ....

(b) nouns that do not regularly take locative class prefixes, e.g.

gae ....

kgakala ....

tlase ....

3. The structure of nouns

As can be derived from the preceding discussion, the structure of the nouns is:

(a) Original nouns

		class prefix	+	nominal root	
mo**simane**	<	mo-	+	-simane	....
le**kgarebe**	<	le-	+	-kgarebe	....
nku	<	n-	+	-ku	....
bo**jalwa**	<	bo-	+	-jalwa	....
go**dimo**	<	go-	+	-dimo	....

In a number of instances the nominal prefixes may be omitted, e.g.

'saka	<	le**saka**	....
'lepe	<	se**lepe**	....
'tlhare	<	di**tlhare**	....
'nala	<	di**nala**	....

(b) Deverbatives

		class prefix	+	verbal root	+	end-ing		
mo**diri**	<	mo-	+	-dir-	+	-i	....	< *dir*a
mo**disa**	<	mo-	+	-dis-	+	-a	....	< *dis*a
mo**lao**	<	me-	+	-lay-	+	-ô	....	< *lay*a
le**bitso**	<	le-	+	-bits-	+	-ô	....	< *bits*a
se**bini**	<	se-	+	-bin-	+	-i	....	< *bin*a
lo**rato**	<	lo-	+	-rat-	+	-ô	....	< *rat*a

8

bo**felo**	<	bo-	+	-fel-	+	-ô	....	<	*fel*a
go **dira**	<	go		dir-	+	-a	....	<	***dir**a*
n**twa**	<	n-	+	-lw-	+	-a	....	<	*lw*a
kepu	<	n-	+	-ep-	+	-u	....	<	*ep*a
se**bodu**	<	se-	+	-bol-	+	-u	....	<	***bol**a*

The structure of polysyllabic deverbatives of the **N- diN-** classes is not so obvious, e.g.

tiro	–	di**tiro**	....	<	***dir**a*
karabo	–	di**karabo**	....	<	***arab**a*
kepu	–	di**kepu**	....	<	***ep**a*

The deverbative stems can also contain the **verbal extensions** (see Chapter 9). In this case the structure is:

	class prefix	+	verbal root	+	exten-sion	+	end-ing			
mo**romiwa**	<	mo-	+	-rom-	+	*-iw-*	+	-a	....	<	rom*iw*a
mo**kwaledi**	<	mo-	+	-kwal-	+	*-el-*	+	-i	....	<	kwal*el*a
ba**sekisi**	<	ba-	+	-sek-	+	*-is-*	+	-i	....	<	sek*is*a
bo**rulelo**	<	bo-	+	-rul-	+	*-el-*	+	-ô	....	<	rul*el*a

The inclusion of **verbal prefixes** like the **objectival concords** (see Chapter 9) and the **reflexive prefix** (see Chapter 9) is discernible in the following:

mo**itaodi**	....	<	*i*taola	....	<	laola
mo**ithati**	....	<	*i*thata	....	<	rata
ba**digami**	....	<	go **di** gama, dipodi
mo**mmatli**	....	<	go **m**matla, motho

Exercise 1.10

For communicative purposes you should find additional examples of these kinds of deverbatives.

9

4. Adopted nouns

The culture contact between the Tswana and Europeans led to mutual influences as far as vocabulary was concerned. The words that were adopted filled a need for naming new concepts or actions that were not originally known in Tswana.

The European languages, Afrikaans and English, are the major sources of adopted words.

In this section we are going to pay attention to the foreign acquisitions from Afrikaans and English to Tswana.

The words that were adopted are mainly nouns and a number of verbs. The reason for this is that the material culture of the Europeans introduced a great number of things foreign to the traditional Tswana, e.g.

galase..   kofi...
baki..   beine...
buka...   pene..
hempe..   peipe...

Foreign words are not adopted into a new language without change. The changes are usually changes of the sounds and the structural elements in order to fit into the sound and structural laws governing Tswana.

(a) The sound changes that some words undergo:

beine	< wyn	(A = Afrikaans)
galase	< glas	(A)
hamole	< hamer	(A)
jase	< jas	(A)
sekepe	< skip	(A)
Mokeresete	< Christen	(A)

Would you agree that some sounds are:

(i) changed, e.g. beine   < wyn
                   hamole   < hamer

(ii) added to the adopted word, e.g.

galase   < glas   (A)
sekepe   < skip   (A)

(b) The structural changes that some words undergo:

mmotorokara	< motorkar	(A)
mmaene	< mine	(E = English)
setempe	< stamp	(E)
borotho	< brood	(A)

10

Do you notice a correspondence between the initial consonant of the European word and the noun class prefix of Tswana? The initial sound of the European words is therefore used to derive the noun class prefix in Tswana, e.g.

mmepe   – mebepe < map   (E)
boleke – maleke < blik (A)

We should now take a closer look at the structure of adopted nouns:

1. The majority of adopted nouns are incorporated into the **N- diN-** classes, e.g.

watše	– diwatše	< watch	(E)
rulara	– dirulara	< ruler	(E)
jeke	– dijeke	< jug	(E)
jokwe	– dijokwe	< juk	(A)
agtereose	– diagtereose	< agteros	(A)
llere	– dillere	< leer	(A)

2. When the original noun commences with **m** it is usually placed in the **mo- me-** classes and the initial **m** is changed to **mm**, e.g.

mmidi	– mebidi	< mielie	(A)
mmetshe	– mebetshe	< mat	(E)

Alternatively these nouns may occur in the **N- diN-** classes without doubling the initial **m**, e.g.

maene	– dimaene	< mine	(E)
mepe	– dimepe	< map	(E)

3. When the original noun commences in a consonant cluster starting with **s** it is adopted as a noun of the **se- di-** classes, e.g.

sekere	– dikere	< skêr	(A)
setempe	– ditempe	< stamp	(A)
sekurufu	– dikurufu	< skroef	(A)
sepanere	– dipanere	< spanner	(E)

4. When the original noun commences in a consonant cluster starting with **b** it is usually adopted as a noun of the **bo- ma-** classes, e.g.

boriki	– mariki	< briek	(A)
borokgo	– marokgo	< broek	(A)
boratše	– maratše	< brush	(E)
borotho	– marotho	< brood	(A)

5. A relatively small number of nouns denoting people are incorporated into the **mo- ba-** classes, e.g.

motoloki	– batoloki	....	< tolk	(A)
molaisi	– balaisi	....	< laai	(A)
mošagi	– bašagi	....	< saag	(A)
moporofeti	– baporofeti	....	< profeet	(A)

Some nouns are adapted as compounds into the **– bô-** classes, e.g.

rralebenkele	– bôrralebenkele	....	< winkel	(A)
rraselaga	– borraselaga	....	< slag	(A)
mmasetena	– bommasetena	....	< steen	(A)

Examples of adopted nouns can also be found by looking up English words in the English – Tswana section of your dictionary.

5. Diminutives

Diminutives are formed by means of the suffixes **-ana** and **-nyana** and they denote:

(a) smallness, e.g.   **kgomo**nyana .... **setlhats**ana ....

(b) immaturity, e.g. **ntšwa**nyana .... **kokw**ana ....

(c) derogation, e.g. **monna**nyana .... **kgosi**nyana ....

(d) tenderness, e.g. **ngwana**nyana .... **mosadi**nyana ....

The forming of diminutives with **-ana** implies a number of sound changes, e.g.

b	> ***jw***	in tse**b**e	> tse***jw***ana
r	> ***tsh***	in phi**r**i	> phi***tsh***ana
l	> ***j***	in mme**l**e	> mme***j***ana
p	> ***tsw***	in sele**p**e	> tshe***tsw***ana
ph	> ***tshw***	in tshe**ph**e	> tshe***tshw***ana
m	> ***ngw***	in kgo**m**o	> kgo***ngw***ana
t	> ***ts***	in leba**t**i	> leba***ts***ana
ng	> ***ny***	in leno**ng**	> leno***ny***ana
f	> ***šw***	in phe***f***o	> phe***šw***ana
d	> ***ts***	in mo**d**i	> mo***ts***ana
n	> ***ny***	in motwa**n**e	> motwa***ny***ane

12

If the final vowel is **u**, **o**, or **ô**, it becomes consonantalised to **w** and **-ana** is suffixed, unless the preceding consonant is bilabial or is the alveolar **d**, e.g.

tau	+	-ana	>	ta**wana**
ntlo	+	-ana	>	ntl**wana**
poo	+	-ana	>	po**wana**
seolo	+	-ana	>	seol**wana**
mokôrô	+	-ana	>	mokor**wana**

If the final vowel is **i**, **e**, or **ê**, the final vowel is elided and **-ana** is substituted, unless the preceding consonant is bilabial or one of the alveolars **t, d, r, l**, or **n**, e.g.

kgosi	+	-ana	>	kgos**ana**
ntšhi	+	-ana	>	ntšh**ana**
motse	+	-ana	>	mots**ana**

Exercise 1.11

Examples like these are scattered throughout the dictionary. In the course of time you should try to expand this list.

6. Collective nouns and nouns denoting aggregations, volumes and masses

Nouns answering to these descriptions include the following:

(i) Collective nouns, e.g. **phuthego** ....

                            mo**tshitshi** ....

                            bo**idiidi** ....

(ii) Aggregations, e.g. **tshadi** < **mosadi** ....

                          le**rolo** < **tholo** ....

                          nna < **monna** ....

(iii) Volumes, e.g. ma**šwi** ....

                   ma**the** ....

                   ma**fura** ....

13

(iv) Masses, e.g. bo**upe** ....

bo**loko** ....

bo**gobe** ....

Exercise 1.12

You should add to this list by looking up this type of noun in the English–Tswana section of the dictionary.

7. Compounds

Compounds are formed by means of different combinations of **roots** and **stems**, e.g.

(a) reduplicated nominal roots, e.g. mo**sese** ....

(b) different nominal roots, e.g. mmale**leme** ....

(c) verb stem + nominal root, e.g. mo**sitatlou** ....

(d) verb stem + adverb, e.g. mo**tsalwapele** ....

Exercise 1.13

You are encouraged to find more examples of this kind in your dictionary.

8. The use of nouns

(i) In sentences the main function of nouns is to act as the subject and the object of sentences, e.g.

Modumedi o tsena **kereke**

(ii) Nouns also have a secondary function as adverbs, e.g.

Re ya **go malome** ....

Ba ile **Gauteng** ....

Ba tla bua **le ntate** ....

Ba kgaola kala **ka šaga** ....

8.1 Adverbs of place

The addition of the disjunctively written locative prefixes **go** and **ga** give nouns an adverbial application as adverbs of place, e.g.

Re tla lebelela *go bôPule* phakela ....

....

Ba ngwegetse *ga Ngwaketse* ....

....

The conjunctively written locative suffix *-ng*, which may be used together with the disjunctively written prefixes *kwa, fa* and *mo*, also gives nouns an application as adverbs of place, e.g.

Bôtshwene ba nna *kwa thabeng* ....

....

Fa sakeng ga go na bojang ....

....

Baya thipa *mo tafoleng* ....

Mme o ile *toropong* ....

Rona re ya *kgonnye* ....

8.2 Adverbs of manner and time

Nouns form adverbs of manner and time when used together with the disjunctively written instrumental prefix *ka*, e.g.

Magodu a tsene *ka fesetere* ....

Ka moso re tla boa *ka terena* ....

Ba gorogile *ka mahube* ....

Adverbs of time are also formed by means of the disjunctively written locative prefix *mo* and the conjunctively written *-ng*, e.g.

Mo bosigong go diragala bogodu ....

....

Bana ba robala *mo mosong* ....

....

Without the addition of prefixes, nouns may be used as adverbs of time, e.g.

Bogologolo batho ba ne ba agile fa ....

....

Ntate o gorogile *maabane* ....

....

8.3 Adverbs of manner

Nouns form adverbs of manner when used together with the disjunctively written instrumental prefix **ka** or the disjunctively written connective prefix **le**, e.g.

Ka moso o boe **le Pule** ....

Ka nnete, ga ke mo itse! ....

Ke mmone **ka matlho** ....

Ba dumalane **le mme** ....

Without the addition of prefixes nouns may also be used as adverbs of manner, e.g.

Motlhabani o sule **senku** ....

Mosimane yo, o itshotse **sesadi** ....

SELF-ASSESSMENT

1. Divide the following nouns into:

   (a) concrete nouns:

   (b) abstract nouns:

borokhu	boikarabelo ....
bogale	pitso ....
ngwao	tetla ....
kilo	phenyo ....

2. Select the plural nouns from the following list:

Masarwa	bobedi ....
mmusi	malau ....
beng	lonyena ....
mmitlwa	bôTawe ....
mhago	dikgole ....

3. Give the structure of the following nouns:

mokgwaro	sešabo ....
monato	phologolo ....
boikarabelo	mosetsana ....
seopedi	moitaodi ....
phiri	moila ....

16

4. Read the following sentences and make a list of the nouns used as:

   (a) subjects: ....

   (b) objects: ....

        Pule o sa ntse a epa sediba.

        Banna ba nosa metlhape ya bona.

        Monna o tsamaya le noka, mosimane o ya ka tsela.

5. Explain the concept "noun" in your own words.
6. On what basis are the pairs of noun classes grouped together?
7. What are the semantic groupings of the nouns classified under each pair of noun class?
8. What are the most common noun class structures?
9. Give your own examples of the following:

   (a) abstract nouns: ....

   (b) concrete nouns: ....

10. (a) Rewrite the following words and mention the sound changes that they underwent in their adoption:

       (i) tafole ....

       (ii) watšhe ....

       (iii) bikiri ....

       (iv) keriibana ....

   (b) Can you divide the sound changes occurring in these words into:

       (i) actual changes of specific sounds: ....

       (ii) newly added sounds: ....

11. Some initial consonants of the European nouns determine their adoption into a particular noun class. Give your own examples.

   ....

   ....

12. Name two main functions of nouns in sentences. Give examples.

13. Nouns may be used for secondary functions as well. Give examples to illustrate.
14. Explain the forming of diminutives as well as the sound changes that occur in the process.
15. Do diminutives express diminution only? Give reasons for your answer.
16. Name three types of compound noun structures.
17. What are the diminutive suffixes and give four examples of their use?
18. Identify the sound changes in the following diminutives:

    kojwana ....

    tshetshwana ....

    potsane ....

    mmutshana ....

19. What kind of nouns are the following?

    motlhape ....

    tshimane ....

    modulasetulo ....

    mositatlou ....

20. (a) As what kind of word are the bold italicised parts used?
    (i) Pule o tabogetse *go ntatemogolo.*
    (ii) Ba ile *Tlhabane maabane.*
    (iii) O tloga o mo kgarameletsa *mo isong!*
    (iv) *Mo metlheng* ena, o boloke madi.
    (v) Ke tla bua *le rrago ka ntlha* e.
    (b) Explain the structures of these bold italicised parts.

21. Read the following paragraph and make lists of nouns used as:
    (a) subjects: ....

    ....

    (b) objects: ....

    ....

    (c) adverbs: ....

    ....

18

Sello o rata dijo thata. Phakela, fa a tsoga, o ya kwa lapeng go ya go kopa dijo. Mme o mo fa bogobe. O futswela bogobe ka metsi. Basimane ba rata bogobe. Basadi ba apaya bogobe mo pitseng. Bogobe bo jewa ka diatla.

22. In what respects are adopted words changed to fit into Tswana?
23. Why do adopted words undergo sound changes and structural changes when adopted?
24. The adoption of words by changing their sounds implies two kinds of changes to their sounds. Can you name these changes?
25. Into what noun classes are the majority of nouns adopted?
26. Do the original European sounds of adopted nouns play a role when these nouns are adopted into Tswana?
27. Mention the two types of words adopted into Tswana.

CHAPTER 2

Absolute pronouns

OBJECTIVES

On completion of this chapter you should be able to:
1. explain the meaning of the term "absolute pronoun";
2. describe the structure and use of absolute pronouns;
3. identify the different uses of absolute pronouns in a paragraph.

---

1. The meaning of the term *absolute pronoun*

The absolute pronouns refer to a noun or a person and are used:

(a) when, because of stylistic reasons, one does not wish to repeat the subject or the object, e.g.

A o gopola monna yo re mmatlang? **Ena**[1] ke legodu le le sentseng.

....

(b) when one wishes to emphasise a subject or an object, e.g.

Legodu lena **lona**, ke **ena** mosenyi yo motona.

....

(c) when one wishes to contrast two nouns, e.g.

Bana ba a dira. Basadi **bona**, ba robetse.

....

From the preceding examples it is also clear that the absolute pronouns have a qualificative application on the noun from which they are derived.

2. The structure of absolute pronouns

The absolute pronouns of the 1st and 2nd person singular and plural are mainly used in conversations and in examples of direct speech, e.g.

Nna ke tla go thusa, mme **wena** o tla patelesega go ntefa.

....

---

1) *Cf. dictionary p. 20.*

A *lona* le a lemoga gore *rona* re ka se kgone tiro re le rosi.

....

The absolute pronouns of the 3rd person are by nature referential, e.g.

Tswene le legakabe di kile tsa bo di le ditsala. Tshwene *yone* e

....

ne e rata diphepheng, mme legakabe *lona* le ne le rata tsie. *Tso-*

....

na dijo tse, di kile tsa bakela ditsala tse, mathata a a boitshegang.

....

The structure of the absolute pronouns is based on:

a prefix resembling the subjectival concord + a stem *-êna* or *-ôna*. Because of sound changes the derivation of the pronouns *nna, wena* and *tsona* are difficult to explain. However, the rest can easily be derived by means of the formula given above, e.g.

Absolute Pronoun		Prefix	+	Stem		
rona	<	re	+	ôna	Re a bua	....
lona	<	le	+	ôna	Le a bua	....
bôna	<	ba	+	ôna	Ba a bua	....
sôna	<	se	+	ôna	Se a bua	....
tsôna	<	di	+	ôna	Di a bua	..................etc.

With the stem *-êna* the derivation is obscured by sound changes:

Absolute Pronoun		Prefix	+	Stem		
wêna	<	o	+	êna	O a bua	....
êna	<	o	+	êna	O a bua	....
nna	<	ke	+	êna	Ke a bua	....

TABLE OF ABSOLUTE PRONOUNS

SINGULAR		PLURAL	
1st Person	nna	1st Person	rona
2nd Person	wêna	2nd person	lona
3rd Person			
mo-	êna	ba-	bôna
—	êna	bô-	bôna
mo-	ôna	me-	yôna
le-	lôna	ma-	ôna
se-	sôna	di-	tsôna
N-	yôna	diN-	tsôna
lo-	lôna	di-	tsôna
bo-	bôna	ma-	ôna
go	gôna	—	—
fa- go- mo- }	gôna	—	—

3. The use of absolute pronouns

Absolute pronouns may be used:

(a) as subjects and objects, e.g.

Rona re ithuta Setswana. ....

Re ithuta **sona**. ....

(b) to qualify subjects and objects by emphasising them, e.g.

Barutwana **bona**, ba ithuta Setswana.

....

Setswana **sona**, ba a se ithuta.

....

In these examples you will notice that the absolute pronoun appears **after** the subject and the object. The absolute pronoun may however appear before the subject and object as well, e.g.

Bona barutwana, ba ithuta Setswana.

....

Sona Setswana, ba a se ithuta.

....

22

Ba a se ithuta, **sona** Setswana.

The following is however not possible:

*Ba a se ithuta, Setswana **sona**.[2]

(c) to contrast two subjects or two objects, e.g.

Tshwene e rata diphepheng. Legakabe **lona** le rata **yona** tsie.

Besides these applications of the absolute pronouns they are commonly used in adverbial constructions to describe verbs. In the following adverbial constructions the prefixing of certain prefixes give the absolute pronouns an adverbial application, e.g.

Adverbs of place

By means of the **disjunctively written** locative prefix **go** the absolute pronouns acquire an adverbial application, e.g.

Ntlo e ne e šwa, mme rotlhe ra tabogela **go yona.**

Malome o a lwala, jaanong ke ya **go ena.**

Adverbs of manner

By means of the **disjunctively written** instrumental prefix **ka** the absolute pronouns also acquire an adverbial application, e.g.

Ke dirisa šaga go kgaola kala. **Ka yone** go ntsaya metsotsonyana fela.

Adverbs of manner are also formed by means of the prefixes **na-** and **le**, e.g.

Ke bua **le** mme. ⎧Ke bua **nae**.[3]

⎩Ke bua **le** ena.

You will notice that the prefix **na-** is written **conjunctively** with the **first syllable** of the absolute pronoun, e.g.

na- + sona > naso, e.g. Ke bua **naso.**

na- + bona > nabo, e.g. Re bua **nabo.**

2) Where * indicates an ungrammatical sentence.
3) Cf. dictionary p. 100.

The connective prefix **le** is disjunctively written, e.g.

Ke tsamaya **le lona**, lekgarebe. ....

Ba rulagantse **le ona**, morafe. ....

Exercise 2.1

Can you use these absolute pronouns in sentences of your own?

SELF-ASSESSMENT

1. Name the structural elements of the bold italicised parts of the following sentences:
   (i) Pitse **yona** ke ya ga Modise.
   (ii) **Rona** re tla kgatlhana **nabo** kwa gae.
   (iii) Boitaodi **bona** ga bo batlege mono.
   (iv) Ba ile **go Pule**.
   (v) Kgosi yona e rerisane **le ona** morafe.
   (vi) Palama pitse! **Ka yona** o tla fitlha ka nako.
2. The adverbial application of absolute pronouns is made possible by the use of certain prefixes. Name these prefixes and give examples of their use.
3. Absolute pronouns are used pronominally and adverbially. Identify instances of these two applications in the following paragraph:

   Phiri le Phokojwe ba kile ba re ba batla go ya go utswa dinku. Phiri a ya fela, mme Phokojwe ena a iketla. A tsaya seletswana a rema dikala ka sona. Fa Phiri a goroga fa lesakeng la dinku a epa mosima. Dinku tsona tsa nna fela. Fa Phokojwe a goroga a bitsa Phiri. Dinku tsa tshoga.

4. Name the two common stems used in the derivation of absolute pronouns.
5. Explain the term **absolute pronoun** in your own words.
6. Name the structural elements used in the derivation of absolute pronouns.
7. In the use of absolute pronouns one can distinguish between **two** distinct applications. Name these two and give two examples of each.
8. Name the two **types** of adverbs that use absolute pronominal stems as a basis.
9. Can an absolute pronoun be used:
   (a) as a subject or an object of a sentence?
   (b) to denote emphasis?
   (c) to contrast?
   Give two examples of each.

CHAPTER 3

Demonstratives

OBJECTIVES

On completion of this chapter you should be able to:
1. explain the meaning of the term "demonstrative";
2. describe the structure and use of demonstratives;
3. identify examples of demonstratives when used in a paragraph.

---

1. The meaning of the term *demonstrative*

The **demonstratives** are words that are used to:

(a) **qualify** subjects or objects that are spoken of and are physically present in the vicinity of the speaker, e.g.

A thipa *eo* ke ya gago? ....

Re ya go tshela noka *e*. ....

In these examples the demonstratives have a qualificative application.

(b) **refer** to subjects or objects that the speaker has just referred to or that were referred to earlier, e.g.

Thipa *ele* ya maabane e ne e se ya gago.

....

Noka *ele* ya maloba e kgadile jaanong.

....

In these examples the demonstratives have a referential application.

2. The structure of the demonstratives

The demonstratives can be divided into five different groups, viz.

1. demonstratives denoting subjects or objects that are **equally near** the **first** and the **second person**, e.g.

   Setlhako **se**,[1] ke sa ga mang? ....

   Bogobe **bo**, bo tswa kae? ....

2. demonstratives denoting subjects or objects that are **near** the **first person**, e.g.

   Setlhako **sena**,[2] ke sa ga mang? ....

   Bogobe **bona**, bo tswa kae? ....

3. demonstratives denoting subjects or objects that are **in the environment** of the **first** and **second** person or **in the environment** of which the **first** and **second** person form a part, e.g.

   Lefatshe **leno**, ke la ga mang? ....

   Mo ntlong **eno**, ga go jewe nama? ....

4. demonstratives denoting subjects or objects that are **near** the **second person**, e.g.

   Setlhako **seo**,[3] ke sa ga mang? ....

   Bogobe **boo**, bo tswa kae? ....

5. demonstratives denoting subjects or objects that are **equally remote** from the **first** and **second** person, e.g.

   Setlhako **sele**,[4] ke sa ga mang? ....

   Bogobe **bole**, bo tswa kae? ....

Let us now consider each of these five demonstrative positions on their own.

POSITION 1 — *equally near the first and second person*

The demonstratives of this position are **derived from the subjectival concord** and they are called the **basic demonstratives** because the demonstratives of the other positions are derived from them. The **basic** demonstratives and the noun classes which they **qualify** or to which they **refer** are the following:

1) *Cf. dictionary p. 149.*
2) *Cf. dictionary p. 150.*
3) *Cf. dictionary p. 151.*
4) *Cf. dictionary p. 150.*

26

SINGULAR		PLURAL	
mo-	yô	ba-	ba
—	yô	bô-	ba
mo-	ô	me-	ê
le-	lê	ma-	a
se-	sê	di-	tsê
N-	ê	diN-	tsê
lo-	lô-	diN-	tsê
bo-	bô/jô	ma-	a
go	gô		
fa-	fa		
go-	gô		
mo-	mô		

With the exception of the locative **gô** the basic demonstratives are used to:
(i) **qualify** subjects or objects that are **equally near** the **first** and the **second person**, e.g.
Re fitlhetse bana ba jele magapu **a**. Le gale basimane **ba**, ga ba

....

a ja sepe. Jaanong matlape re ka a fa dikolobe **tsê**. Di ka a jela **fa**.

....

(ii) denote subjects or objects that have **just been referred to** by the **first person**, e.g.
Ga twe ka letsatsi lengwe monna o kile a ipopela setlhare, le kga-

....

bo, le mmotorokara ka mmopa. O ne a tsaya gore setlhare **se**, le

....

kgabo **e**, le mmotorokara **o**, di tla fetoga di bo di nna tsa mmatota.

....

In the case of the locative **gô** the **demonstrative meaning was lost** and now it expresses **endearment** or **disparagement** concerning subjects or objects **near** the **first** and the **second person**, e.g.
Ntate, a ke re o setse o itse golo **go** (when introducing a girlfriend).

....

A golo **go**, go ka mphenya! Le ka moso!

....

27

POSITION 2 — *near the first person*

The demonstratives of this position are **derived from the basic demonstratives** of position 2 + the **suffix -na**, e.g.

SINGULAR		PLURAL	
mo-	yôna	ba-	bana
—	yôna	bô-	bana
mo-	ôna	me-	êna
le-	lêna	ma-	ana
se-	sêna	di-	tsêna
N-	êna	diN-	tsêna
lo-	lôna	diN-	tsêna
bo-	bôna/jôna	ma-	ana
go	gôna		
fa-	fana		
go-	gôna		
mo-	môna		

With the exception of the locative **gôna** these demonstratives are used to:

(i) **qualify subjects or objects that are near** the **first person**, e.g.
"Pule, tsaya šaga **êna**, o nkgaolele setlhare **sêna**, se se re kgo-

....

reletsang go aga lorako **lôna**."

....

(ii) denote subjects or objects that have **just been referred to** by the **first person**, e.g.
Mosadimogolo o kile a jwala lebelebele le mmidi le maraka. Ka

....

gore o ne a tlhokomela dijwalo tse 'lebelebele **lena**, le mmidi **ona**,

....

le maraka **ana**, a gola. A gola a ungwa.

....

The demonstrative **gôna** of the locative class **go-** has added to **its demonstrative meaning** and is now also used to express **endearment** or **disparagement** concerning subjects or objects **near** the **first person**, e.g.

Mme, ke go reketse golo **gona** kwa toropong (when referring to a desired object).

....

Rra, golo **gona**, go re utswetse madi.

....

POSITION 3 — *in the environment of the first and second person or in the environment of which the first and second person form a part*

The demonstratives of this position are **derived from the basic demonstratives** of position 1 + the **suffix -no**, e.g.

SINGULAR		PLURAL	
mo-	yô**no**	ba-	ba**no**
—	yô**no**	bô-	ba**no**
mo-	ô**no**	me-	ê**no**
le-	lê**no**	ma-	a**no**
se-	sê**no**	di-	tsê**no**
N-	ê**no**	diN-	tsê**no**
lo-	lô**no**	diN-	tsê**no**
bo-	bô**no**/jô**no**	ma-	a**no**
go	gô**no**		
fa-	fa**no**		
go-	gô**no**		
mo-	mô**no**		

With the exception of the locative **gôno** these demonstratives are used to:

(i) **qualify** subjects or objects that occur in the environment of the first and second person as well as subjects and objects of which the first and second persons form a part, e.g.

Lefatshe **leno**, ke la Batswana.

....

Ngwana **yono**, ke wa me wa gofejane.

....

(ii) denote subjects or objects that have **just been referred to** by the **first person**, e.g.

Maabane ke ne ke tla go thiba diphatla mo legoreng leno. Ke ne ka

....

tla ke tshotse selepe le ngakale le mofago. Jaanong phatlha *êno*

ke ya go e thiba pele ka gore mo malatsing *ano* dibata ga di

tlhole di tshaba batho.

The demonstrative *gôno* of the locative class *go* has **lost its demonstrative meaning** and is now used to express **endearment** or **disparagement** concerning subjects or objects nearest to the **first person**, e.g.

Bagaetsho golo *gôno*, go ntsholetse mosimane (referring to a beloved wife).

Mo iketlele! Golo *gôno*, ke tla go kabolola ditsebe.

POSITION 4 — *near the second person*

The demonstratives of this position are derived from the basic demonstratives of position 1 + the **suffix -o**, e.g.

SINGULAR		PLURAL	
mo-	yô*o*	ba-	ba*o*
—	yô*o*	ba-	ba*o*
mo-	ô*o*	me-	ê*o*
le-	lê*o*	ma-	a*o*
se-	sê*o*	di-	tsê*o*
N-	ê*o*	diN-	tsê*o*
lo-	lô*o*	diN-	tsê*o*
bo-	bô*o*	ma-	a*o*
go	gô*o*		
fa-	fô*o* }	In the case of *fa* the *a* is
go-	gô*o*	replaced by *-ôo* to give *fôo*.
mo-	mô*o*	

With the exception of the locative *gôo* these demonstratives are used to:

30

(i) **qualify** subjects or objects that are **near** the **second person**, e.g.

A hempe *eo* ke ya gago? ....

Se atumele! Ema teng *foo*! ....

(ii) denote subjects or objects that have **just been referred to**, e.g.

Bathusi ba gagwe ba ne ba tlhoka motlhaba le samente le

....

ditena. O ba reketse motlhaba *oo*, le samente *seo*, le ditena *tseo*.

....

The demonstrative *gôo* of the locative class *go* has **lost its demonstrative meaning** and is now used to express **endearment** or **disparagement** concerning subjects or objects near the **second person**, e.g.

Golo *goo*, o se ka wa go lebala. Ke mpho ya ga mme.

....

Golo *goo*, go tla go raela ka mosese!

....

POSITION 5 — *equally remote from the first and second person*

The demonstratives of this position are derived from the basic demonstratives of position 1 + the **suffix -lê**, e.g.

SINGULAR		PLURAL	
mo-	yô*lê*	ba-	ba*lê*
—	yô*lê*	bô-	ba*lê*
mo-	ô*lê*	me-	ê*lê*
le-	lê*lê*	ma-	a*lê*
se-	sê*lê*	di-	tsê*lê*
N-	ê*lê*	diN-	tsê*lê*
lo-	lô*lê*	diN-	tsê*lê*
bo-	bô*lê*/jô*lê*	ma-	a*lê*
go	gô*lê*		
fa-	fa*lê*		
go-	gô*lê*		
mo-	mô*lê*		

With the exception of the locative *gôlê* these demonstratives are used to:

(i) **qualify** subjects or objects that are **equally remote** from the **first** and **second person**, e.g.

Dikgomo *tsele*, ke tsa ga mang? ....

Tlhola teng *fale*, ke bone noga teng!

....

(ii) denote subjects or objects that had **been referred to earlier**, e.g.

Bagwebi ba ne ba rekisa dibuka, sesepa le boupe ka Sontaga,

....

mme dibuka *tsele*, le sesepa *sele*, le boupe *bole*, ba ne ba di

....

rekisa ka tlhwatlhwa e e kwa godimo thata.

....

The demonstrative *gôlê* of the locative class *go* has **lost its demonstrative meaning** and is now used to express **endearment** or **disparagement** concerning subjects or objects that are equally remote from the **first** and **second person**, e.g.

Golo *gole*, go nkwaletse lokwalo lo loleele (referring to a lover).

....

Golo *gole*, ga go thulege. Ke tlhobogile!

....

Besides the abovementioned **five** kinds of demonstratives you should also take note of the locative demonstratives: **kwa, kwana, kwano, koo** and **kwale**.[5]

These demonstratives are also used to:

(i) **qualify** a locality at the moment of speaking,
(ii) **refer** to a locality previously mentioned.

The meanings of positions 1 and 2 of the locative demonstratives: **kwa, kwana, kwano, koo** and **kwale** differ from those of the demonstratives discussed at the beginning of this section because they do not denote positions near the first or second person, e.g.

5) *Cf. dictionary pp. 79–80.*

POSITION 1 AND 2 — *far away from the first and second person*

Kgomo e e fulang **kwa**, ke ya ga mang?

....

Poo e e bopang **kwana**, ke ya ga mang?

....

POSITION 3 — *in a locality encompassing the first person*

Kwano pula ga e na. ....

Kwano re a tlhagola, mme kwa re a tlogela.

....

POSITION 4 — *near the second person*

Ema gone **koo**! Se atumele! ....

Wa re **koo** ga o a bona sepe? ....

POSITION 5 — *equally remote from the first and second person*

Ke mang yo o fetang **kwale**? ....

Batlhodi ba re **kwale** ga go na mafulo.

....

3. The use of demonstratives

Thus far it was illustrated that demonstratives are used to:

(a) **qualify** subjects and objects in respect of their distance from the speaker,
(b) **refer** to people or things that the speaker has just referred to or that were referred to earlier.

In addition it was shown that the locative demonstratives **go, gona, gono, goo** and **gole**[6] have lost their demonstrative meaning in favour of the expression of endearment or disparagement.

To continue it should however be demonstrated that the demonstratives of the other locative classes also have the application as adverbs of place, e.g.

6) *Cf. dictionary p. 37.*

Position 1	Position 2	Position 3	Position 4	Position 5
fa	*fana*	*fano*	*fôo*	*falê*
ka *fa*	ka *fana*	ka *fano*	ka *fôo*	ka *falê*
fano *fa*	—	*fano* fa	—	—
gônê *fa*	gônê *fana*	gone *fano*	gônê *fôo*	gônê *falê*
fa le *fa*	*fana* le *fana*	*fano* le *fano*	*fôo* le *fôo*	*falê* le *falê*
kwa	*kwana*	*kwano*	*kôo*	*kwalê*
ka *kwa*	ka *kwana*	ka *kwano*	ka *koo*	ka *kwalê*
gônê *kwa*	gônê *kwana*	gônê *kwano*	gônê *kôo*	gônê *kwalê*
mô	*môna*	*môno*	*môo*	*môlê*
ka *mô*	ka *môna*	ka *môno*	ka *môo*	ka *môlê*
gônê *mô*	gônê *môna*	gônê *môno*	gônê *môo*	gônê *môlê*

Exercise 5.1

Can you form sentences of your own illustrating the use of demonstratives as adverbs of place?

SELF-ASSESSMENT

1. (a) Classify the following list of demonstratives according to the five demonstrative positions:
seo, tse, bale, fana, bono, ele, yole, o, seno, koo, gona and leo.
   (b) Which of these are basic demonstratives?
   (c) Mention four demonstrative suffixes and give one example each of their application.
2. Discuss the derivation of the following demonstratives:
bo, bona, bono, boo, bole.
3. Explain the term **demonstrative** in your own words.
4. Name the structural elements used in the derivation of demonstratives.
5. Demonstratives are used in:
   (i) a qualificative sense
   (ii) a referential sense
   Explain what is **qualified** and what is **referred** to in:
   Position 1, Position 2, Position 3.
6. In what way do the demonstratives derived from the **go** locative class differ from those of the other noun classes? Give examples.
7. Explain the term **demonstrative** in your own words.

34

8. Mention the different demonstrative positions and name the structural elements comprising each.
9. In the use of demonstratives one can discern different applications. Mention these and give an example of each.
10. In what way do the demonstratives of the **go** locative class differ from the rest?
11. The demonstratives **kwa** and **kwana** can be set apart. Why?

CHAPTER 4

Adjectives

OBJECTIVES

On completion of this chapter you should be able to:
1. explain the meaning of the term "adjective";
2. describe the structure of adjectives;
3. identify examples of adjectives when used in a paragraph.

---

1. The meaning of the term *adjective*

The **adjectives** are words that **qualify** those words that can be used as subjects or objects of sentences. They qualify in respect of **appearance, nature, number** and **colour**, e.g.

Dikgong *tse dikima*[1] ga di tuke.

....

Tsona *tse dikima* ga di tuke.

....

Tseo *tse dikima* ga di tuke.

....

Tsotlhe *tse dikima* ga di tuke.

....

Dingwe *tse dikima* ga di tuke.

....

The colour adjectives, as will be illustrated, have a dual function in that they also qualify subjects and objects in respect of:

(a) sex in the case of animate things, e.g.

Tlhaola *e tuba* le *e tubana* o di tlise kwano.

....

---

1) *Cf. dictionary p. 72. When adjectives are looked up in the dictionary they will be found under their first or third letter.*

(b) the intensity or beauty of a colour, e.g.

Mosetsana *yo mosetlhana* o apere mosese *o mosetlhana.*

....

2. The structure of the adjective

The structure of the adjective is built up around the adjectival root and is made up of:

  (i) the basic demonstrative of the qualified word which acts as a prefix,
 (ii) the class prefix of the qualified word which acts as a prefix,
(iii) the adjectival root, and if required
(iv) the suffixes *-ana* or *-nyana*, e.g.

The structural elements mentioned above are numbered in the following examples and although the demonstrative in (i) below is written disjunctively it is very much part of the structure of the **adjective as a word**:

Mosetsana *yo mo*sesane*nyana.*
       (i) (ii)   (iii)   (iv)

....

Legodu *le le*be.
   (i) (ii) (iii)

....

Dikgomo *tse di*namagadi*nyana.*
     (i) (ii)   (iii)   (iv)

....

Bojang *jo bo*ntsi.
   (i) (ii) (iii)

....

Elements (i) and (ii) are called the adjectival concords and they are prefixed to the adjectival root which is (iii).

The *-ana* and *-nyana* are the diminutive suffixes of the noun classes.

2.1 Adjectival concords

Can you give the adjectival concords for all the noun classes?
  Use the following to check your own list:

ADJECTIVAL CONCORDS

SINGULAR		PLURAL	
Noun class	**Adjectival concord**	**Noun class**	**Adjectival concord**
mo-	yô mo-	ba-	ba ba-
—	yô mo-	bô-	ba ba-
mo-	ô mo-	me-	ê me-
le-	lê le-	ma-	a ma-
se-	sê se-	di-	tsê diN-
N-	ê N-	diN-	tsê diN-
lo-	lô lo-	diN-	tsê diN-
bo-	bô bo-/jo bo-	ma-	a ma-
go	gô go-		
fa-	fa go-		
go-	kwa go-		
mo-	mô go-		

2.2 Adjectival roots

The adjectival concords combine with adjectival roots. In the following list you will notice that the roots are hyphenated. This indicates that these roots are incomplete and they require the adjectival concords to complete them. The roots are divided into:

2.2.1 General adjectival roots

The following is an incomplete list of these roots:

-tona	-kima	-lelele	-tonanyana
-šwa	-ntle	-nana	-be
-gologolo	-tsiang	-kgaraga	-botlana
-nnye	-sesane	-khutshwane	-namagadi

38

-golwane	-nnyennyane	-phaphathi	-tshegadi
....	....	....	....
-tonna	-nnyennye	-potokwane	-potokwe
....	....	....	....

Exercise 4.1

Can you add more examples to this list of general adjectival roots? Use the English/Tswana section of the dictionary to add to your list.

These adjectival roots can be used in examples like:

(i) Motho yo mo**s**esane.[2]   Batho ba ba**s**esane.

....

(ii) Thupa e **tsh**esane.[3]   Dithupa tse di**tsh**esane.

....

(iii) Legodu le le**b**e.   Magodu a ma**b**e.

....

(iv) Tau e m**p**e.   Ditau tse dim**p**e.

....

(v) Selepe se se**g**olo.   Dilepe tse di**kg**olo.

....

(vi) Thipa e **kg**olo.   Dithipa tse di**kg**olo.

....

Exercise 4.2

You should now try to form your own examples by using the general adjectival roots.

Have you noticed the plosivation caused by the "hidden" nasal, or **N-** prefix, of the **N- diN-** classes? This **N-** prefix combines with some initial consonants of adjectival roots to produce plosivated versions of these roots, e.g.

2) *Cf. dictionary p. 151.*
3) *Cf. dictionary p. 194.*

39

-**b**e	>	-**p**e	....
-**g**olo	>	-**kg**olo	....
-**s**esane	>	-**tsh**esane	....

In sentences (ii), (iv) and (vi) the **N-** prefix is therefore actually "hidden" in the sound change affected on the initial consonant of the adjectival stem. Plosivation applies to adjectival roots commencing with:

b-	**s-**	**h-**
d-	**š-**	**w-**
r-	**g-**	
l-	**f-**	

Adjectival roots commencing with **other consonants cannot** undergo plosivation and the **N-** is elided in the case of the **polysyllabic stems**, e.g.

Thupa e **khutshwane** ....

Tau e **tona**nyana ....

Thipa e **tona** ....

In the case of sentence (iv) above

Tau e m**pe**.   Ditau tse dim**pe**.

....

this nasal prefix of the **N- diN-** class is retained as the **m-** in the monosyllabic root **mpe**.

Another sound change, viz. consonant assimilation, takes place in the case of nouns of the **mo- ba-** classes singular and adjectival stems commencing in **b-**, e.g.

Mosetsana yo **mob**otlana   >   Mosetsana yo **mm**otlana

....

Mosadi yo **mob**e   >   Mosadi yo **mm**e

....

2.2.2 Numeral adjectival roots

The following is a complete list of these roots:

-bêdi	-nê	-rataro	-kae?
....	....	....	....
-raro	-tlhano	-ntsi	
....	....	....	

40

These adjectival roots can be used in examples like:

   (i) Mesese e me**b**edi ....

  (ii) Diopedi tse **p**edi ....

 (iii) Makgarebe a ma**r**aro ....

  (iv) Dikgong tse **th**aro ....

   (v) Basimane ba ba**n**e ....

  (vi) Dipodi tse **nn**e ....

Exercise 4.3

Use these adjectival roots to form examples of your own.

In sentences (ii) and (iv) you will notice that the **N-** prefix is once again "hidden" in the sound changes. The numeral adjectival roots that can undergo plosivation are:

     -bedi   > -pedi ....

     -raro   > -tharo ....

     -rataro > -thataro ....

The nasal prefix of the **N- diN-** classes is retained as **n-** in the monosyllabic root **nne of sentence (vi) above. This nasal prefix of the N- diN-** classes is elided in the case of polysyllabic adjectival stems that cannot be plosivated, e.g.

    Ntate o rekile dipodi **tse tlhano.** ....

    Ntate o rekile dipodi **tse kae?** ....

The interrogative adjectival root **-kaé** is used in phrasing questions regarding number, e.g.

    Ba rekile mesese **e mekae?**

....

    Khwaere ya bone e na le diopedi **tse kae?**

....

    Le laleditse makgarebe **a makae?**

....

    Tiro ena e ka dirwa ke basimane **ba bakae?**

....

2.2.3 Colour adjectival roots

As was stated earlier, these roots qualify subjects and objects in terms of colour and sex. For this reason and because of certain irregularities both the masculine and the feminine forms of the roots are given below. The feminine roots, as you will notice, take the suffix *-ana*. When used to qualify people or inanimate things, this suffix also denotes the beauty or intensity of a particular colour:

MASCULINE	FEMININE
-bududu	-budutswana
-ramaga	-ramagana
-tshumo	-tshunyana
-fatshwa	-fatshwana
-tshega	-tshegana
-šampa	-šampana
-nkgwe	-gwana
-khukhwa	-khukhwana
-tlhaba	-tlhabana
-gwaripa	-gwaripana
-gweba	-gwebana
-tilodi	-tilotsana
-ngolo	-ngolwana
-nala	-naana
-fitshwa	-fitshwana
-tuba	-tubana
-putswa	-putswana
-ntlhwa	-tlhwaana
-rokwa	-rokwana
-webu	-otswana
-hunou	-hunwana
-setlha	-setlhana
-hibidu	-hibitswana

-sweu	-swaana ....
-birwa	-birwana ....
-fifadu '	-fifatswana ....
-ntsho	-tshwana ....

Exercise 4.4

By using the dictionary you should now study the use of those adjectival roots that suit your particular needs.

In the case of the roots:

| **-šotšwa**[4] .... | **-šotšwana** .... |
| **-tšhotšwa** .... | **-tšhotšwana** .... |

you should notice that the adjectival roots also indicate **gender** but **not colour**. The reason being that this root denotes hornlessness, e.g.

Poo **e tšhotšwa** ....

Ngaka **e tšhotšwa** ....

The colour adjectival roots can be used in examples like:

(i) Motho yo mo**ntsho** ....

(ii) Kgomo e **ntsho** ....

(iii) Podi e **tshwana** ....

(iv) Moroba o mo**swana** ....

(v) Mokodue o mo**bududu** ....

(vi) Mokodue o mo**budutswana** ....

(vii) Namane e **putswa** ....

(viii) Namane e **putswana** ....

In the examples (v) – (viii) the presence or absence of **-ana** makes the difference between the sex of the blue grey animals.

These examples also illustrate the plosivating effect of the hidden nasal of the **N- diN-** classes. Other examples illustrating this are:

-**b**irwa   > -**p**irwa ....

-**f**ifadu   > -**ph**ifadu ....

4) *Cf. dictionary p. 160.*

43

-ḣunwana > -kḣunwana ....

-šampana > -tšhampana ....

Exercise 4.5

Can you use these colour adjectival roots in examples of your own?

2.3 Adjectival suffixes

The suffixes that may be used with adjectival roots are **-ana (-ane)** and **-nyana**.

2.3.1 The suffix **-ana (-ane)**

(i) This suffix, as has been illustrated, expresses **feminine gender** when suffixed to colour adjectival roots qualifying **animals**. In some cases it causes a sound change called palatalisation, e.g.

Kgomo *e pududu* > Kgomo *e pudutswana*

....

Namane *e tilodi* > Namane *e tilotswana*

....

Podi *e tshumo* > Podi *e tshunyana*

....

(ii) When suffixed to colour adjectival roots qualifying **people** or **inanimate** things, the suffix **-ana** expresses **affection** or **appreciation** for the colour in question. Palatalisation is evident in the two examples in bold print:

Mmala *o mohibidu* > Mmala *o mohibitswana*

....

Mosese *o mosweu* > Mosese *o moswaana*

....

Ngwanyana *yo mosetlha* > Ngwanyana *yo mosetlhana*

....

Khai *e tuba* > Khai *e tujwana*

....

44

2.3.2 The suffixes *-ana (-ane)* and *-nyana (-nyane)*

Depending on the context, these suffixes can express:

(i) the diminution of the idea expressed by the adjectival roots, e.g.

Ntate, a re ka kgetla dinamune *tse pets**ana***?

....

Bana *ba bagolw**ane*** ga ba itshole jaana.

....

Mosadi *yo montle**nyana*** ke mme.

....

*Yo mokhutshwa**nyane*** ga se malome.

....

(ii) derogation or deprecation is usually expressed by the suffix
-nyana, e.g.

Kgomo *e tshwana**nyana*** e, ke ya ga mang?

....

A mosadinyana *yo mokima**nyana***!

....

Ba leka go ntefa ka dikoko ***tse pedinyana***.

....

Exercise 4.6

Can you give more examples of the use of suffixes with the adjectival roots?

On structure in general it can be said that:

(i) intricate animal colours are expressed by means of compound
adjectives, e.g.

Kgomo ***e nkgwekhibidu***.

....

Namane ***e tshungwanaphifatshwana***.

....

45

(ii) intensification of the adjective idea can be expressed by the reduplication of the stem, e.g.

Mosetsana *yo montlentle*.

....

Lofofa *le letalatala*.

....

3. The use of adjectives

Adjectival roots may be used for a number of purposes as can be seen from the following:

3.1 The adjectival use of adjectival roots

(i) Adjectives, as we have seen, are used to qualify these words, appearing in subject or object position, in respect of their **appearance, nature, number** and **colour**.

(ii) The **addition** of the suffix *-ana* to colour adjectival roots qualifying animals expresses **feminine gender** while the **absence** of *-ana* denotes **masculine gender**.

(iii) When suffixed to colour adjectival roots qualifying people, the suffix *-ana* expresses **affection** or **appreciation**.

(iv) Depending on the context the suffixes *-ana (-ane)* and *-nyana (-nyane)* express the **diminution of the idea** expressed by the adjectival root, or the adjectival idea may be used in a **derogatory or deprecatory sense**.

3.2 The normal use of adjectival roots

(i) All adjectival roots can combine with the class prefix **bo-** to form abstract nouns, e.g.

bo**kima**	bo**bedi**	bo**tuba**
bo**namagadi**	bo**raro**	bo**sweu**
bo**golo**	bo**rataro**	bo**ramagana**

46

(ii) A limited number of adjectival roots can combine with other class prefixes to form nouns, e.g.

mo*golo* .... *pedi* .... mo*ntsho* ....

ba*golo* .... *tharo* .... ba*ntsho* ....

ba*šwa* .... *nne* .... ba*sweu* ....

n*tona* .... *rataro* .... mo*setlha* ....

din*tona* .... me*setlha* ....

Some of the nouns formed from colour adjectival stems are more commonly used in possessive constructions as figures of speech, e.g.

tshetlha ya metsi ....

tshetlha ya dipoa ....

Thamaga ya boJesu ....

di*thamaga* tsa legodimo ....

tilodi ya dikgopa ....

tilodi ya ga malome ....

(iii) in the context of a conversation or a written text the adjectives may be used alone as subjects or objects of indidivudal sentences. When used like this the adjective only replaces the original noun, e.g.

Jaanong, ka gore **yo motona** o ne a sa itse gore **yo mokima** o

....

tsene mo tlung, le ena o bo a tsena. **Yo motona** a bo a utlwa se-

....

ngwe se hema —. Ya nna: "Mma wee!" A bokola a sutlha ditlha-

....

tsana tsa mokgalo. **Yo mokima** a sala fale a ntse a re: "Hê-hê-hê."

....

When used nominally the adjectives acquire other nominal qualities as well and they may be used adverbially, e.g.

Letsatsi le le latelang, yo mokima a ya **go yo motona** a mo fitlhela

....

47

a ntse a itlhomola. A mmotsa gore go diragetse eng? Tidimalo!

A leka gape go bua **le yo motona**.

This adverbial application is achieved by prefixing the adverbial prefixes **ka, le** and **go**, e.g.

Ke rema **ka** *se setona* ....

Ba bua **le** *ba babe* ....

Re ya **go** *yo moleele* ....

Exercise 4.7

Can you use the adjectival roots nominally in examples of your own?

3.3 The syntactic position of adjectives

(i) Adjectives always follow the subjects or objects qualified by them, e.g.

Monna **yo mosesane**, o bua le mosadi **yo mokima**.

....

(ii) More than one adjective may be used to qualify the same subject or object, e.g.

Dinamane **tse pedi tse dintsho**.

....

Lekolwane **le lekgaraga le lethata**.

....

(iii) Emphasis of the adjectival idea is achieved by reversing the abovementioned sequence, e.g.

Yo mosesane, monna, o bua le **yo mokima**, mosadi.

....

This sequence is characterised by a pause in speech and by a comma in writing.

SELF-ASSESSMENT

1. Name the structural elements appearing in the following adjectives:

   Metsi a mantsi ....

   Dimao tse kae? ....

   Khai e tala ....

   Basimane ba barataro ....

   Podi e pirwana ....

   Ngwanyana yo montlenyana ....

   Bojalwa bo bonnye ....

2. Identify examples of sound changes in the adjectives appearing in:

   Thupa e telele ....

   Kgole e ntšhwa ....

   Namane e potlana ....

   Mmolai yo mme ....

   Ngwana yo mmotlana ....

3. Classify the following adjectival roots into three groups:

   -bedi .... -tuba ....

   -khutshwane .... -kae? ....

   -sweu .... -gologolo ....

4. Explain the term **adjective** in your own words.
5. Describe the structure of an adjective. Give examples.
6. What sound changes occur in adjectives? Give examples.
7. Give examples of three kinds of adjectival stems.
8. (a) Name the structural elements of the following adjectives that have undergone sound changes:

   Khai e khibidu ....

   Namane e tujwana ....

   Podi e tshunyana ....

   Dinamune tse petsana ....

49

(b) Name the sound changes that occurred in (a) above.

9. Classify the following adjectival roots into three groups:

-sesane .... -ntle ....

-tlhano .... -nala ....

-rokwana .... -raro ....

10. What is the function of the adjectives?

11. Describe the structure of the following adjectives:

Ntate o rekile moroba o mošampana.

....

O ne a apere hempe e talanyana.

....

12. Name three kinds of sound changes that occur in adjectives. Give examples of each sound change.

13. Explain the meaning of adjectival suffixes when used to qualify:
    (i) the colour of animals, people or things.
    (ii) the appearance of animals, people or things.
    (iii) the number of animals, people or things.

14. Do adjectival stems have a nominal application? Give examples.

15. What is the usual position of adjectives in a sentence?

16. Can more than one adjectival stem be used to qualify a subject or an object?

17. How is emphasis of the adjectival idea achieved?

CHAPTER 5

Enumeratives

OBJECTIVES

On completion of this chapter you should be able to:
1. explain the meaning of the term "enumerative";
2. describe the structure and use of enumeratives;
3. identify the different kinds of enumeratives in a passage.

---

1. The meaning of the term *enumerative*

The enumeratives are used to qualify the subject or the object of a sentence, e.g.

Motho **mongwe**[1] o ntseetse madi.

....

Monna, o batla dikgomo **dife**?

....

Go gorogile batho **basele**.

....

Ga go na bana **bape** mono.

....

Let us now take a closer look at each of these enumeratives.

2. The structure of the enumeratives

The enumeratives are divided into two groups on the grounds of the prefixes taken by the roots:

GROUP 1	GROUP 2
-ngwe	*-fe* **-sele** *-pe*

1) *Cf. dictionary p. 108.*

2.1 The enumerative *-ngwe*

The root *-ngwe* combines with prefixes that closely resemble the noun class prefixes, e.g.

SINGULAR	PLURAL
mo**ngwe**	ba**ngwe**
mo**ngwe**	me**ngwe**
le**ngwe**	ma**ngwe**
se**ngwe**	di**ngwe**
n**ngwe**	di**ngwe**
lo**ngwe**	di**ngwe**
bo**ngwe**	ma**ngwe**
go**ngwe**	
go**ngwe**	

In the singular the enumerative *-ngwe* expresses the meaning of "a certain" while in the plural it expresses the meaning of "some", e.g.

Podi **nngwe** e bolailwe ke phokojwe.

....

Dilepe **dingwe** di fa setlhareng sele.

....

The root *-ngwe* is monosyllabic and therefore **retains** the prefix **n-** of the **N- diN-** class singular in the example:

Podi **nngwe.**

Exercise 5.1

You should now attempt to use the enumerative root -ngwe in practical examples of your own.

2.2 The enumerative *-fe*

The root *-fe* combines with a set of prefixes from which the nasal elements of the noun prefixes have been elided, e.g.

SINGULAR	PLURAL
o*fe*	ba*fe*[2]
o*fe*	e*fe*
le*fe*	a*fe*
se*fe*	di*fe*
e*fe*	di*fe*
lo*fe*	di*fe*
bo*fe*	a*fe*
go*fe*	
go*fe*	

This enumerative expresses the meaning of "which"? Therefore the predominant use of the enumerative **-fe** is that of an interrogative, e.g.

Rra, o batla ngwana **ofe**?

....

Ke dikgomo **dife** tse di suleng?

....

The enumerative **-fe** can however be used in statements as well, e.g.

Ga re itse gore ke **bafe** ba ba sentseng.

....

Ga ke itse gore ke tla dirisa buka **efe**.

....

Exercise 5.2

*Can you use the enumerative root **-fe** in examples of your own?*

2.3 The enumerative -sele

The root **-sele**, like **-fe**, combines with a set of prefixes from which the nasal elements of the noun prefixes have been elided, e.g.

2) *Cf. dictionary p. 6.*

SINGULAR	PLURAL
o**sele**	ba**sele**[3]
o**sele**	e**sele**
le**sele**	a**sele**
se**sele**	di**sele**
e**sele**	di**sele**
lo**sele**	di**sele**
bo**sele**	a**sele**
go**sele**	
go**sele**	

The enumerative **-sele** expresses the meaning of "foreignness", e.g.

Dikgomo tseo ke **disele.**

....

Selepe se, ke a se itse. **Sesele** se, ga ke se itse.

....

Rona re bua ka ga batho **basele.**

....

In the case of **gosele** of the locative classes the enumerative may also be used adverbially, e.g.

Ntate o ile **gosele.** ....

Exercise 5.3

*You should now attempt to use the enumerative root **-sele** in examples of your own.*

2.4 The enumerative -pe

The root **-pe**, like **-fe** and **-sele**, combines with a set of prefixes from which the nasal elements of the noun prefixes have been elided, e.g.

3) *Cf. dictionary p. 7.*

SINGULAR	PLURAL
o**pe**	ba**pe**[4]
o**pe**	e**pe**
le**pe**	a**pe**
se**pe**	di**pe**
e**pe**	di**pe**
lo**pe**	di**pe**
bo**pe**	a**pe**
go**pe**	
go**pe**	

This enumerative expresses the meaning of "none" or "not any".
The enumerative *-pe* is almost exclusively used in negative sentences, e.g.

Ga go na motho **ope** fano.

....

Ga go a tlhabiwa dinku **dipe**.

....

The enumeratives taking the root *-pe* are very commonly used alone, the nouns qualified by them are omitted, e.g.

Ga go na **ope** fano.

....

Ga go a tlhabiwa **dipe**.

....

This also applies to **gope** of the locative classes which is used adverbially, e.g.

Ba teng, ga ba a ya **gope**.

....

Ga o ye **gope**! Nna teng foo!

....

4) *Cf. dictionary p. 7.*

The following idiomatic application of **-pe** is noteworthy:

Ga go na **le fa e le ope**.

....

Ga ba na **le fa e le sepe**.

....

Ga o itse **sepe**.

....

Exercise 5.4

You should now attempt to use the enumerative root -pe in examples of your own.

3. The use of the enumeratives

It is relatively rare to use different enumerative roots together in the same sentence because their meanings are mutually exclusive, e.g.

O raya motho osele ofe?

....

Can you think of further examples?

However, the enumerative roots can be used together with other words that also qualify the subject or the object of the sentence. In the following examples the enumeratives are used together with:

Possessives: Ntlo *nngwe* **ya bona** e thubilwe.
Adjectives: Setlhare *sengwe* **se sekima** se kgaotswe.
Relatives: Ngwana *mongwe* **yo o botlhale** of falotse.
O raya monna **yo o lwalang** *ofe*?

Exercise 5.5

You should now find more examples illustrating this use of the enumeratives.

56

SELF-ASSESSMENT

1. Identify the words containing the enumerative roots in the following sentences. Write down the enumerative underlining the roots:

    Bogobe bongwe bone bo tsenne.
    Setlhare se o se remang, ke sefe?
    Bao ke batho basele.
    Mo motseng ona, ga go na ntšwa epe.

2. In what way do the prefixes of the following enumeratives differ?

    A: Mosetsana mongwe o rekile mosese.
    B: O rekile mosese ofe?
    C: O bua maaka, ga a a reka ope.
    A: Ao, wena o motho osele. O rata kganetso!

3. What kind of word is implied by the term "enumerative"?

4. In what way does the structure of the different enumeratives differ?

5. The enumerative **gosele** is used in a special way. Explain.

6. Can enumeratives be used together in a sentence? Motivate your answer and give examples.

7. Name examples of other qualificatives that may be used together with enumeratives.

CHAPTER 6

Quantitatives

> **OBJECTIVES**
>
> On completion of this chapter you should be able to:
> 1. describe the structure of the inclusive and the exclusive "quantitatives";
> 2. describe the function of these quantitatives in sentences;
> 3. identify these quantitatives in a passage.

1. The meaning of the term *quantitative*

The quantitatives are used to qualify the subject or the object of a sentence, e.g.

(i) Batho **botlhe**[1] ba rata dijo.

....

(ii) Ke beditse bona **bosi.**[2]

....

The quantitatives are divided into two types on the grounds of the meaning of the two quantitative roots. We distinguish between **inclusive** and **exclusive** quantitatives.

Let us now take a closer look at the structures of each of these two kinds of quantitatives.

2. The structure and use of the inclusive quantitative

The inclusive quantitatives show a structural relationship with the subjects or the objects that they qualify, e.g.

(iii) **S**etlhare **s**otlhe se tletse dinonyane.

....

(iv) Basadi ba rekisitse **b**ojalwa **b**otlhe.

....

---

1) *Cf. dictionary p. 14.*
2) *Cf. dictionary p. 14.*

Because of the sound changes that take place and because of the omission of some of the sounds the structural relationship between subject, object and quantitative is not always as clearly demonstrable as in examples (iii) and (iv) quoted above, e.g.

(v) Morafe *otlhe* o ya pitsong ka moso.

....

(vi) Re tla lema tshimo **yotlhe.**

....

From the preceding examples it is clear that the initial element of the inclusive quantitative is derived from a noun or an absolute pronoun which is used as the subject or object of a sentence.

The following is the full list of quantitatives giving examples of the nouns and pronouns from which they are derived:

SINGULAR			PLURAL		
1st p. nna	—		**r**ona	>	**r**otlhe
2nd p. wena	—		**l**ona	>	**l**otlhe
3rd p. motho	—		**b**atho	>	**b**otlhe
motse	>	otlhe	metse	>	yotlhe
lerapo	>	**l**otlhe	marapo	>	otlhe
setšhaba	>	**s**otlhe	ditšhaba	>	tsotlhe
thaba	>	yotlhe	dithaba	>	tsotlhe
logare	>	**l**otlhe	dikgare	>	tsotlhe
bojalwa	>	**b**otlhe	majalwa	>	otlhe
go bua	>	**g**otlhe			
felo	>	**g**otlhe			

From these examples it is clear that the structure of the inclusive quantitative is made up of **a prefix + a root**, e.g.

prefix + root

setswalo	>	s-	+ -otlhe
dinku	>	ts-	+ -otlhe
bojang	>	b-	+ -otlhe

Exercise 6.1

You should now be able to use the abovementioned quantitatives in practival sentences of your own.

The 1st and the 2nd person singular do not take a quantitative. Their plurals however do take a quantitative, e.g.

Rona rotlhe le *lona lotlhe* re tla ya sekolong.

....

Nna ke tla thapa *lona lotlhe.*

....

From these examples it is clear that the quantitative is used to qualify the subjects and the objects of sentences.

3. The structure and use of the exclusive quantitative

This kind of qualificative can be used:

(a) qualificatively, e.g.

Ke romile **b**ona **b**osi.

....

Ba rekisitse **d**ikgomo tsa bona *ts*osi.

....

Yona **y**osi e ka se kgone.

....

(b) in copulative sentences, e.g.

Ba tlile ba le **b**osi.

....

Re ikwadisitse re le *r*osi.

....

Fa **d**inku di le *ts*osi mafulo a ka di lekanela.

....

The derivation of the initial structural element of the exclusive quantitative is noticeable in the following examples. The table also gives examples of nouns and pronouns from which the deriviation takes place:

60

SINGULAR			PLURAL		
1st p.	nna	> nosi	rona	> rosi
2nd p.	wena	> wesi	lona	> losi
3rd p.	ena	> esi	bona	> bosi
	mokgalo	> osi	mekgalo	> yosi
	lesaka	> losi	masaka	> osi
	sekgwa	> sosi	dikgwa	> tsosi
	tlhogo	> yosi	ditlhogo	> tsosi
	lonaka	> losi	dinaka	> tsosi
	bojang	> bosi/josi	majang	> osi
	go laola	> gosi		
	golo	> gosi		

From these examples it is clear that the structure of the exclusive quantitative is made up of a prefix + a root, e.g.

		prefix	+ root
kgole	>	y-	+ -osi
leselo	>	l-	+ -osi
rosi	>	r-	+ -osi

Exercise 6.2

You should now be able to add to these examples that illustrate the structural relationship between the exclusive quantitative and the subjects or objects qualified by them.

The full list of exclusive quantitatives is not used by all speakers. Many people however use **nosi** in copulative constructions, e.g.

Rona **re nosi.**

....

Maagwe **o nosi.**

....

Bona **ba le nosi** ba tla kgona.

....

Pula **e le nosi** e tla re thusa.

....

61

From these examples it is clear that **nosi** is used without regard to the noun class or singularity or plurality of the noun or pronoun qualified by it.

4. Quantitatives with a numerical base

We will now introduce you to yet another type of quantitative as demonstrated by the following examples:

(i) Rona **roobabedi**[3] re ba bone ba feta.

....

(ii) Lona **loobabedi** le fetse tiro ena.

....

(iii) Bona **boobabedi** ba adimile mmotorkara wa me.

....

(iv) Mekgalo **yoomebedi** ena e se ka ya kgaolwa.

....

(v) Makau **oomabedi** a ile go ithekela diaparo tsa moletlo.

....

Exercise 6.3

Would you agree that the bold printed words are derived from an adjectival root?

The structure of the quantitative with a numeral base is:

	prefix	+	adjectival prefix	+	adjectival root
rona **roobabedi** <	roo-	+	-ba-	+	-bedi

In the examples mentioned previously you will notice:

(i) that the sound change rules applicable in the case of the adjectives of the **diN-** classes are still operative, e.g.

diphuka **tsoopedi** < -**b**edi

3) *Look up under the first letter. Cf. dictionary p. 143 under **roo-**.*

(ii) that the first prefix is derived from the subject or object qualified, e.g.

*L*ona *loo*babedi, tlayang kwano.

....

*D*inku *tsoo*pedi di timetse.

....

(iii) that the second prefix of the 1st, 2nd and 3rd persons are derived
from the **ba-** class, e.g.

Rona roo**babedi**.

....

Lona loo**babedi**.

....

Bona boo**babedi**.

....

In the case of the other noun classes you will notice that the second
prefix corresponds with the adjectival prefix which is derived from
the noun class prefixes, e.g.

Basimane boo**babedi**.

....

Mekgalo *yoo***me**bedi*.

....

Dinku *tsoo***pedi*.

....

In the case of the **diN-** classes the second prefix is "hidden" in the
sound changes.
 The quantitative with a numeral base can therefore be classified
with the inclusive quantitatives.

SELF-ASSESSMENT

1. What are the structural elements constituting the two kinds of quantitatives? Give examples.
2. What is the function of the quantitatives in a sentence? Give examples.
3. Is there a structural relationship between the quantitative and other words within sentences? Give examples to illustrate this.
4. What is the position of the quantitative **nosi** in sentences? Give examples.
5. Identify and name the prefix and the root in the following items:
   - (i) tsosi
   - (ii) lotlhe
   - (iii) bosi
   - (iv) gotlhe
6. What is the structure of the quantitatives with a numeral base?
7. What is the function of the quantitatives with a numeral base?
8. Do the prefixes of the quantitatives with a numeral base show any structural relationships with the subjects or the objects that they qualify?
9. Identify and name the structural elements of the bold italicised items:
   - (i) Rona **roobabedi** re ya gae.
   - (ii) Lona **loobabedi** le tswa kae?
   - (iii) Dintšwa **tsoopedi** di mo lomile.
   - (iv) Ba rekile mefuta **yoomebedi.**

CHAPTER 7

Possessives

OBJECTIVES

On completion of this chapter you should be able to:
1. explain the term "possessive";
2. describe the structure and use of possessives;
3. identify possessives when used in a passage.

1. The meaning of the term *possessive*

The term possessive refers to the relation that exists between a **possession** and a **possessor**, e.g.

    thipa *ya*[1] *monna*

The **man** is the **possessor** and the **knife** is the **possession** and the possessive relationship is expressed by means of the possessive concord *ya*. In our example *ya monna* is a disjunctively written word called a **possessive.**

  Possessives are commonly used to denote a possessive relationship, e.g.

    Selepe *sa monna*

    Mosadi *wa gago*

    Kobo *ya ole*

They may however also be used in a qualificative sense when the possessor is inanimate, e.g.

    Selepe *sa magagane*

    Mosadi *wa mmopa*

    Kobo *ya mariga*

    Diaparo *tsa senna*

    Letsatsi *la bone*

    Lebotlele *la tšhefi*

1) *Cf. dictionary p. 208 under yá.*

The possessor, in these examples, does not actually own the **possession**. In actual fact the **possessor** qualifies the **possession**. In other words:

>*sa magagane* qualifies *selepe*
>*wa mmopa* qualifies *mosadi*
>*ya mariga* qualifies *kobo* etc.

Exercise 7.1

You should now be able to give examples of your own of possessives denoting a possessive relationship and of possessives used in a qualificative sense.

2. The structure and use of possessives

To commence with one should draw a distinction between the **possessive construction** and the **possessives as independent words**. This can be explained as follows.

The italicised parts of the following examples are **possessive constructions**:

(i) ***Ntlo ya mosadi*** e agilwe.

....

(ii) ***Ngwana wa gago*** o a lwala.

....

(iii) ***Setšhaba sa gaetsho*** se a ikanngwa.

....

The **possessive construction** consists of a **noun** which is the **possession**, i.e.

>*ntlo* ....

>*ngwana* ....

>*setšhaba* ....

From each of these nouns a **possessive concord** is derived, i.e.

>ntlo ***ya*** ....

>ngwana ***wa*** ....

>setšhaba ***sa*** ....

66

These possessive concords link the possessions to the **possessors**, i.e.

Ntlo ya *mosadi* ....

Ngwana wa *gago* ....

Setšhaba sa *gaetsho* ....

The **possessive concords** + the **possessors** form the **disjunctively written word** called the **possessive**, i.e.

Ntlo *ya mosadi* ....

Ngwana *wa gago* ....

Setšhaba *sa gaetsho* ....

The possessive is therefore a word consisting of a **possessive concord** + a **noun which is the possessor**. Let us now take a closer look at the **possessive concords** and the **noun classes from which they are derived**:

SINGULAR		PLURAL	
Noun class	**Possessive concord**	**Noun class**	**Possessive concord**
mo-	wa	ba-	ba
mo-	wa	me-	ya
le-	la	ma-	a
se-	sa	di-	tsa
N-	ya	diN-	tsa
lo-	lwa	diN-	tsa
bo-	ba/jwa	ma-	a
go	ga		
go-	ga		

These possessive concords, as will be shown, can be prefixed to a number of word categories.

2.1 Possessive concords prefixed to nouns

1. The possessive concords may be prefixed to nouns of all types, excluding the subclass of the *mo- ba-* classes singular, to form possessives, e.g.

67

Lebotana **la ditena.**

....

Batho **ba Botswana.**

....

Sentlhaga **sa thaga.**

....

Go opela **ga banyana.**

....

Fa pele **ga ntlo.**

....

Felo **ga basimane.**

....

Pene **ya modulasetulo.**

....

Loso **lwa moitaodi.**

....

Exercise 7.2

Can you give additional examples of possessive concords prefixed to different kinds of nouns?

2. The nouns of the subclass of the **mo- ba-** classes behave differently from those in 1 above. They require an additional prefix **ga** to complete the possessive, e.g.

Bana *ba* **ga** *rakgadi.*

....

Loso *lwa* **ga** *Kgama.*

....

Buka *ya* **ga** *mang?*

....

Diaparo *tsa* **ga** *nneu.*

....

Exercise 7.3

Can you add to these examples of the use of the subclass singular of the **mo- ba-** *classes when used in possessives?*

3. A **contracted** and conjunctively written version of the possessive concord is used when the possessive construction expresses relationship e.g.

Kgaitsadi**a** *Pule* ....

Rakgadi**a** *Dikeledi* ....

Maloma**a** *Shole* ....

Monna**a** *Mpho* ....

Would you agree that originally these possessive constructions contained the full form of the possessive concord? e.g.

Kgaitsadi **wa** Pule, etc.

....

Another contracted form is:

rraagwe Modise   <   rra **w**a **ga**gwe

....

mmaagwe Pholo   <   mma **w**a **ga**gwe

....

malomaagwe Kabelo < malom**e w**a **g**agwe

Would you agree that the contraction took place after the elision of the parts in bold print?

Exercise 7.4

You should now try to give more examples of the use of the contracted possessive concords.

2.2 Possessive concords prefixed to pronominal possessive stems

A special type of pronominal stem is used in possessive constructions. These possessive pronominal stems **differ** from the absolute pronouns only in respect of the italicised 1st and 2nd and 3rd person singular, e.g.

69

SINGULAR		PLURAL	
Pronominal possessive		**Pronominal possessive**	
1st person	*me*	1st person	rona
2nd person	*gago*	2nd person	lona
3rd person	*gagwe*	3rd person	bona
mo-	ona	me-	yona
le-	lona	ma-	ona
se-	sona	di-	tsona
N-	yona	diN-	
lo-	lona	diN-	
bo-	bona/jona	ma-	
go	gona		
go-	gona		

These possessive pronominal stems are written disjunctively, e.g.

Diaparo *tsa **me*** di kae?

....

A nka adima buka *ya **gago***?

....

Batsadi *ba **gagwe*** ba nna kwa Gauteng.

....

Tlhatlhela dikgomo mme e seng dinamane *tsa **tsone***.

....

Ke eng se se suleng? Ga ke rate go nkga *ga **gone***.

....

Exercise 7.5

Can you give more examples of the use of the possessive concords when prefixed to pronominal possessive stems?

2.3 Possessive concords prefixed to communal possessive pronominal stems

Things that are the communal possessions of a group of people also feature in the expression of possessive relationships. The communal possessive pronominal stems by means of which this is expressed, are made up by two groups of stems, viz.

etsho[2]	*gaetsho*
eno	*gaeno*
gaabo	*gagabo*

Various forms of elision occur with the application of these stems, e.g.

(i) mosadi **wa gaetsho** ....

    mosadi **wa etsho** ....

    mosadi **wetsho** ....

(ii) bana **ba gaeno** ....

    bana **ba eno** ....

    bana **beno** ....

(iii) selepe **sa gagabo** ....

    selepe **sa gaabo** ....

    selepe **saabo** ....

Exercise 7.6

You should now try to find your own examples of the full and elided forms of the communal possessive construction.

2.4 Possessive concords prefixed to demonstratives

Mafoko *a **bale*** ga a njese monate.

....

Batho ba motse o, ga ba lwale. *Ba **ole***, ba a lwala.

....

Mosadi yo, o kgonne mme tiro *ya **yona***, ga e a fela.

....

O segile dikala tse sentle. Tswelela le *tsa **sena***.

....

Exercise 7.7

You should now be able to form your own examples of the use of the possessive concords when prefixed to demonstratives.

2) *Cf. dictionary p. 22.*

2.5 Possessive concords prefixed to adjectives

A mesese e mentle! Nna ke rata *wa* **yo mosetlhana.**

....

Diaparo tse, ga di ye go go lekana. Leka *tsa* **yo mokima** yole.

....

Bophokojwe ba a boitshega. Ba bolaile namane *ya* **e tshwana.**

....

A le na le dibuka? Le ka adima *tsa* **ba bararo** bale.

....

Exercise 7.8

Can you give more examples of the use of the possessive concords when prefixed to adjectives?

2.6 Possessive concords prefixed to enumeratives

Maitseo *a* **bangwe** mo go lona ga a jese monate.

....

O raya namane *ya* **efe**? ....

Ga ke a tsaya madi *a* **ope.** ....

Ke dibuka *tsa* **basele.** ....

Exercise 7.9

Can you give your own examples of the use of the possessive concords prefixed to enumeratives?

2.7 Possessive concords prefixed to pronominal possessive stems

Diaparo *tsa* **ba gago** di kae?

....

Molemo *wa* **ya me**, o tla go alafa.

....

Mofeng *wa* **sa gagwe**, o robegile.

....

Ke tla boa le bana *ba* **sa lona**, sekolo.

....

Exercise 7.10

Can you give more examples of possessive concords prefixed to possessive stems?

2.8 Possessive concords prefixed to relative constructions

Namane *ya* **e e suleng** maabane e kae?

....

Bana *ba* **yo o bonolo** ba ka se senye.

....

A o itse mekgwa *ya* **ba ba utswang**?

....

A o lemoga tiro *ya* **ba ba tlhaga**?

....

Exercise 7.11

Can you form your own examples of possessive concords prefixed to relative constructions?

2.9 Possessive concords prefixed to adverbs of time and place

Merafe *ya* **kwa moseja** e humile.

....

Leuba *la* **ngogola** le bolaile diruiwa.

....

Manku *a* **mono**, a bolawa ke sekaname.

....

Ditiro *tsa* **gompieno** le di fetseng.

....

Exercise 7.12

Can you give more examples of possessive concords prefixed to adverbs of time and place?

2.10 The possessive concords in idiomatic expressions

Motho **wa** bogolo ....

Mosadi **wa** Modimo ....

SELF-ASSESSMENT

1. Explain the terms **possessive** and **possessive construction** in your own words.
2. What is the function of the possessive construction?
3. Can the possessives be used in a qualificative sense?
4. Is the possessive concord derived from the possession or the possessor?
5. The possessive concords may appear before a number of word categories. Name these categories and give an example of each.
6. In what way does the structure of the following possessive construction differ from that of the other with nominal possessors?

    Mosese wa ga mme.
7. Name the singular, plural and communal possessive pronominal stems of the 1st, 2nd and 3rd person.
8. Name the constituents of the following possessive constructions:

    Ke metsi a pula a a ka thusang.

    Tsaya, o tlotse menwana ya leoto.
9. What would you say are the full forms of the following contracted possessive constructions?

    rangwanaa Motsei

    rakgadiagwe Pule.

CHAPTER 8

Interrogatives

OBJECTIVES

On completion of this chapter you should be able to:
1. explain the meaning of the term "interrogative";
2. explain the use of interrogatives as words belonging to different word categories;
3. identify interrogatives when occurring in a passage.

---

1. The meaning of the term *interrogative*

The interrogatives are a group of words by means of which statements may be changed to questions, e.g.

O a lwala   >   **A** o a lwala?

....

Ba a opela   >   Ba dira **eng**?[1]

....

Ba batla Modise   >   Ba batla **mang**?

....

Le tsere tse pedi   >   Le tsere **di le kae**?

....

Besides particular words that may be used to phrase interrogative sentences, one can change a statement into a question by simply raising the sentence intonation at the end of a sentence, e.g.

Mang? ....

Leng? ....

Ba gorogile? ....

Fa ba ka boa? ....

O bone mme? ....

1) *Cf. dictionary p. 20.*

2. The kinds of interrogatives

Sentences are composed of a number of word categories like **nouns, verbs, adverbs, adjectives,** etc. In order to communicate, the speaker sometimes needs **to ask questions about these word categories** when they are used by the second or a third person in a conversation.

Questions are asked for numerous reasons, e.g. disbelief, to ascertain a word which is not clearly pronounced, etc.

1. A: Ntate o batla *Papiso*. ....

   B: Wa re ntate o batla **mang**? ....

2. A: Ba ya toropong *ka moso*. ....

   B: Ba ya **leng** toropong? ....

3. A: Ke batla buka *e tala*. ....

   B: O batla buka ya mmala **ofe**? ....

4. A: Moagi o batla matlapa *a a kana*. ....

   B: Moagi o batla matlapa **a a kae**? ....

Would you agree that the italicised interrogatives ask questions pertaining to a number of different word categories, e.g.

- In sentence 1 a question is asked about a noun, *Papiso*, by means of an interrogative noun **mang?**
- In sentence 2 a question is asked about an adverb of time, *ka moso*, by means of an interrogative adverb **leng?**
- In sentence 3 a question is asked about an adjective, *e tala*, by means of an interrogative enumerative **ofe?**
- In sentence 4 a question is asked about a relative construction, *a a kana*, by means of an interrogative relative construction **a a kae?**.

One can therefore conclude that **different kinds of interrogatives** are used to phrase questions about **different kinds of words** in a sentence.

Let us now take a closer look at the different kinds of interrogatives.

2.1 The nominal roots *mang, -káe* and *-kaé*

2.1.1 The root **mang**[2]

The word **mang** is a noun and it can be used in **statements** as well as in **interrogatives**, e.g.

2) *Cf. dictionary p. 91.*

76

(i) Ke itse gore o batla **mang**. ....

(ii) Monna, wena o batla **mang**? ....

(iii) Ke setlhare **mang** se ba se remang?

....

(iv) Wena **o mang**? ....

(v) Ga ke itse gore **ke mang**. ....

(vi) **Ke bômang**, batho bale? ....

From these sentences it is clear that **mang** and **bômang** are used to state or to establish the **identity** of a person or persons. In sentences (iv) – (vi) they are used as part of the **identifying** copulative, i.e. **ke**. In sentence (iii) **mang** is used together with the noun **setlhare**. Whenever the noun **mang** is used in conjunction with another noun it expresses the meaning of "what kind", e.g.

Selo se, ke phologolo **mang**?

....

Ga ke itse gore ke nonyane **mang** eo.

....

The idiomatic expression:

Ke nako **mang**? ....

could also be grouped with these examples.

The following application of **mang** together with the connective prefix **le** is also noteworthy:

Mang **le** mang a ka tla go rapela. ....

Exercise 8.1

You should now try to give your own examples of interrogatives with the nominal root **mang**.

2.1.2 The root **-káe**[3]

The nominal root **-káe**, note the tone, can be used in **statements** as well as in **interrogatives**. The use of this root is furthermore restricted to a few noun class prefixes, viz. **bo-, mo- ba-** and **se-**, e.g.

---

3) *Cf. dictionary p. 54.*

Ga ke itse gore ke reke **bo**kae jwa nku.

....

Ba mo abetse **bo**kae jwa kgomo?

....

Ga ke itse gore wena o **mo**kae.

....

Batho ba ba nnang mono, ke **ba**kae?

....

Ke ba reeditse, mme ga ke itse gore ba bua **se**kae.

....

A dijo tse di monate! O ne o apeile **se**kae?

....

Exercise 8.2

*Can you give more examples of the use of the nominal root -**káe**?*

2.1.3 The root -**kaé**[4]

The nominal root -**kaé**, note the tone, can be used in **statements** as well as in **interrogatives**. The use of this root is furthermore restricted to two noun classes, viz. **bo-** and **di-**, e.g.

Ke tla ba botsa gore ba batla **bo**kae.

....

Sukiri ya lona e ja **bo**kae?

....

Ba laetswe gore ba boe ka **di**kae?

....

A o itse gore ke **di**kae gompieno?

....

Exercise 8.3

*Can you form your own practical examples illustrating the use of the nominal root -**kaé**?*

4) *Cf. dictionary p. 54.*

2.2 The enumerative -*ng*[5]

1. The root -*ng* nowadays only occurs with a few noun class prefixes in forming **statements** as well as **interrogatives**, e.g.

    (i) Ngwana ke ***mong***?

....

   (ii) Ga ke itse gore ba batla **eng**[6] (***batlang***)

....

  (iii) Dinaka tse ke tsa **eng**? (***tsang***)

....

  (iv) Ke bana ***bang*** bao?

....

   (v) Ke **eng**?

....

  (vi) A o itse ***bong*** jwa ngwana yoo?

....

In the previous examples we have witnessed the use of the root -*ng* in the ***mo- ba-, bo-*** and ***N- diN-*** classes.

From these sentences it is also clear that the root -*ng* is used to profess knowledge or to ask about information about the "being" of an object. Hence the frequent use of the identifying copulative ***ke***.

The root -*ng* can be used to enquire about the **colour** or **sex** of animals, e.g.

 (vii) Namane e e tsetsweng e ***tsiang***?

....

(viii) Kgomo e e suleng e ***jabang***?

....

Example (vii) enquires about the colour, but as we have seen in Chapter 4, the answer will also include information about the sex, e.g.

    E thokwa ....

    E thokwana ....

5) *Cf. dictionary p. 103.*
6) *Cf. dictionary p. 20.*

Example (viii) only enquires about the sex and the answer will be:

E namagadi ....

E tonanyana ....

Exercise 8.4

Can you give more examples of the use of the enumerative -ng as an interrogative?

2. The following application of **eng** together with the connective prefix **le** is also noteworthy:

O ka dirisa *eng* **le** *eng* go thiba phatla.

....

3. The root **-ng**, when used after a verb as **eng**, can appear in the full form, e.g.

Ba batla **eng**?
O dira **eng**?

This full form is commonly used when the question is asked with a measure of annoyance. The elided form **-ng** is more commonly used for unemphasised questions and is written conjunctively, e.g.

Ba batla**ng**? ....

O dira**ng**? ....

This alternation between **-ng** and **eng** is also to be seen in the interrogative construction asking about the comparative size, length, thickness or amount (i.e. how much) of something. In less emphatic questions the elided form is more popular, e.g.

Letlapa leo le **kana ka**ng?

....

Ke kgole e e **kana ka**ng e e neng e tlhaela?

....

Buka ya me e kima, ya gago e **kana ka**ng?

....

Peterolo e **kana ka**ng mo tankeng eo?

....

Besides the interrogative use of **kana kang** there is of course its use in statements, e.g.

Ga ke itse gore letlapa leo le **kana kang**.

....

Mmotse gore kgole e e tlhaelang e **kana kang**.

....

This elided form also appears in **goreng**, which is formed by the infinitive **go**, the verb stem **-re** and -ng. The word **goreng**[7] can be used in **statements** as well as **interrogatives**, e.g.

Goreng o sa nkarabe?

....

Ga ke itse gore ke **goreng** o sa fetse.

....

2.3 The adverbs *leng, kae* and *jang*[8]

The words **leng, kae** and **jang** are adverbs and they can be used in **statements** as well as **interrogatives**, e.g.

Ga ke itse gore o tla tla **leng**.

....

Ba tla fetsa tiro **leng**?

....

Ke tla mmotsa gore madi a **kae**.

....

Rraagwe o ile **kae**?

....

Ke itse gore legodu le tsene **jang**.

....

O tla dira **jang** go nthusa?

....

7) *Cf. dictionary p. 40.*
8) *Cf. dictionary pp. 85, 54, 51.*

From these examples it is clear that:

(i) *leng* is an **adverb of time** which may be used to ascertain the **time** at which an action or process takes place.

(ii) *kae* is an **adverb of place** which may be used to ascertain the **place** at which an action or process takes place. (The tone of this adverb is *káe*.)

(iii) *jang* is an **adverb of manner** which may be used to ascertain the **manner** in which an action or process takes place.

The following application of these adverbs with the connective prefix *le* is noteworthy:

Ka moso o ka tla *leng* **le** *leng*, o tla re fitlhela.

....

Re batlile *kae* **le** *kae*, ga re bone sepe.

....

O ka ganela *jang* **le** *jang*, ga re dumele se o se buang.

....

In the case of **kae** you will find that it also takes the locative prefixes *fa,* *kwa* and *mo*, e.g.

Ba eme *fa* kae? ....

Lo ya **kwa** kae? ....

O se beile **mo** kae? ....

To conclude with the adverbial interrogatives, mention should be made of the idiomatic expression used to enquire about a person's health, i.e.

O **kae** rra? ....

Exercise 8.5

*You should now give your own examples to gain experience in the use of the adverbs **leng, kae** and **jang**.*

2.4 The root -kaé[9]

The root **-kaé** occurs in quite a number of word categories where it can be used in **statements** and **interrogatives**.

9) *Cf. dictionary p. 54.*

2.4.1 The root -**kaé** in relative constructions

This root can be used in relative constructions to phrase questions about size, thickness, length or amount (i.e. how much), e.g.

Moagi o batla matlapa **a a** kae?

....

The answer to this question can be:

O batla matlapa **a a** kana le **a a** kalo.

....

In this sentence, as you can see, the roots **kana** and **kalo** are used demonstratively as relative constructions. The root -**kaé**, in this application, is used interrogatively as a relative root.

Exercise 8.6

*You should now give examples of your own to gain experience in the use of the root -**kaé** in relative constructions.*

2.4.2 The root -**kaé** in adjective constructions

This root can be used in adjective constructions to phrase questions about number (i.e. how many), e.g.

Moagi o batla matlapa **a ma**kae?

....

The answer to this question can be:

O batla matlapa **a ma**kana le **a ma**kalo *(i.e. showing the numbers).*

....

In the preceding example, as is evident, the roots -**kana** and -**kalo** are used demonstratively as adjective constructions. The root -**kaé**, in this section, is used interrogatively as an adjectival root.

Exercise 8.7

*You should now attempt to give more examples of the use of the root -**kaé** in adjectival constructions.*

2.4.3 The root -**kaé** in copular constructions

This root can be used in descriptive copular constructions to phrase questions about:

(i) size, thickness, length or amount (i.e. how much), e.g.

Moagi o batla matlapa **a** *kae?*

....

The answer to this question can be:

Moagi o batla matlapa **a** *kana* le **a** *kalo.*

....

(ii) number (i.e. what number or how many), e.g.

Matlapa ao, **a ma***kae?* ....

The answer to this question can be:

Matlapa a, **a ma***kana.* ....

In the preceding examples, as was shown, the root -**kana** was used in descriptive copular constructions. The root -**kaé**, in this section, is also used in descriptive copular constructions.
   The following idiomatic application of -**kaé** is noteworthy.

Malome o na le dikgomo **di se** *kae.*

....

Exercise 8.8

*You should now give examples of your own to gain experience in the use of the root -***kae*** in copular constructions.*

2.4.4 The root -**kaé** in the possessive construction

In possessive constructions this root can phrase a question about the number in a sequence (Afr. "die hoeveelste"), e.g.

Ke kgomo **ya bo***kae* e ntse e feta fa?

....

The answer to this question can be:

Ke kgomo **ya** *boraro.* ....

Exercise 8.9

You should now attempt to give more examples of the use of the root *-kaé* in the possessive construction.

2.5 The enumerative root *-fe*

The enumerative root *-fe* can be used in **statements** as well as in **interrogatives**, e.g.

Ke tla ba botsa gore ba batla *sefe*.[10]

....

Ntate, o batla thipa *efe?*

....

A great number of possible answers can be given to this question, e.g.

Adjective: Ngwanaka, ke batla e ntšhwa.

....

Relative: Ngwanaka, ke batla e e bogale.

....

Relative: Ngwanaka, ke batla e e looditsweng.

....

Possessive: Ngwanaka, ke batla ya me.

....

Enumerative: Ngwanaka, ga ke batle epe.

....

This demonstrates that the enumerative *-fe* can be used to phrase questions about the qualificatives.

Exercise 8.10

You should now attempt to give examples of the use of the enumerative root *-fe* in interrogatives as well as statements.

2.6 The conjunctives *a* and *naa* or *naare*[11]

2.6.1 The conjunctive *a*

The word *a* is a conjunctive and it can be used in **statements** as well as in **interrogatives**, e.g.

10) Cf. dictionary p. 149.
11) Cf. dictionary pp. 1, 100.

Ga ke itse gore **a** ba go senyeditse.

....

A go riana ga o dumele se ke se begileng?

....

In the first of these two sentences the conjunctive application of **a** is clearly illustrated. The interrogative function of **a** is aimed at the predicate of the sentence, e.g.

Ba a opela   >   **A** ba a opela?

....

Tsamaya!   >   **A** o a tsamaya?

....

Mosimane o rata dimonamone   >   **A** mosimane o rata dimonamone?

....

Exercise 8.11

*You should now attempt to give your own examples of the use of the conjunctive **a**.*

2.6.2 The conjunctive **naa** or **naare**

The word **naa** or **naare** is a conjunction and it can be used in **statements** as well as in **interrogatives**, e.g.

Ke tla tlhomamisa gore a ba a go itse **naa**.

....

Ga ke itse gore a ba tla go thusa **naare.**

....

Naa motho yole o ile kae?

....

Naare o mang? ....

From these examples it is clear that **naa** and **naare** are used with other interrogatives like **a, kae** and **mang** thus emphasising the question.

These words may however be used in sentences that do not contain another interrogative. In these instances they serve as an alternative for **a** but they are more emphatic than **a**, e.g.

Naa ga o ise o fetse? ....

Naare o mo fitlhetse? ....

Naa o Pule? ....

Exercise 8.12

*You should now attempt to give your own examples of the use of the conjunctives **naa** and/or **naare** as interrogatives.*

SELF-ASSESSMENT

1. Explain the term "interrogative" in your own words.
2. To what word categories do the following words and roots belong?

   leng   jang

   -fe   a

   káe   naare
3. The root **-kaé** can appear in a number of word categories. Name them and give examples.
4. Can interrogatives be used in statements? If so, make a survey of the situation in this and the preceding lesson on interrogatives.
5. Would you agree that there are **different interrogatives** that can be used to clear up uncertainties about **any word** appearing in a sentence?
6. Can interrogatives be expressed by changing the intonation of sentences?
7. To what word categories do the roots **mang, -káe, -kaé** and **-ng** belong?
8. With which of the roots in 7 above can the identifying copulative **ke** be used?
9. What is implied with the term "interrogative"?
10. To what word categories do the interrogatives in the following sentences belong?
    (i) Motabogi o tshotse mong?
    (ii) Ntate o re reketse bokae jwa nku?
    (iii) Re ya go simolola kgaisano leng?
    (iv) Banna bao ba re ba batla mang?
    (v) Basetsana bao ba a bo ba ile kae?
    (vi) Mmotorokara ona o ja bokae?

87

(vii) Go tlile jang gore a go fore?
(viii) Matlapa ao, o a batlang, a kaé?
(ix) Noga e tsene mo káe?
(x) Ke semonamone sa bokae o se ja?
(xi) Nka go neela buka dife?
(xii) Mesese eo, e mekae?
(xiii) O batla matlapa a a kae?
(xiv) A o a mo itse naa?
(xv) Naa ba ile?

CHAPTER 9

Verbs

OBJECTIVES

On completion of this chapter you should be able to:
1. explain the meaning of the term "verb";
2. describe the structure of verbs;
3. identify the prefixal verb structures when used in a paragraph;
4. explain the meaning of the term "adopted verbs."

---

1. The meaning of the term *verb*

Would you agree that the italicised elements of the following sentences are verbs and that they denote a process or action?

Barutwana **ba dirisa**[1] dibuka. ....

Ditlhare **di a tlhoga**. ....

Monna **o besa** dikgong. ....

Ntate **o a di batla**, dibuka tseo.

....

The verb is therefore the word expressing:

(i) the process or action performed by the subject, e.g.

Pula **e a na**. ....

Banna **ba tla lema**. ....

(ii) the action undergone by the object, e.g.

Banna **ba tla lema** tshimo. ....

Monna **o besa** dikgong. ....

Verbs that **imply** an object or actually **take** an object are called **transitive verbs**, e.g.

1) *Cf. dictionary p. 18.*

Ntate *o a rema*. ....

Ntate *o rema* setlhare. ....

Rona *re a bala*. ....

Rona *re bala* buka. ....

In the case of transitive verbs, the action is therefore carried over on the implied object or on the actual object.

Verbs that only denote a process without requiring an object are called **intransitive verbs**, e.g.

Mmemogolo *o a lwala*. ....

Barutwana *ba a tlhalefa*. ....

2. Verbal structures

All verbal structures are built up **around** the **verbal root** which is the part printed in bold in the following italicised verbs:

Malome *o a* **gam***a*. ....

Malome *o* **gam***a* leradu. ....

Malome *o a le* **gam***a* leradu. ....

Leradu *le* **gam***elelwa* ntate kwa sakeng.

....

The -*a* in the preceding examples is a **verbal ending** and is discussed in section 2.1.1.

It is not always this easy to identify the verbal root. The reason is that some consonant sounds are written with more than one symbol, e.g.

tl	*tsh*	*tshw*
kh	*kgw*	*jw*

In the following examples the roots are once more represented by the parts printed in bold italics, e.g.

Mosimane o ***tlats***a kgamelo ....

Mosadi o ***tshwar***a koko ....

Mosetsana o ***tlhatsw***a diaparo ....

Monna o ***jwal***a mmidi ....

90

Monosyllabic verbs pose a different problem because in their case the verbal root consists of a consonant only, e.g.

Mosimane o *ja* bogobe ....

Mosadi o *ga* metsi ....

Tshaba! Setlhare *se a wa* ....

Naga *e a šwa* ....

Some verbal roots on the other hand commence with vowels, e.g.

Mosimane o **araba** rraagwe ....

Ntšwa *e* **utlwa** sengwe ....

Mmotorokara o **ema** mo tseleng ....

Ntate o **epa** mosima ....

In your dictionary the **uninflected form** of the verb **is not** followed by abbreviations like *perf, caus, appl, pass, neut,* etc. (see section 2.1.2).

An example of this kind is to be found on p. 20 of your dictionary, viz.

ema ....

emela *appl* ....

emisa *caus* ....

emetse *perf* ....

Exercise 9.1

By first looking up the uninflected form of a verb stem you should now have no difficulty in identifying twenty verbal roots.

2.1 Verbal prefixes

The bold italicised morphemes to the **left** of the **root** are called **prefixes**, e.g.

o a *gama* ....

o a le *gama* ....

The verb has quite a number of verbal prefixes. The verbal prefixes are **mostly** written **disjunctively. Only three** kinds, as you will observe later on in this chapter, are written **conjunctively.**

91

The verbal prefixes consist of the following:

2.1.1 Present tense **a**[2)]

This prefix is used when the process or action of the verb is in the present tense, e.g.

Bana ba **a** tshameka. ....

Makolwane a **a** e ja, nama. ....

This structure of the verb is called the **long form** of the present tense.

Exercise 9.2

You should now attempt to use the long form of the present tense in similar sentences.

2.1.2 The future tense **tla**[3)]

This prefix denotes a process or an action that will take place in the future, e.g.

Bana ba **tla** tshameka. ....

Makolwane a **tla** e ja, nama. ....

Exercise 9.3

You should now attempt to use the prefix **tla** in sentences of your own.

2.1.3 Negatives **ga, sa** and **se**[4)]

These prefixes are used to form negatives in different moods, e.g.

(a) **Indicative mood**[5)]

Lekgarebe le a kgaba   > Lekgarebe **ga** le kgabe.

....

(b) **Participial mood**

Fa a goroga, o tla itse   > Fa a **sa** goroge, o tla itse.

....

2) Cf. dictionary p. 1.
3) Cf. dictionary p. 173.
4) Cf. dictionary pp. 29, 147, 149.
5) The concept mood is explained in Chapter 11.

(c) **Imperative mood**

Tsamaya!   > **Se** tsamaye!

....

Exercise 9.4

*You should now attempt to give your own examples of the negation of verbs by means of the prefixes **ga, sa** and **se**.*

2.1.4 Reflexive **i-**[6]

This **conjunctively written** prefix usually appears immediately next to the verbal root, e.g.

Bona *ba tla **i**thapisa*. ....

The objectival concord of the 1st person may appear between the reflexive and the verb stem and is also written conjunctively, e.g.

Ke rapela gore *o **i**ntshwarele*.

....

Exercise 9.5

*You should now attempt to give your own examples of these two applications of the reflexive **i-**.*

2.1.5 Progressive **sa**[7]

This prefix denotes a continued process or action, e.g.

Bana *ba **sa** robetse*. ....

Bana *ba **sa** ntse ba robetse*. ....

Exercise 9.6

*You should now give your own examples of the progressive **sa**.*

2.1.6 Potential **ka**[8]

This prefix denotes that a process or action can or may take place, e.g.

Nonyane *e **ka** fofa*. ....

Ngwanaka, *o **ka** ya jaanong*. ....

6) *Cf. dictionary Preface par. 4.*
7) *Cf. dictionary p. 147.*
8) *Cf. dictionary p. 53.*

Exercise 9.7

You should now attempt to form your own sentences containing the potential prefix.

2.1.7 Subjectival concords

The subjectival concords of the **1st and 2nd persons** are derived from the absolute pronouns used as subjects, e.g.

Nna **ke**[9] *ya gae.* ....

Lona **lo**[10] *dira eng?* ....

The full list of these subjectival concords is:

	SINGULAR		PLURAL	
	Abs. pron.	Subj. concord	Abs. pron.	Subj. concord
1st person	Nna	*ke*	Rona	*re*
2nd person	Wena	*o*	Lona	*lo*

The subjectival concords of the **3rd person** are derived from the class prefix of a subject, e.g.

Segole **se** *tlhoka madi.* ....

Basadi **ba** *tlhoka madi.* ....

The full list of these subjectival concords is:

SINGULAR		PLURAL	
Class prefix	Subj. concord	Class prefix	Subj. concord
mo-	*o*	ba-	*ba*
—	*o*	bô-	*ba*
mo-	*o*	me-	*e*
le-	*le*	ma-	*a*
se-	*se*	di-	*di*
N-	*e*	diN-	*di*
lo-	*lo*	diN-	*di*
bo-	*bo*	ma-	*a*
go	*go*		
fa-			
go- }	*go*		
mo-			

9) *Cf. dictionary p. 58.*
10) *Cf. dictionary p. 87.*

Exercise 9.8

By using the dictionary, you should now find an example (singular and plural) of each of the noun classes and then derive their appropriate subjectival concords.

2.1.8 Objectival concords

The objectival concords of the **1st and 2nd persons** are derived from the absolute pronouns used as objects, e.g.

Ntate *o a go bitsa*, wena. ....

Nna, bagaetsho *ba a ntirela.* ....

	SINGULAR		PLURAL	
	Abs. pron.	Obj. concord	Abs. pron.	Obj. concord
1st person 2nd person	Nna Wena	*n-* or *m-*[11] *go*	Rona Lona	*re* *lo*

The **conjunctively written** concords of the 1st person singular assimilate with the first consonant of the verb stem, e.g.

Nna *ba tla mpetsa.*

....

Bomme *ba tla nkaraba,* nna.

....

The objectival concords of the 3rd person are derived from the class prefix of an object, e.g.

Mothudi *o se baakantse* setswalo se.

....

Mapodisa *ba tla mmatla,* mosimane yoo.

....

Mapodisa ba tla *mo* tshwara, mosimane yoo.

....

11) *Cf. dictionary pp. 90, 99.*

The objectival concord of the 3rd person singular is **mo-** and it may assimilate to the **conjunctively written m-** if the first letter of a verb stem commences with **b-**, e.g.

Ke *tla **mo** bitsa*, mosimane > Ke *tla **m**mitsa*, mosimane.

The full list of the objectival concords is:

SINGULAR		PLURAL	
Class prefix	Obj. concord	Class prefix	Obj. concord
mo-	*mo* or *m-*	ba-	*ba*
—	*mo* or *m-*	bô-	*ba*
mo-	*o*	me-	*e*
le-	*le*	ma-	*a*
se-	*se*	di-	*di*
N-	*e*	diN-	*di*
lo-	*lo*	diN-	*di*
bo-	*bo*	ma-	*a*
go	*go*		
fa- ⎫			
go- ⎬	*go*		
mo- ⎭			

Exercise 9.9

(a) *By using the dictionary, you should now find your own examples (singular and plural) of each of the noun classes and then derive their appropriate objectival concords.*

(b) *Can you identify and name the abovementioned* **eight** *kinds of verbal prefixes in the following examples?*

Bojalwa bo ka se tlogelwe fana!
Kgosi e sa ntse e le laya, lekgotla.
Ke tla le ikwalela, lekwalo leo.
Mme o a lwala.

2.2 Verbal suffixes[12]

The morphemes to the **right** of the **root** are called suffixes, e.g.

12) *Cf. dictionary Preface par. 3.*

Leradu *le gamelelwa* ntate kwa sakeng.

....

Ntate *o gamisa* basimane ba ba tshabang.

....

The verb has quite a number of **conjunctively written** suffixes. They are known by different names like *ending, extension, imperative -ng* and the *relative -ng*.

2.2.1 Verbal ending

The **root** plus the **ending** of one of the moods (see Chapter 11) gives us **a verbal stem**, e.g.

root + ending = stem

bits- + *-a*   = bitsa, e.g. Mogokgo *o bitsa* wena.

....

kwal-+ *-e*   = kwale, e.g. Bana *ga ba kwale* sepe.

....

seny-+ *-ê*   = senyê, e.g. Satane o batla gore *re senyê*.

....

Verb stems may be reduplicated **in full** or **partly** giving the significance of repeated, careless or actions performed on a small scale, e.g.

tlola   >   ***tlolatlola***[13] ....

gasa   >   ***gasagasa*** ....

ja   >   ***jaaja*** ....

wa   >   ***waawa*** ....

tsamaya >   ***tsamatsamaya*** ....

tlhanya >   ***tlhakatlhakanya*** ....

Exercise 9.10

*You should now be able to find **ten** verb stems listed in the dictionary and in each case you should be able to identify their endings.*

13) Cf. dictionary p. 187.

2.2.2 Extensions

These verbal suffixes appear **between the verbal root** and **one of the endings** and are called **verbal extensions**, e.g.

root + exten- + end- = stem
       sion   ing

kwal- + **-el-** + -a = kwal**el**a, e.g. Rona *re a mo kwalela.*

bon- + **-an-** + -e = bon**an**e, e.g. Basadi *ba bonane.*

rem- + **-il-** + -ê = rem**il**ê, e.g. Banna *ba remile.*

The following will serve as examples of verbal extensions:

1. NEUTER

This form of the verb denotes a subject that is entering or already is in a particular state or condition without mentioning the cause. The neuter can best be translated by means of the English "become". Alternatively the English suffixes "-ible" and "-able" account for the following neuter suffixes, e.g.

-êg-, -agal- and **-al-**, e.g.

senya > seny**eg**a ....

dira > dir**agal**a ....

bona > bon**al**a ....

Jaanong *go tlhokega* madi fela. ....

Thipa eo *e tla latlhega.* ....

2. APPLIED

This form of the verb is used to denote an action carried out on behalf of somebody, to the detriment of somebody or in the direction of somebody or a place. The following applied suffixes commonly occur, e.g.

-êl- and **-êts-**, e.g.

roma > rom**êl**a ....

besa > bes**êts**a ....

*Ke tla go kwal**ela** lekwalo.* ....

Bona! Ntšwa *e j**ela** ngwana.* ....

Ngwanaka, *tabog**ela** kwano!* ....

3. RECIPROCAL

This form of the verb is used to denote actions performed mutually by separate individuals. The English "each other" or "one another" is expressed by means of **-an-**, e.g.

utlwa > utlw**an**a. ....

rata > rat**an**a. ....

Fa dikokwana di timetse, *di a bits**ana**.* ....

4. REVERSIVE

This form of the verb signifies that the action denoted by the infinitive form of the verb is undone or reversed.
The suffixes of the reversive transitive are: **-ol-** and **-olol-**, e.g.

rwala > r**ol**a. ....

bofa > bof**olol**a. ....

Ntšwa *e ep**olol**a lerapo.* ....

The suffixes of the reversive intransitive are: **-og-** and **-olog-**, e.g.

tla > tl**og**a. ....

bofa > bof**olog**a. ....

Lerapo la ntšwa le gana *go ep**olog**a.* ....

5. CAUSATIVE

This form of the verb denotes that the subject causes or brings about the action. In English this can be rendered as "cause to do" or "make to do". The suffixes expressing the causative are: **-is-, -s-, -ts-, -tsh-** and **-y-**, e.g.

rema > rem**is**a. ....

tloga > tl**os**a. ....

fela	>	fe**ts**a.	....
bona	>	bon**tsh**a.	....
tsena	>	tsen**y**a.	....

Mafoko ao, *a gakgamatsa* batho. ....

6. PERFECT

This form of the verb denotes an action that has been completed and is expressed by means of the suffix **-il-**,

reka	>	rek**il**e.	....

Depending on their final syllables the perfect form of verbs may assume a number of suffixes, e.g.

robala	>	rob**ets**e.	....
gotlhola	>	gotlho**ts**e.	....
fufula	>	fufu**ts**e.	....
apaya	>	ape**il**e.	....
tshosa	>	tshos**its**e.	....
senya	>	sen**ts**e.	....
gana	>	gan**n**e.	....
kopana	>	kopa**ny**e.	....
apara	>	ap**er**e.	....

Pula e ne e gana go na. Maabane *e nele.*

....

7. PASSIVE

This form of the verb signifies that the subject undergoes the action of the verb and is expressed by means of the suffixes **-w-** and **-iw-**, e.g.

bona	>	bon**w**a.	....
besa	>	bes**iw**a.	....

Molelo *o gotsiwa* ke mang? ....

8. DENOMINATIVE

Verb stems can be derived from nominal and adjectival stems by the suffixation of *-f-* and *-fal-*. Denominatives can usually be translated as "become . . .", e.g.

bo*gale* .... > *galef*a ....

bo*leo* .... > *leof*a ....

ntsho .... > *ntshofal*a ....

le*sedi* .... > *sedifal*a ....

Fa letsatsi le phirima, *go a tsidifala.* ....

Exercise 9.11

You should now be able to consult your dictionary to find your own examples of verbs containing the different verbal extensions. You should also attempt to use your examples in practical sentences.

2.2.3 Imperative *-ng*

This suffix is required when a command is given to more than one person, e.g.

Taboga**ng** basimane! ....

Tlaya**ng** kwano balekana! ....

Exercise 9.12

Can you give examples of your own to illustrate the use of the imperative -ng?

2.2.4 Relative *-ng*

This suffix occurs in relative constructions qualifying subjects or objects of sentences, e.g.

Monna *yo o buang* ke malome.

....

Rrangwane ena, ke *yo o emeng* fale.

....

Exercise 9.13

Can you distinguish between the relative -ng and the imperative -ng? Illustrate the difference between the two by means of your own examples.

2.2.5 Deideophonic suffixes -la, -ga, -ma, -mela, -metsa and -sela

Verb stems are derived from ideophones by suffixing a number of suffixes, e.g.

IDEOPHONE	DEIDEOPHONIC VERB STEMS
dike!	> dike**la**[14] ....
kgothu!	> kgothu**ga** ....
phatsi!	> phatsi**ma** ....
khuru!	> khuru**mela** ....
nene!	> nene**sela** ....

Exercise 9.14

By consulting your dictionary you should be able to give more examples of deideophonic verb stems.

3. Adopted verbs

The verbs adopted into Tswana denote:

(a) new kinds of actions as well as
(b) familiar actions which have acquired new meanings, e.g.

(a) New actions

These words denote actions associated with European technology, e.g.

tipa[15] (dikgomo)	< dip	(A)
tipa (llori)	< tip	(E)
posa	< pos	(A)
kurufela	< inskroef	(A)

---

14) *Cf. dictionary p. 17.*
15) *Cf. dictionary p. 173.*

Exercise 9.15

Can you give more examples like these?

(b) **Familiar actions**
Although Tswana verbs exist for the following, the adopted words have a special meaning and therefore justify their inclusion in the language, e.g.

ORIGINAL WORD	ADOPTED WORD			
dira	bereka	....	< werk	(A)
thapa	hira	....	< huur	(A)
duela	patala	....	< betaal	(A)
fetolela	toloka	....	< tolk	(A)

Exercise 9.16

Can you give more examples like these?

4. The predicate

A predicative sentence normally consists of two main components, viz.

(i) a predicate denoting the action.

(ii) a subject performing the action.

The predicate is italicised in the following examples;

Monna *o a kwala.*

....

Monna *o kwala lokwalo.*

....

Monna *o kwala lokwalo jaanong.*

....

Monna *o kwala lokwalo lo loleele jaanong.*

....

Monna *o sa ntse a kwala lokwalo lo loleele.*

....

From these examples it is clear that the predicate can be simple or fairly extensive. What one should realise is that **the object of a sentence also forms an integral part of the predicate**. This is illustrated by the use of the objectival concord as a verbal prefix in the following example, e.g.

Monna *o sa ntse a* **lo** *kwala lokwalo lo loleele.*

The verb stem or perhaps the *verbal root* can be regarded as the element around which the predicate, as a syntactic element, is structured. In the abovementioned sentence the root is **-kwal-**.

SELF-ASSESSMENT

1. Explain the following concepts in your own words:
   (a) verb
   (b) transitive
   (c) intransitive
   (d) prefix
   (e) root
   (f) ending
   (g) stem
2. Explain the concept "suffix" in your own words and name five kinds of suffixes.
3. Give your own examples of a verb stem containing one of the extensions.
4. To what part of a sentence does the term predicate refer? Give examples.
5. Explain the concept "verb" in your own words.
6. Explain the term "prefix" and name eight kinds of prefixes.
7. In what way do transitive and intransitive verb stems differ in their use?
8. How are subjectival concords derived? Give examples of this derivation.
9. How are objectival concords derived? Give examples of this derivation.
10. Name the verbal prefixes that are written:
    (a) conjunctively;
    (b) disjunctively.
11. How is a verbal stem formed?
12. Identify and name the **suffixal** structural elements of the verbs in the following sentences:

   (i) Ga ke mo kwalele lokwalo.
  (ii) Dikeledi le Kabelo ba a ratana.
 (iii) Sukiri ga e utlwale mo kofing ena.
 (iv) Moruti o tla sokolola basiamolodi.
  (v) Kwa gae batho ba a tlhabologa.
 (vi) Ema pele! Ke sa ntse ke jesa ngwana.
 (vii) Kopi e ole, mme ga e a thubega.
(viii) Itlhaganeleng! Ke batla go tsamaya.
 (ix) A phamola thipa, a re phamo!
  (x) Legodu le tiketse, la re tike!

13. Rewrite the following sentences underlining the predicate.
    Motsomi o ratela tholo.
    Tholo ga e mmone.
    Motsomi o tsoma ka kobi le metsu.

14. Divide the following verb stems into:
  (a) transitive
  (b) intransitive

lema	bebenya	thula	opela
rora	boa	fala	rata
fenya	lala	bona	sia

15. Identify and name the **prefixal** structural elements of the verbs in the following sentences:
    (i) Fa o sa kgone, o kope thuso.
   (ii) Tau ga e bonale mo thlageng.
  (iii) Terena e ka go isa gae ka bonako.
  (iv) Batlhabani ba tla palamela mo godimo.
   (v) Se bofololeng ntšwa eo!
  (vi) Barutwana ba a se ithuta, Setswana.
 (vii) Batlhatlhobiwa ba sa ntse ba di kwala, ditlhamo.
(viii) Mo marigeng naga e a setlhafala.
  (ix) Baganani ba tla sokologa.
   (x) Bannabagolo ga ba rate morogano.

16. Adopted verbs were responsible for the derivation of a number of new deverbatives, e.g.
    moferefi < verf
Can you give more examples like these?

17. European technology introduced a new set of verbs. Give examples of these.

18. Familiar actions that acquired new meanings necessitated the adoption of new words, e.g.
    jwala – polanta < plant
Give more examples like these.

CHAPTER 10

Auxiliary verbs

OBJECTIVES

On completion of this chapter you should be able to:
1. explain the meaning of the term "auxiliary verb";
2. explain the difference between an auxiliary verb and a main verb;
3. identify examples of auxiliary verbs in a paragraph and explain the structure of compound predicates.

In the following sentences the predicate appears in *medium* and **bold** italic print. Would you agree that the part appearing in *medium italic print* adds to or expands the meaning of the part appearing in **bold italic print?**

(i) Monna *o ne*[1] ***a tsamaya*** ka bonako.

....

(ii) Tshwene *a bo* ***a phamola*** Mmutle.

....

(iii) Batho bao *ga ba kitla* **ba fetsa**.

....

(iv) Basimane *ga ba ise* **ba boe**.

....

(v) Nna *ke tle* ***ke etele*** mmemogolo.

....

(vi) Tsamayang! *Ke tla sala* **ke bala**.

....

(vii) Tumelo *o tlhola* ***a re tshwenya***.

....

1) *Cf. dictionary p. 102.*

(viii) Badiri *ba tloga **ba fetsa*** tiro.

....

(ix) Ngwanaka, *ga o a tshwanela **go dira*** jaana.

....

(x) *Re tsoga **re ya*** toropong.

....

Let us now evaluate the situation sentence by sentence:

  (i) *o ne* refers to the time of walking and therefore expands the meaning of the verb ***tsamaya***.
 (ii) *a bo* refers to the sequence of events and therefore expands the meaning of the verb ***phamola***.
(iii) *ga ba kitla* expresses the negation of the verb ***ba fetsa***.
 (iv) *ga ba ise* expresses the negation of the verb ***ba boe***.
  (v) *ke tle* refers to the occasional performance of the verb ***ke etele***.
 (vi) *ke tla sala* refers to the continued performance of the verb ***ke bala***.
(vii) *o tlhola* refers to the continued performance of the verb ***a re tshwenya***.
(viii) *ba tloga* refers to the time at which the verb ***ba fetsa*** will take place.
 (ix) *ga o a tshwanela* refers to the way things ought not be done.
  (x) *re tsoga* refers to the time at which the verb ***re ya*** will take place.

The words printed in medium italics in the preceding examples add shades of meanings to the basic meanings of the main verbs. These words in medium italics are called **auxiliary verbs** and they precede the **main** or **complementary verbs** which appear as the words in bold italic type. Together the auxiliary and the main verb form **a compound verb**.

The auxiliary verbs can be divided into two groups of stems, viz. those that can:

(a) usually function together with a main or complementary verb, as in the case of examples (i) – (v);
(b) function together with a main verb or independently as a verb as in the case of examples (vi) – (x).

The following examples will illustrate the use of the medium italicised verb stems in (vi) – (x) as independent verbs:

107

Tsamayang! *Ke tla sala* fa.

....

Tumelo *o tlhola* mo gae.

....

Badiri *ba tloga* phakela.

....

Ngwanaka, *ga o a tshwanela* mosimane ole.

....

Re tsoga phakela.

....

When verb stems like these are used as auxiliaries they perform the functions of auxiliaries in the full sense of the word. Both groups of auxiliary verbs are characterised by the following:

(i) They are dependent and do not constitute complete predicates, e.g.

Monna *o setse* ....

Mosadi *o tlhola* ....

Bathusi *ba bo* ....

Tau *e batlile* ....

(ii) The auxiliary verbs are seldom used alone. They are commonly followed by a main verb to complete the predication. This main verb functions as a **complement** and together with the auxiliary verb it forms a **compound predicate**, e.g.

Monna *o setse **a ile.***

....

Mosadi *o tlhola **a bopa*** nkgwana.

....

Bathusi *ba bo **ba fetsa*** tiro.

....

Tau *e batlile **go tswara*** pitse ya me.

....

We can now proceed to the discussion of the two types of auxiliary verbs, viz. those that can:

(a) usually function together with a main or complementary verb and they are called the **original auxiliary verbs**;
(b) function as auxiliary verbs but which also have the function of an independent verb — this group is also known as **deficient verbs** or **derived auxiliary verbs**.

1. Original auxiliary verbs

This group of auxiliary verbs will now be discussed in terms of their:

(a) morphological characteristics;
(b) semantic function;
(c) syntactic position.

In order to facilitate our discussion you will now be provided with a list of original auxiliary verbs. You will notice that they do not resemble any independent verb.

ba	bisa	ke	nte
be	ise	kile	ne
bo	kitla	ka	tle
bile	kete	mmê	
bolo	kê	mpa	

Exercise 10.1

You should now look up these original auxiliary verbs in your dictionary to get examples of their use.

1.1 The morphology of original auxiliary verbs

At a first glance it is obvious that this list of original auxiliary verbs differs from independent verbs. The original auxiliary verbs end in a number of vowels while the basic form of verb stems ends in **-a** only, e.g. *go dira*.

1.1.1 The use of subjectival concords

Like ordinary verbs, the auxiliary verbs require the use of subjectival concords. In the following examples these concords appear in **bold italics** while the stems of the auxiliary verbs appear in *medium italics*. The subjectival concord of the auxiliary verb is usually repeated in the structure of the main verb or complement, e.g.

(i) Bona! Noga *e* *ne* *e* kgabaganya fa.

....

(ii) Ga *ba* *ise* *ba* fetse.

....

(iii) Rangwane *a* *bo* *a* mmitsa.

....

(iv) Ga *ba* *kitla* *ba* feta ke sa ba bone.

....

(v) Rona *re* *tle* *re* ye toropong fa gare ga beke.

....

Exercise 10.2

Select five auxiliary verb stems from the list above and use them to illustrate the use of the subjectival concords.

In the case of the auxiliary verb stem you should note that the invariable (indefinite) subjectival concord *e*[2] is sometimes used, e.g.

Monna, *e* *kete* ga *o* nkutlwe.

....

1.1.2 The use of the suffix *-ng* of the relative construction

The suffix *-ng* of the relative construction forms subordinate clauses and they appear in complex sentences, e.g.

Monna *yo* *o* *buang*, ke ntate.

....

When the subordinate clause also contains an auxiliary verb, **the whole compound predicate** is part of the subordinate clause, e.g.

2) *Cf. dictionary p. 19.*

110

Monna **yo o neng a bua**, ke ntate.

....

Exercise 10.3

Can you recognise the subordinate clauses in these examples?

(i) Batho *ba ba kileng ba nna fa*, ba ne ba aga lebotana le.

(ii) Ngwano *yo o se kitlang a bala*, ga a ka ke a falola.

(iii) Wena *yo o tleng o ba thuse*, ga o lalediwe.

(iv) Kgosi *e e neng e busa*, ke mang?

(v) *Ba ba iseng ba leme*, ga ba ye go kotula.

Exercise 10.4

Select five auxiliary verb stems from the list in 1 above and use them to illustrate the use of the verbal relative -**ng** in subordinate clauses.

1.1.3 The expression of negatives by means of the negative prefixes **sa, se** and **ga**

In the case of **sa** and **se** the negative prefixes occur **between** the subjectival concord and the auxiliary verb stem, e.g.

(i) Batho bao *ba se kile* ba lema, ka jalo ga ba na dijo.

(ii) Molwetse *a se ka* a robala.

In the case of **ga** the negative prefix **ga** precedes the subjectival concord of the auxiliary verb, e.g.

Ga *ba kitla* ba re thusa.

In the case of a few auxiliary stems the negative prefix **sa cannot** enter the structure of the auxiliary verb and the main or complementary verb is used to express the negation, e.g.

Bana *ba ne* ba **sa** tlhaloganye.

Tau *a bo* a **sa** kgone tiro eo.

Exercise 10.5

Select five auxiliary verb stems from the list in 1 above and form sentences representative of the different negative structures that have been illustrated.

1.1.4 The use of the future prefix **tla**

This prefix occurs **between** the subjectival concord and the auxiliary verb stem, e.g.

Ka nako eo, *ke **tla** bo* ke feditse.

*Lo **tla** mpa* lwa boa go re thusa.

Exercise 10.6

*Select five auxiliary verb stems from the list in 1 above and use them in examples to illustrate the use of the future prefix **tla**.*

1.1.5 The use of the potential aspectual prefix **ka**

This prefix occurs **between** the subjectival concord and the auxiliary verb stem, e.g.

Ba feta *ba **ka** kete* ga ba mpone.

*Re **ka** mma* ra ya gae jaanong.

Exercise 10.7

*Select five auxiliary verb stems from the list in 1 above and use them in examples to illustrate the use of the potential aspectual prefix **ka.***

1.1.6 The use of the present tense prefix **a**

In conjunction with auxiliary verbs this prefix forms "the long form" of the auxiliary predicate, e.g.

Monna, *o bo* o dirang?

....

Monna, *o **a** bo* o dirang?

....

Re ne re gama dipodi.

....

*Re **a** ne* re gama dipodi.

....

Exercise 10.8

*Select five auxiliary verb stems from the list in 1 above and use them to illustrate the use of the present tense prefix **a.***

SELF-ASSESSMENT

1. Identify the types of auxiliary verbs appearing in the following:

   (i) Mosimane o ne a wa ka mpa ya sebete.

   ....

   (ii) Radinku ga a kitla a tlhaloganya dipalo.

   ....

   (iii) Raselokwane ga a ise a gorose dikgomo.

   ....

   (iv) Rapula o tlhola a tshameka le bana.

   ....

113

(v) Mmule o tsoga a ya sepetlele.

....

(vi) Mpotokwe ga a a tshwanela go tlhapatsa batho.

....

2. Identify the structural elements of the auxiliaries appearing in the following:
   (i) A ga ba ise ba wetse dikgang tsa bona le monna yo o buang bobe yole?
   (ii) Modise a se ka a goa.
   (iii) Re tla mpa re boeletsa ditlhatlhobo.
   (iv) Re tla mpa re boeletsa ditlhatlhobo gonne barutwana ba ne ba sa tlhaloganye.
   (v) Re ka mpa ra ba okeletsa maduo.
3. What is the function of auxiliary verbs in a sentence?
4. Is the auxiliary verb independent?
5. What is the verb called which follows on an auxiliary verb?
6. Name the two kinds of auxiliary verbs that have been distinguished.
7. Name four prefixes that may enter the structure of the compound predicate.

1.2 The semantic function of original auxiliary verbs

The meanings conveyed by the original auxiliary verbs are difficult to classify into specific categories. For the purposes of this section we will concentrate on the role of the auxiliary verb when expanding the meaning of the main verb in terms of the:

(a) time of the action or process.
(b) negation of the action or process.
(c) expression of the hortative.
(d) expression of conjunctives.

1.2.1 The time of the action or process

Some auxiliary verbs that expand the meaning of the main verb in terms of time are the following:

Ga *ba kitla* **ba boa** gompieno.

....

Ntate *o kile* **a ya** Gauteng.

....

114

*O ne **a tsaya** thipa a bo **a itshegela.***

....

*Ka ba **ka reka** nama ka boa.*

....

Exercise 10.9

Can you give more examples of auxiliary verbs expanding the meaning of the main verb in terms of time?

1.2.2 The negation of the action or process

A number of auxiliaries have an inherent negative connotation, e.g.

*Go bisa **go itse** dithuto go kotsi.*

....

*Ga ba ka ke **ba re duela.***

....

*Ga re kitla **re dumelana.***

....

*Ga e ise **e swe**, kgomo eo.*

....

*Ga ba bolo **go tla.***

....

Exercise 10.10

Can you give more examples of auxiliary verbs expanding the meaning of the main verb in terms of negation?

1.2.3 The expression of the hortative

The hortative refers to expression of pleas, supplications and requests, e.g.

*A re nke **re mo tseise.***

....

*Ntate, o mme **o nne** fa.*

....

A *re nte* **re mo etele.**

....

Ba ka mpa **ba tsamaya.**

....

Exercise 10.11

Can you give more examples of auxiliary verbs expressing the hortative?

1.2.4 The expression of conjunctives

Some original auxiliary verbs can be used as conjunctives between independent sentences, e.g.

(i) Monna a tsaya selepe. Monna a palama kariki. Monna a ya kgonnye.

....

These sentences can be joined by means of the auxiliary verb, **ba**, e.g.

(ii) Monna a tsaya selepe *a* **ba** a palama kariki *a* **ba** a ya kgonnye.

....

Another example of the expression of conjunctives can be seen in:

(iii) Nna ke ratana le Montle. Ke ya go mo nyala.

....

These independent sentences can be joined by means of the auxiliary stem **bile**. You will notice that **bile** may be preceded by either the subjectival concord **ke** or the invariable subjectival concord **e**, e.g.

(iv) Nna ke ratana le Montle *ke* **bile** ke ya go mo nyala.

....

(v) Nna ke ratana le Montle *e* **bile** ke ya go mo nyala.

....

Exercise 10.12

Can you give more examples of original auxiliary verbs used as conjunctives?

116

1.3 The syntactic position of original auxiliary verbs

The syntactic position assumed by the original auxiliary verb stem in the compound predicate, is before (i.e. to the left of) the main verb or complement, e.g.

(i) Pule *o ne* **a feta** fa. ....

(ii) Mosadi *a bo* **a kwala** lekwalo.

....

More than one auxiliary verb stem may be used in such a compound predicate, e.g.

(iii) Pule *o ne a ise a ke* **a fete** fa.

....

As you can see, this compound predicate contains the auxiliary stems **ne, ise** and **ke.** The next sentence also contains a compound predicate with more than one auxiliary verb stem, e.g.

(iv) Mosadi *o ne a ise a ke a bo* **a kwale** lekwalo.
        (i)   (ii)   (iii)   (iv)

....

Exercise 10.13

Can you give similar examples of more than one auxiliary verb stem used in a compound predicate?

This concludes the description of the original auxiliary verb stems.

SELF-ASSESSMENT

1. Combine the following sentences using auxiliary verbs:

(i) Mmalekutu o utswile madi. Mmalekutu o tsaya diaparo tsa ga rraagwe. Mmalekutu o inaya naga.

....

....

(ii) Ga ke ye gae. Mme a nthekele ditlhako.

....

117

(iii) Mmapule o ntlhapaditse. Ke ya go mo tlalea.

....

(iv) Mphe madi ao. Ke reke nama.

....

2. Rewrite the following underlining the roots of auxiliaries:

  (i) Rangwane o ne a ise a tlhabe.

....

  (ii) E bile fa a ka bo a kile a go itsise, o ne o se kitla o mo du-
medisa. ....

3. What is the function of the auxiliary verb in a compound predicate?

4. In what respect does an auxiliary verb differ from an independent verb?

5. The semantic function of the original auxiliary verbs deals with:
  (a) the time of the action or process.
  (b) the negation of the action or process.
  (c) the expression of the hortative.
  (d) the expression of conjunctives.
Illustrate these semantic functions by means of two sentences for each function.

6. What is the syntactic position of auxiliaries in a sentence? Give examples.

7. Can more than one auxiliary verb occur in a sentence? Give two examples.

8. Give an example of a subordinate clause containing a compound predicate. The following example might help you:
    Podi e e neng e lwala, e sule

2. Derived auxiliary verbs (deficient verbs)

In the previous section it was pointed out that quite a number of independent verbs can function as dependent auxiliary verbs. In the following examples this will be illustrated by means of *medium italic type* in the case of auxiliaries and ***bold italic type*** in the case of independent verbs, e.g.

  (i) Mosimane *o setse* pitse morago.

....

Mosimane *o setse **a itse** mafulo a yona.*

....

(ii) Ntate **a feta** ka bonako.

....

Ntate *a feta **a nna** fa fatshe.*

....

In these examples you will have noticed that there are differences in the meanings of the verb stems, when used as auxiliary verbs or as main verbs.

The derived auxiliary verbs will now be discussed in terms of their:

(a) morphological characteristics;
(b) semantic function;
(c) syntactic position.

You will have noticed that the headings that are used in this discussion are similar to those used in 1.1–1.3 on original auxiliaries.

2.1 The morphology of derived auxiliary verbs

The first morphological aspect that concerns us is the fact that the derived auxiliary verbs retain some of the structural features associated with their independent verbal counterparts. This is illustrated by the entries in the following list:

PRESENT	PERFECT	PRESENT	PERFECT
aga	— agile	rata	— ratile
batla	— batlile	re	— rile
dika	— dikile	senka	— senkile
feta	— fetile	sala	— setse

119

PRESENT	PERFECT	PRESENT	PERFECT
fitlha	— fitlhile	tla	— tle
lala	— letse	tlhola	— tlhotse
nama	— namile	tsoga	— tsogile
nna	— nntse	tloga	— tlogile
nne	— nnile	tshwanela	— tswanetse

The suffixes *-il-* and *-ts-* are clearly discernible. These verbal suffixes are of course associated with independent verbs.

2.1.1 The use of subjectival concords

Like ordinary independent verbs, the derived auxiliary verbs also require the inclusion of subjectival concords in their structure, e.g.

Lekgarebe leo *le* tlhola *le* kgaba.

Re letse *re* opela dipina tse di monate

Bana ba me *ba* tla dika *ba* falotse.

Bana ba me *ba* dikile *ba* falotse.

Ntate *o* tla tsoga *a* ya morakeng.

Ntate *o* tsogile *a* ya morakeng.

120

In the preceding example you will notice that the subjectival concord of the main verb or complement is **a** instead of the usual **o**. This **a** is an example of the subjectival concord of the subjunctive mood and will receive more attention in a future section on the subjunctive mood.

Exercise 10.14

Select five auxiliary verb stems from the list given in 2.1 above and use them to illustrate the use of the subjectival concords.

2.1.2 The use of the suffix -ng of the relative construction

As in the case of the original auxiliary verbs the **-ng** of the verbal relative construction combines with the auxiliary stems in subordinate clauses, e.g.

Ngwana *yo o tlholang* a bala, o a tlhalefa.

....

Ntšwa *e e agang* e re senyetsa, e sule.

....

Lekgarebe *le le tsogileng* le apaya, le ile.

....

Exercise 10.15

Select five auxiliary verbs from the list that appears earlier to illustrate the use of the verbal relative -ng in subordinate clauses containing auxiliary stems.

2.1.3 The expression of negatives by means of prefixes and suffixes

When the negative of compound predicates is to be expressed, it is done by:

(i) prefixing the negative prefix **ga** to the auxiliary stem; and replacing the positive ending of the auxiliary stem, viz. **-a** with a negative ending **-e**, e.g.

Ditlou **ga** *di tlhole* di bonala fa.

....

Ga *re fete* re bua mmaaka.

....

Phokojwe *ga a age* a re tshwarela dinku.

Bana *ga ba lale* ba tlhodia.

(ii) prefixing the negative prefix *sa* to the auxiliary stem; and by replacing the positive ending of the auxiliary stem, viz. *-a* with the negative ending *-e*, e.g.

Fa *re sa dike* re dira, re tla ja eng?

Fa *ba sa sale* ba robala, ba tla fetsa.

Fa *ba sa fete* ba bua maaka, re tla gololwa.

Fa *re sa name* ra iphemela, re tla fengwa.

(iii) by prefixing the negative *se* when the potential aspectual prefix appears in the structure of the compound verb, e.g.

Bana *ba ka se tsoge* ba ikapesa.

Mmaago *a ka se lale* a go emetse.

O tenne balemi. Ba *ka se tlhole* ba lema.

Balemi *ba ka se name* ba go direla.

Exercise 10.16

Select any five auxiliary verbs from the list given above to illustrate the negation of compound predicates.

2.1.4 The use of the future prefix **tla**

When the future tense prefix **tla** appears as a structural element in a compound verb, only the present tense form of the derived auxiliary stems is used, e.g.

Ntšwa e **tla** tloga e go loma.

....

Ke **tla** sala ke robetse.

....

Wena o **tla** tswa o re apeela.

....

Ntatemogolo o **tla** nna a ora molelo.

....

Exercise 10.17

Select any five auxiliary verbs from the list given above in 2.1. to illustrate the use of the future tense prefix **tla.**

2.1.5 The use of the potential aspectual prefix **ka**

This prefix occurs between the subjectival concord and the auxiliary verb stem, e.g.

Ditshwene di **ka** tlhola di senya mmidi.

....

Mosadi yo, a **ka** aga a go leofela.

....

Exercise 10.18

Select any five auxiliary verb stems from the list given above to illustrate the use of the potential prefix **ka**, e.g.

2.1.6 The use of the present tense **a**

Unlike the original auxiliary verbs the present tense **a** is not used in the case of the derived auxiliary stems.

2.2 The semantic function of derived auxiliary verbs

It is important to realise that the auxiliary verbs express time or tense such as **the present, the past** and **the future**. They do however expand the meaning of main verbs in respect of the:

(i) time of the action or process, e.g.

Ba thola *ba aga* lebotana leo.

......

Rona *re sa ntse* **re ba emela.**

......

(ii) negation of the action or process, e.g.

Madi ao, *ga a tlhole* **a batlega.**

......

Fa *ba sa tlhole* **ba lema**, ga ke ba duele.

......

Kgomo eo, *e ka se lale* **e amusitse.**

......

(iii) completeness or incompleteness of an action or process, e.g.

Basimane *ba tlhola* **ba rema** dikgong.

......

Basimane *ba tlhotse* **ba rema** dikgong.

......

Basimane *ba tlhotse* **ba remile** dikgong.

......

2.3 The syntactic position of derived auxiliary verbs

1. The derived auxiliary verbs precede the main verb or complement. Together the derived auxiliary verb and the main verb form a compound predicate, e.g.

Malome *o tla tsoga* **a goroga** mono.

......

2. Should the complement be left out, then the auxiliary verb assumes the meaning of an ordinary verb, e.g.

Malome *o tla tsoga.*

....

3. Only one **derived** auxiliary stem can occur in a compound predicate. In the case of the **original** auxiliary stems more than one stem may be used, e.g.

Malome *o ne a ise a ke **a tsoge.***
     (i)   (ii)   (iii)

....

4. When **original** and *derived* auxiliary stems occur in the same compound predicate, the *derived* auxiliary stems occur **next to the complement**, e.g.

Re ka bo *re setse* **re rutilwe.**

....

Ga o kitla *o tlhola* **o mo laola.**

....

Exercise 10.19

Select eight derived auxiliary stems and use two each, as in the case of the previous examples, to illustrate their syntactic position.

SELF-ASSESSMENT

1. Rewrite the following sentences and identify the structural elements of the derived auxiliary verbs that appear in them:

   (i) Mosimane yo o agang a re tlhodia, o robetse.

   ....

  (ii) Rrapula o dikile a falotse dikerii ya gagwe.

   ....

 (iii) Mmapula a ka se tsoge a go direla sepe.

   ....

 (iv) Le gale, barwao ba tla sala ba go tlhokometse.

   ....

  (v) Bana ba tlhola ba rema dikgong.

   ....

---

2. Explain the term auxiliary verb in your own words.
3. Would you say that an auxiliary has an independent meaning and function?
4. Do auxiliary verbs require subjectival concords as prefixes?
5. Do the suffixes **-il-** and **-ts-** occur with original auxiliary verbs?
6. Give two examples for each of the two types of auxiliaries to illustrate the use of the **-ng** of the verbal relative construction.
7. Give three examples of negative forms of the derived auxiliary stems.
8. Can original and derived auxiliary stems occur as members of the same compound predicate?

CHAPTER 11

The use of the verb

In Chapter 9, dealing with the verb, you were introduced to:

  (i) the **meaning** of the term "verb";
 (ii) the **constituents** of the verb;
(iii) **adopted** verbs and
 (iv) the **predicate**.

Because it is so lengthy the **use** of the verb was not discussed in Chapter 9. The use of the verb will be attended to in this chapter and each **way of using the verb** (mood) will be discussed in detail. Each section will therefore contain the **objectives** as well as the **self-assessment** questions of a particular mood. The moods that will be discussed in the following sections are:

1. Infinitive
2. Indicative
3. Imperative
4. Participial
5. Subjunctive
6. Habitual.

1. The inifitive mood

> **OBJECTIVES**
>
> On completion of this section you should be able to:
> 1. describe the structure and use of the "infinitive mood positive and negative";
> 2. explain the semantic application of the infinitive mood positive and negative;
> 3. identify examples of the infinitive mood when used in a passage.

1.1 The infinitive as a mood expressing processes or actions

Would you agree that each of the following parts in medium italics express a process or an action?

127

(i) Lorato *o itse* go loga. ....

(ii) Simane *o rata* go tshameka. ....

(iii) Pula *e batla* go na. ....

(iv) Moleofi *o tshwanetse* go sekisiwa.

....

The medium italicised part in these sentences is called the **main verb or the complement** of the auxiliary verb which appears in bold italics. The auxiliary verbs that appear in these sentences are **derived auxiliary** verbs and **together with** the main verb or complement they form **a compound predicate**, i.e.

. . . *o itse* go loga. ....

. . . *o rata* go tshameka. ....

. . . *e batla* go na. ....

. . . *o tshwanetse* go sekisiwa. ....

The main verb or the complement in these structures is said to be in the infinitive mood which expresses processes or actions.

1.2 The structure of the infinitive mood

The infinitive mood commonly occurs as a main verb or complement after the following derived and original auxiliary verb stems:

tshwanela	— tshwanetse	bolo
senka	— senkile	bisa
rata	— ratile	sena
batla	— batlile	
ya	— ile	
itse	— itsile	

128

In the following examples of the use of the main verb or complement are included a number of familiar structural elements in bold italics. Do you recognise them?

(i) Ga ba bolo *go le em**e**la.*

....

(ii) Ke batlile *go **i**kgobatsa.*

....

(iii) Ntšwa ga e a tshwanela *go bofel**w**a.*

....

(iv) Ba batla *go **tla** falola.*

....

(v) Ga a bolo *go **ka** bala buka.*

....

(vi) Le tshwanetse *go **sa** jele losea.*

....

(vii) Modisa ga a bolo *go **sa** senka letimela.*

....

Exercise 11.1

You can now proceed with forming your own examples of the infinitive mood and at the same time make use of the aforementioned structural elements.

From the preceding examples and from your own examples it should be clear that the infinitive as the main verb or complement of a compound predicate may consist of:

(a) the disjunctively written infinitive prefix **go** + the verb stem ending in **-a**, e.g. **go** *direla.*

....

(b) the verb stem may be preceded by the conjunctively written reflexive prefix **i-**, e.g. *go **i**tirela.*

....

(c) the reflexive prefix may be preceded by:

    (i) the disjunctively written objectival concord, e.g. *go **ba** itirela*;

    (ii) the disjunctively written potential prefix ***ka*** and the progressive prefix ***sa***, e.g. *go **ka** iponela, go **sa** itirela;*

(d) the verb stem may be preceded by the disjunctively written future tense prefix ***tla***, e.g. *go **tla** dira*

(e) the disjunctively written negative prefix ***sa*** also precedes the verb stem, e.g. *go **sa** dire*

You should note that the negative ***sà*** is low toned while the progressive ***sá*** is high toned.

    In addition to the formation of the negative by means of ***sa*** there is also the negative ***se*** with the verb stem ending in *-ê*, e.g.

*go **se** dirê*

(f) the verb stem of the infinitive may contain all the verbal extensions that were discussed in Chapter 9, e.g. *go di**re**ga, go di**ro**lola, go di**ri**sa*, etc.

Exercise 11.2

Can you make your own sentences accounting for the various verbal extensions used as part of the infinitive structure?

1.3 The use of the infinitive mood

The main verb or complement in these compound predicates may be described by any adverb or adverbial clause, e.g.

    (i) Ga ba bolo *go le emela **fa sakeng.***

    (ii) Ke batlile *go ikgobatsa **maabane.***

(iii) Ntšwa ga e a tshwanela *go bofelwa* **ke ngwana.**

....

(iv) Ba batla *go tla direla* **kwa ba leng teng.**

....

(v) Ga a bolo *go ka bala buka* **a ise a ye sekolong.**

....

Exercise 11.3

Can you form similar sentences in which the infinitive is described by adverbs?

1.4 The confusion between class 15 nouns and the infinitive

Because of the remarkable structural similarity between **the nouns of class 15** and **the main verb or complement of the infinitive mood** it is difficult to keep these structures apart. The infinitive mood forms part of **the predicate** while the nouns of class 15 function as **subjects** and **objects** of sentences, e.g.

(i) **Go palama pitse** go kgatlha basimane.

....

(ii) Le nna ke leka **go e palama.**

....

(iii) Mme o kgona **go apaya le go roka diaparo.**

....

(iv) Nna ke palelwa ke **go itirela.**

....

(v) **Go ka tlhaloganya Segerika** go a retela.

....

Do you recognise the different **go** prefixes appearing in the previous sentences? e.g.

Go palama pitse **go** kgatlha basimane.

....

Le nna ke leka **go** e palama.

....

131

The **go** in **go** *palama* is of course the disjunctively written class prefix of a class 15 noun used as **a subject** while the **go** in **go** *kgatlha* is the subjectival concord derived from the noun **go** *palama*. Similarly the **go** in **go** *e palama* is the class prefix of the class 15 noun used as **the object** of the sentence.

Can you now explain the **go** prefixes of sentences (iv) and (v) above?

Exercise 11.4

*You should now be able to form your own examples in which nouns of the **go** or infinitive noun class are used as **subjects** and **objects** of sentences.*

The nouns of the **go** class, as you have seen, may be used as subjects and objects of sentences. In addition, like all other nouns, they may be qualified by means of the following qualificative structures:

(a) **demonstratives**, e.g.

Go aka *gole*, go ne ga dira gore botlhe ba mo tlhokomologe.

....

(b) **adjectives**, e.g.

Basetsana ba ratelwa **go opela** *go gontle* le **go se senye** *go gobe*.

....

(c) **enumeratives**, e.g.

Mme o utlwa **go tlhodia** *gofe*?

....

(d) **quantitatives**, e.g.

Go ja *gosi* go monate.

....

(e) **possessives**, e.g.

Letsatsi lotlhe re ne re utlwa **go duma** *ga pula*.

....

(f) **relative** or **qualificative clauses**, e.g.

Go ithuta *go go thabisang* le **go bala** *go go monate* ke ditiro tsa

morutwana. ....

....

132

Exercise 11.5

Can you supply additional examples to illustrate how each of the abovementioned structures may be used to qualify nouns of the **go** class?

SELF-ASSESSMENT

1. For what purpose is the infinitive mood used?
2. The infinitive mood customarily appears together with a number of auxiliary verbs:
   (a) Give four sentences containing such auxiliary verbs.
   (b) Name four additional auxiliary verb stems that precede the infinitive mood.
3. Identify the following items in the next sentence: *main verb* or *complement; auxiliary verb* and *compound predicate:*
   Noga e batlile go ntoma maabane.
4. Why are the nouns of class 15 easily confused with the infinitive mood?
5. Can the class 15 nouns be qualified by other structures? Give six examples of such qualificatives.
6. Name the structural elements of the infinitive appearing in italics in the following examples:
   (i) **Ke batla *go ya* gae.**
   (ii) **Ga ba bolo *go tsamaya.***
   (iii) Ke itse **go** letsa phala.
   (iv) Ntate o ya go **i**kagela lorako.
   (v) Malome o ya go thusa ntate go **lo** aga.
   (vi) Bagaetsho ba rata go **sa** ikagela ka gobo mongwe le mongwe o tshwanetse go **ka** itirela.
   (vii) Bana ba gaetsho ba tshwanetse go **se** senye.
   (viii) Rona re ya go rut**iw**a ke morutabana.
   (ix) Ba tla boa fa ba sena **go fetsa *kwa morakeng***.
   (x) ***Go bisa*** go reetsa **sentle** go tla go bakela mathata.
7. (a) Which of the following are examples of the infinitive mood?
      (i) Go tsamaya ka bonako go lapisa thata.
      (ii) Basimane ba tlhola ba batla go tshameka fela.
      (iii) Legodu le ne le kopa go itshwarelwa.
   (b) Give three more sentences illustrating the use of the infinitive mood.
   (c) Give two examples using the class 15 nouns in subjectival and objectival positions.

2. The indicative mood

The indicative mood, as will be seen in 2.3 and 2.4, is discussed under the following headings:

(i) The indicative mood positive

(ii) The indicative mood negative

2.1 The indicative as a mood expressing statements and facts

Would you agree that the following sentences are statements or express facts?

(i) Nna ke rata nama ya koko. ....

(ii) Morutabana o a bala. ....

(iii) Rangwane o sa ntse a lwala. ....

(iv) Bana ba ka ya gae. ....

(v) Balemi ba jwetse mmidi monongwaga.

....

(vi) Baagi ba tla fetsa lebotana ka moso.

....

Sentences like these are said to be in the **indicative mood** because this mood is used when one wishes to make a statement or to express a fact in the **present, perfect** and **future tenses.**

2.2 The indicative as a mood expressing questions

Let us rephrase the sentences of 2.1 as questions in this section, e.g.

(i) A wena o rata nama ya koko? ....

(ii) A morutabana o a bala? ....

(iii) A rangwane o sa ntse a lwala? ....

(iv) Bana ba ka ya kae? ....

(v) Balemi ba jwetse mmidi leng?

....

(vi) Baagi ba tla fetsa lebotana leng?

....

From this it is clear that the **indicative mood** is also used to express questions. The answers to such questions are again statements or the expression of facts.

Exercise 11.6

You should now be able to supply your own examples of interrogatives which are used to phrase questions in the indicative mood, e.g.

Ba tla boa **jang**? ....

Mosenyi yoo, o sietse **kae**? ....

Lo dira **eng** jaanong? ....

Baeng ba batla **mang**? ....

Namane eo, e **kana kang**? ....

Rraago o rekile pitse **efe**? ....

Gore eng o sa re thuse? ....

Would you agree that the answers to these questions are statements or the expression of facts?

From the preceding it is clear that the **indicative mood** expresses statements or facts as well as questions in the present, perfect and future tenses.

2.3 The indicative mood positive

OBJECTIVES

On completion of this section you should be able to:
1. describe the structure and use of the "indicative mood positive";
2. explain the semantic application of the indicative mood positive;
3. identify predicates expressing the indicative mood positive in a sentence.

Let us review the sentences given in 2.1 above and then you can try to identify the different tenses represented in these examples:

2.3.1 Present tense

(i) The first sentence of 2.1. above is an example of the **short form** of the present tense, i.e. the verb consists of:

a subjectival concord + a verb stem ending in -a.

135

Exercise 11.7

Can you give your own examples of the **short form** of the present tense as one of the tense forms of the **indicative mood**? e.g.

Ntate *o baakanya* koloi.

....

Pula *e na* thata monongwaga.

....

(ii) The second sentence of 2.1 above is an example of the **long form** of the present tense, i.e. the verb consists of:

a subjectival concord + the present tense *a* + a verb stem ending in -*a*.

Exercise 11.8

Can you give more examples of the **long form** of the present tense as one of the tense forms of the **indicative mood**? e.g.

Ntate o *a lwala.* ....

Tiro e *a fela.* ....

The **long form** can also take the objectival concord, e.g.

Mme o a *e apaya*, nama. ....

Dintšwa *di a e tshaba*, tau. ....

Exercise 11.9

Can you form your own examples of the **long form** of the present tense when taking an objectival concord? e.g.

Magodu *a o utswile*, mmotorokara.

....

Mokoko o *lo adimile*, lomao.

....

(iii) The third sentence of 2.1 above is an example of the *progressive aspectual prefix* **sa** and the *auxiliary verb* **ntse** expressing that an action in the indicative mood is **continuing**, e.g.

Batlhatlhobiwa ba *sa ntse* ba kwala tlhamo.

....

Nnake o *sa ntse* a ja. ....

136

Exercise 11.10

Can you give your own examples of the present tense when taking the **progressive aspect**? *e.g.*

Basadi *ba* **sa ntse** *ba tlhagola.*

....

Mosimane *o* **sa ntse** *a gama.* ....

(iv) The fourth sentence of 2.1 above is an example of the use of the *potential aspectual prefix* **ka** expressing that an action in the present can or may take place, e.g.

Re **ka** *fetsa* go rulela gompieno.

....

Lona *le* **ka** *ya* go re rekela sukiri.

....

Exercise 11.11

Can you give more examples of the present tense when taking the **potential aspect**? *e.g.*

Ngwanaka, *o* **ka** *tsamaya* jaanong.

....

Basadi *ba* **ka** *tlhatswa,* banna *ba* **ka** *gama.*

....

Besides accommodating sentences in the present tense, the indicative mood also makes use of the perfect and the future tenses.

2.3.2 Perfect tense

(v) The fifth sentence of 2.1 above is an example of a sentence expressing that an **action is completed**. This is expressed by the **perfect tense** of the indicative mood, i.e. it takes one of a number of perfect endings, e.g.

Balemi **ba jwetse** mmidi monongwaga.

....

Exercise 11.12

Can you form your own examples of the **perfect tense** *as one of the tense forms of the indicative mood? e.g.*

137

Baeng *ba* **diile** mme.

....

Mong wa rona, *o* **okeditse** madi a rona.

....

Besides completed actions the **perfect tense** also expresses **a state**, e.g.

Pitse *e* **sule.** ....

Ngwana *o* **robetse.** ....

The last tense form occurring in the indicative mood is the future tense.

2.3.3 Future tense

(vi) The sixth sentence of 2.1 above is an example of a sentence expressing that an action will take place in the future. This is expressed by the **future tense** of the indicative mood, i.e. it takes the future tense prefix *tla*, e.g.

Baagi *ba* **tla** *fetsa* lebotana ka moso.

....

Exercise 11.13

Can you give more examples of the **future tense** *as one of the tense forms of the indicative mood? e.g.*

Basimane *ba* **tla** *bolotsa* dinamane.

....

Terena ya rona *e* **tla** *goroga* phakela.

....

SELF-ASSESSMENT

1. What semantic content, i.e. what kind of sentence, is expressed by means of the indicative mood?
2. (a) Name the three tenses occurring in the indicative mood.
   (b) What are the structural elements characterising these tenses?

3. Under what tense would you classify:
   (a) the short form
   (b) the long form
   (c) the progressive aspect
   (d) the potential aspect.
4. The progressive aspectual prefix **sa** and the potential aspectual prefix **ka** may be used in the three tenses of the indicative mood. Can you give six more examples to add to the following sentences and then classify all the sentences according to their tenses?

> Nnake o sa ntse a lela.
> Batlhabani ba ka bo ba tsere kgang pele.
> Matimela a sa ntse a ile.
> Nna nka tla jaanong-jaana.
> Ngwanake o sa ntse a tla fetsa dithuto.
> Ntate a ka tla a re thusa ka madi.

2.4 The indicative mood negative

OBJECTIVES

On completion of this section you should be able to:
1. describe the structure and use of the "indicative mood negative";
2. explain the semantic application of the indicative mood negative;
3. identify predicates expressing the indicative mood negative in a sentence.

In the preceding section it was shown that the **indicative mood** is used to:

(a) express **statements** or **facts**, e.g.

Bona ba ithuta Setswana. ....

(b) express **questions**, e.g.

Bona ba ithuta eng? ....

The **indicative mood** was discussed in terms of the **positive** form of the following tenses:

(a) present
(b) perfect
(c) future

In this section you will be introduced to the **negatives** of these tenses.

2.4.1 Present tense

This tense consists of:

(i) the **short form** of the present tense, e.g.

Moruti *o kolobetsa* ngwana   > Moruti *ga a kolobetse* ngwana

....

A lekgarebe *le apara* mosese? > A lekgarebe *ga le apare* mosese?

....

In these example you will notice that:

- the negative is expressed by means of the *verbal prefix* **ga**
- the *subjectival concord* of the **mo- ba-** class singular is **a** instead of **o**
- the *verb stem* ends in **-e**

Exercise 11.14

Can you give more examples of the negative of the indicative mood in the **short form** *of the present tense? e.g.*

Ntšwa *e rata* nama   > Ntšwa *ga e rate* nama.

....

A bojalwa *bo bela* sentle? > A bojalwa *ga bo bele* sentle?

....

(ii) the **long form** of the present tense has no negative form of its own but uses the negative of the short form, e.g.

Ntšwa *e bogola* legodu   > Ntšwa *ga e bogole* legodu.

....

Ntšwa *e a bogola*   > Ntšwa *ga e bogole.*

....

2.4.2 Perfect tense

This tense cannot be subdivided like the present tense, e.g.

Badisa **ba boloditse** dinamane > Badisa **ga ba a bolodisa** dinamane

Pule **o gamile** mala   > Pule **ga a a gama** mala.

A **lo duetse** monnamogolo?   > A **ga lo a duela** monnamogolo?

In these examples you will notice that:

- the negative is expressed by means of the *verbal prefix* **ga**
- the *subjectival concord* of the **mo- ba-** class singular is **a** instead of **o**
- the *subjectival concord* is followed by a *prefix* **a**
- the *verb stem* ends in **-a**

Exercise 11.15

Can you supply your own examples of the negative of the indicative mood **perfect tense**? *e.g.*

Ba mo emeletse fa kgorong   > **Ga ba a mo emelela fa** kgorong.

Ena **o butse** setswalo   > Ena **ga a a bula** setswalo.

2.4.3 Future tense

As in the case of the perfect tense the **future tense** cannot be subdivided, e.g.

Bona **ba tla re thusa**   > Bona **ga ba ne ba re thusa.**

Ke tla gamela ntate   > **Ga ke kitla ke gamela** ntate.

A mmaago **o tla boa** gompieno? > A mmaago **ga a ne a boa** gompieno?

141

In these examples you will notice that:

- the negative is expressed by means of the *verbal prefix* **ga**
- the *subjectival concord* of the **mo- ba-** class singular is **a** instead of **o**
- the *first subjectival concord* is followed by the *auxiliary verb stem* **ne** or **kitla**
- the *second subjectival concord* is followed by the *main verb ending in* **-a**

From the preceding it is clear that the **indicative mood negative** expresses negative statements and the negation of facts in the present, perfect and future tenses.

SELF-ASSESSMENT

1. Can you identify and name the structural elements of the following:
   (a) Ena yo, ga a tlhaloganye Setswana.
   (b) Badiri bona ga ba a amogela madi.
   (c) Tau ga e ne e tsoma e le nosi.
2. What is the semantic content of the negatives of the indicative mood?
3. In what tenses do the negatives of the indicative mood occur?
4. Can one ask questions by means of sentences in the indicative mood? Give examples of questions in three tenses.

---

3. The imperative mood

OBJECTIVES

On completion of this section you should be able to:
1. describe the structure and use of the "imperative mood positive and negative";
2. explain the semantic application of the imperative mood positive and negative;
3. identify examples of the imperative mood when occurring in a passage.

3.1 The imperative as a mood expressing commands, requests, admonitions and encouragement

Would you agree that the following are examples of the expression of commands, requests, admonitions and encouragement?

(i) Tsaya mosimane!

....

(ii) Le ithuteng sentle monongwaga!

....

(iii) Ba rekele sukiri fa le boa!

....

(iv) Re thuse fano!

....

(v) Nwayang! Dino tse, ke molemo.

....

(vi) Ntla! Ba tloga ba go ronkgela.

....

(vii) Se senye nako mo sekolong!

....

(viii) Mpheng dibuka tsa lona!

....

Sentences by means of which one can express commands, requests, admonitions and encouragement are examples of the **imperative mood.**

Would you agree that some of these examples are phrased politely while some of them are not polite? Sentence (i) for example is not polite, while sentence (viii) is polite.

In the imperative mood there are structural differences between commands formed by means of:

(a) monosyllabic verb stems
(b) polysyllabic verb stems.

3.2 Monosyllabic verb stems and the imperative mood

This kind of verb stem may be used:

(a) unchanged, e.g.

Tla kwano! ....

Tswa fa! ....

143

Ja ka bonako! ....

Nwa, o fetse! ....

(b) by adding a *suffix -a*, e.g.

Tlaa! or *Tlaya*! ....

Tswaa! or *Tswaya*! ....

Jaa! or *Jaya*! ....

Nwaa! or *Nwaya*! ....

Exercise 11.15

Can you give more examples illustrating the use of monosyllabic verb stems in the imperative mood?

3.3 Polysyllabic verb stems and the imperative mood

The polysyllabic verb stems are used unchanged, e.g.

Tsamaya! ....

Didimala mosimane ke wena! ....

Reetsa fa go buiwa! ....

Exercise 11.16

Can you give your own examples illustrating the use of polysyllabic verb stems in the imperative mood?

3.4 General structural characteristics

1. Sentences of the imperative mood may contain **objectival concords** and the **reflexive prefix**. This results in the change of the *verbal ending* from *-a* to *-e*, e.g.

Ba bits**e**!	Iketl**e**! ....
Mmontsh**e**!	Itirel**e**! ....
Nthus**e**!	Itlhatlhob**e**! ....
A nw**e**! (metsi)	Ijel**e**! ....
E j**e**! (nama)	Ithekel**e**! ....

Have you noticed?

(a) the example of assimilation in: ***Mm****ontshe!*

(b) *the examples of plosivation in:*

144

Itirele   <   **direla** ....

Ithekele   <   **rekela** .... etc.

2. When the *objectival concord of the 1st person singular* is used, one can distinguish two forms of the imperative, e.g.

Mpha thipa eo!   **Mphe** thipa eo!

....

Ntshegela nama foo!   **Ntshegele** nama foo!

....

Nkapeela dijo!   **Nkapeele** dijo!

....

3. If a *second objectival concord* or the *reflexive prefix* is used in addition to the objectival concord of the first person then the *verb stem* only ends in *-e*, e.g.

E mphe thipa eo! ....

Di nkapeele dijo tseo! ....

Intshwarele ntate! ....

Exercise 11.17

You should now be able to give your own examples illustrating the use of the imperative in 1 – 3 above.

4. When a command, request, admonition or encouragement is directed at more than one person all imperatives end in the *plural imperative suffix* **-ng**, e.g.

Tlaya**ng** kwano! ....

Ntlang**!** ....

Reetsa**ng!** ....

Mmontshe**ng!** ....

Iketle**ng!** ....

Ntshegele**ng!** ....

Exercise 11.18

You should now be able to give your own examples of commands, requests, admonitions and encouragement when directed at more than one person.

5. The negative of all imperatives is formed by means of the *negative prefix* **se** and the *verbal ending* **-a** is replaced by **-e**:

Se tleng! ....

Se ntleng! ....

Se reetseng! ....

Se mmontsheng! ....

Se iketleng! ....

Se ntshegeleng! ....

Exercise 11.19

You should now be able to give more examples of negative commands, requests, admonitions and encouragement given to:

(a) single persons
(b) more than one person

From the preceding it is clear that the imperative mood expresses **commands, requests, admonitions** and **encouragement** given in the positive and the negative to single and to plural persons. **The imperative mood occurs in the present tense only.**

SELF-ASSESSMENT

1. Identify and name the bold printed structural elements characterising the imperative mood in the following examples:
   (i) **Ya** fale!
   (ii) **Tshwara** jaana!
   (iii) Ja**a** (or jay**a**)! Re batla go tsamaya.
   (iv) Tlay**a** ke bone!
   (v) **N**tswa! O ntenne.
   (vi) **N**tlhalosets**e**! Ga ke tlhaloganye.
   (vii) **I**ketlele**ng** pitse eo!
   (viii) Ijel**e** nama e!
   (ix) **Di n**kadim**e**, dibuka tseo!
   (x) Bana, **se** sale**ng** basenyi morago!

146

2. For what purpose is the imperative mood used?
3. Structurally there are differences in the use of monosyllabic and polysyllabic verb stems in the imperative mood. Give examples of this and comment on the differences.
4. In what way does the addition of objectival concords and the reflexive prefix affect the structure of the verb stem? Give examples.
5. What variations are possible when the objectival concord of the 1st person singular is used in imperatives? Give examples.
6. What structural elements characterise the imperative mood when:
   (a) a command is given in the plural?
   (b) a command is negated?

4. The participial mood

OBJECTIVES

On completion of this section you should be able to:
1. describe the structure and use of the "participial mood positive";
2. explain the semantic application of the participial mood positive;
3. identify predicates expressing the participial mood positive when occurring in a passage.

4.1 The participial as a mood expressing simultaneous actions

Would you agree that each of the following sentences expresses simultaneous actions or an action that coincides with the main action of each sentence?

(i) Ke bona bana **ba thusa** batsadi.

....

(ii) Morekisi o fetile **a rwele** thoto.

....

(iii) Ka **a tla gana** go re thusa, re tla go rapela.

....

147

Would you agree that the bold printed subjectival concords are prefixes of verbs denoting actions that occur simultaneously with the main action, e.g.

- the **assistance** given by the children in (i) above coincides with my **observation** of the situation
- the **passing** of the seller in (ii) above coincided with the **carrying** of a load
- the possibility of a future **refusal** in (iii) above will coincide with a future **plea** for assistance.

Sentences like these by means of which one can express simultaneous actions or an action that coincides with the main action are examples of the **participial mood**.

What tenses are represented in the three abovementioned examples? Would you agree that the bold printed verb of sentence:

(i) is an example of the **present tense**?
(ii) is an example of the **perfect tense**?
(iii) is an example of the **future tense**?

Exercise 11.20

You should now be able to give additional examples to illustrate the structure and use of these tenses in the participial mood.

If you have a problem in doing this on your own, the following will serve as an example. In these examples you should note that the bold italicised verb is the one expressing the participial mood. The other verb can be in the indicative mood.

4.2 The participial mood positive

4.2.1 Present tense

The term present tense only refers to the tense of the bold-printed participial mood. The other verb can appear in any other tense, e.g.

Ka ntate *a re direla*, rona *re tla mo tshepa*.

....

Mapodisa *a rakile* legodu *le thuba* banka.

....

Fa wena *o ba ruta* maitseo, bana ba gago *ba tla kgona*.

....

Mohumi *o lebeletse* batlhanka *ba dira*.

....

Exercise 11.21

Can you add your own examples to these?

4.2.2 Perfect tense

Once again the term perfect tense refers to the bold printed verbs of the participial mood only, e.g.

Bathusi ba rona *ba goroga **re feditse** tiro.*

....

Le fa ***a rekile*** mogoma, mmu ona *ga o lemege.*

....

Ka ***o nthusitse**, ke tla go lefa.*

....

Mosetsana yo, o timetse ***a itse*** tsela.

....

Exercise 11.22

Will you be able to add your own examples to these?

4.2.3 Future tense

The future tense applies to the bold printed verbs of the participial mood only. The second verb may be in any tense, e.g.

Ka ***a tla reka*** mmotorokara, *o tla adima madi.*

....

Fa ***ba tla ntetlelela,** ke tla ba direla.*

....

O ya go nyala mosetsana yo, le fa ***a tla mo tlhala.***

....

Ka ***a tla bolaya*** mabele, *o rekile mmotorokara.*

....

Exercise 11.23

Can you add your own examples to these?

4.3 General characteristics of the participial mood

1. If you review the preceding examples as well as your additions to them you will notice that structurally they show great similarity with the indicative mood. There is one important structural difference, viz; the *subjectival concord* of the **mo- ba-** class singular is **a** in the participial mood and not **o**, e.g.

Fa morutabana **a** lo laela, lo reetse.

Tabogela kwa gae. O tla fitlhela mme **a** go emetse.

Le tla kgona jang ka ena **a** gana go thusa.

Exercise 11.24

Can you give your own examples illustrating the use of the subjectival concord of the **mo- ba-** *class singular in the participial mood?*

2. Apart from this you will notice that the subjectival concords of the participial mood are **high toned** and this affects the tonal pattern of the verb, e.g.

Ke le lebelela *lé senya*.

Le fa *ré ba ruta*, ba gana go ithuta.

Ka *ó nnyatsa*, ga ke go rate.

Compare the tone of the italicised verbs above with the same verbs appearing in the **indicative mood** below:

Basimane, *le senya* nako.

Re ba ruta go bala.

Wena *o nnyatsa* kwa ntle ga lebaka.

Exercise 11.25

You should now give your own examples to illustrate the high toned subjectival concord of the participial mood, e.g.

Fa **ke** *reka* baesekele, ke ya go go pega.

....

Ka rraago **a** *tlhoka* thipa, o ka mo naya ena.

....

Ba dira ka bonako, le fa pula **e** *na*.

....

3. Thus far nothing has been said about the **conjunctives** that precede predicates in the participial mood. You must have noticed that quite a number of sentences commencing in the *conjunctives* **fa, le fa** and **ka** are followed by predicates in the participial mood, e.g.

Ka *ba gana*, ba tlogele.

....

Fa *a goroga*, o mo nee molaetsa o.

....

Le fa *re itse*, ga re kgone go dira sepe.

....

In addition to these the participial mood also follows on the conjunctions **e tswa, abo** and **le mororo**, e.g.

O fulere, **e tswa** *a tshwanetse* go lala fa.

....

Malome o tla go šapa **le mororo** *a le* segole.

....

Abo Motabogi *a le* mosetlhana!

....

Ba jele tsotlhe, **e tswa** *ke kopile* thathanyana.

....

151

O paletswe **le mororo** *a le botlhale.*

....

Abo *a rata* basimane!

....

From the preceding it is clear that the participial mood expresses the occurrence of simultaneous actions or an action that coincides with a main action.

SELF-ASSESSMENT

1. On what structural evidence would you classify the bold printed verb as being an example of the participial mood?
   Nna ke mmone **a phamola** madi.
2. How does the tone of the bold printed verbs differ?
   Ke utlwile tau **e duma.**
   Tau **e duma** mo sekgweng.
3. For what purpose is the participial mood used? Examples of verbs in the participial mood can occur in one of three tenses. Name these tenses and give examples to illustrate them.
4. Can a verb in the participial mood be used together with a verb in another mood?
5. How does the subjectival concord of the **mo- ba-** classes singular change when used in the participial mood?
6. What happens to the intonation of the verb in the participial mood?

4.4 The participial mood negative

OBJECTIVES

On completion of this section you should be able to:
1. describe the structure and use of the "participial mood negative";
2. explain the semantic application of the participial mood negative;
3. identify predicates expressing the participial mood negative when occurring in a passage.

In the previous section it was shown that the **participial mood** is used to express simultaneous actions or an action coinciding with the main action of each sentence, e.g.

(i) Re fitlhetse ntšwa **e re jela** nama.

....

(ii) Ke tlhapisa ngwanake **a eme** mo molapong.

....

(iii) Le fa **o ba fa** madi, ba tla go nyatsa.

....

The **participial mood** was discussed in terms of the positive forms of the following tenses:

(a) present
(b) perfect
(c) future

In this section you will be introduced to the **negatives** of these tenses. The participial mood in the following examples is expressed by the bold printed verb. The other verb can be in the indicative mood.

4.4.1 Present tense

The present tense of the verb only applies to the verb in the participial mood. The other verb may be in any other tense. In order to contrast the positive with the negative, examples of both are given, e.g.

Positive	Negative
(i) Ntate o go bone	(i) Ntate o go bone
o tlhagola.	**o sa tlhagole.**
(ii) Fa ena **a ba ruta**, ba	(ii) Fa ena **a sa ba rute**, ba
tla falola monogwaga.	tla falola monongwaga.
(iii) Mookamedi o fitlhetse	(iii) Mookamedi o fitlhetse
badiri **ba ikhutsa.**	badiri **ba sa ikhutse.**

Positive	Negative
(iv) Ka mme **a ba direla**,	(iv) Ka mme **a se ba direle**,
....	....
rona re a mo direla.	rona re a mo direla.
....	....

Exercise 11.26

You should now be able to add your own examples of the negative of the participial mood present tense to these.

4.4.2 Perfect tense

The term perfect tense refers to the bold printed verbs of the participial mood only, e.g.

Positive	Negative
(i) Re mo tshwere **a**	(i) Re mo tshwere **a sa**
....	....
kgaritlhile pitsa.	**kgaritlha** pitsa.
....	....
(ii) O ngwegile e tswa **a**	(ii) O ngwegile e tswa **a sa**
....	....
laetswe go re tlhokomela.	**laelwa** go re tlhokomela.
....	....
(iii) Abo ntate **a humile**!	(iii) Abo ntate **a sa huma!**
....	....
(iv) Pule o paletswe le mororo	(iv) Pule o paletswe le mororo
....	....
a nnile ngaka.	**a sa nna** ngaka.
....	....

Exercise 11.27

You should now be able to add your own examples of the negative of the participial mood perfect tense to these.

4.4.3 Future tense

The future tense only applies to the bold printed verbs of the participial mood. The second verb may be in any tense, e.g.

Positive	Negative
(i) Ka **ba tla aga** .... ntlo, ba sega bojang.	(i) Ka **ba se ne ba aga** .... ntlo, ba sega bojang. ....
(ii) Fa **o tla nthusa**, ... le nna ke tla go thusa.	(ii) Fa **o se kitla o nthusa**, ... le nna ke tla go thusa. ....
(iii) O ya go mo nyala, le fa .... **a tla mo** tlhala, ...	(iii) O ya go mo nyala, le fa .... **a se kitla a mo tlhala.** ....
(iv) Le mororo **a tla kotula**, ... o tla go bolaisa tlala.	(iv) Le mororo **a se ne a kotula**, ... o tla go bolaisa tlala. ....

Exercise 11.28

Can you add your own examples of the negative of the participial mood future tense to these?

4.5 General characteristics of the participial mood negative

1. A review of the examples quoted above as well as those that you have supplied, will reveal that the negative structure of the participial mood is characterised by:

(i) the *subjectival concord* **a** for the **mo- ba-** classes in positives and negatives, e.g.

Fa **a** *sa lo laele*, le nne fela.

....

Exercise 11.29

You should now give examples of your own to illustrate the use of this subjectival concord in the negative.

(ii) The *subjectival concords* of verbs in the participial mood, positive and negative, are *high toned*. This affects the tonal pattern of the verb, e.g.

Le fa **re** *sa ba rute*, ba na le kitso.

....

Ntate o tla go ema nokeng le mororo **a** *se na thata.*

....

Exercise 11.30

Can you give more examples that will illustrate the use of the high toned subjectival concord in the negative?

(iii) The negative structures of the tenses are the following:

4.5.1 Present tense

The *subjectival concord* of the **mo- ba-** classes is **a** instead of **o**, e.g.

Ke mo fitlhetse **a** **sa** *dire.*

....

As can be seen in the previous example, the negative prefix is **sa** and the verb ends in **-e**.

Exercise 11.31

You should now be able to give similar examples of your own while using nouns from other noun classes.

4.5.2 Perfect tense

The *subjectival concord* of the **mo- ba-** classes is **a** instead of **o**, e.g.

Ke mo fitlhetse *a sa dira*.

....

As can be seen in the previous example, the negative prefix is **sa** and the verb ends in **-a**.

Exercise 11.32

You should now be able to give similar examples while using nouns from other noun classes.

4.5.3 Future tense

The *subjectival concord* of the **mo- ba-** classes is **a** instead of **o**, e.g.

Ke mo fitlhetse **a se ne a dira.**

....

As can be seen in the previous example, the negative prefix is **se** and it occurs before the *auxiliary verb stems* **ne** and **kitla**. The *main verb* also takes the *subjectival concord* **a** and ends in **-a.**

Exercise 11.33

You should now be able to give similar examples using nouns from the other noun classes.

SELF-ASSESSMENT

1. On what structural evidence would you classify the bold italicised verbs as examples of the participial mood?
   (i) Le mororo **a rata** Motabogi, ga a ye go mo nyala.
   (ii) Ke ba rakile **ba sa solofele** gore ke teng.
2. How does the tone of the bold italicised verbs differ?
   (i) Ke utlwa sengwe **se tsamaya**.
   (ii) Sengwe **se tsamaya** mo lefifing.
   (iii) Fa lekgarebe **le go rata**, o tshabe.
   (iv) Lekgarebe leo **le go rata** mo go maswe.
3. When does one use the participial mood?
4. The participial mood accommodates sentences in three different tenses. Name these tenses and give examples of each in the positive and negative.
5. In what way is the subjectival concord of the **mo- ba-** classes changed in the participial mood?
6. What is peculiar about the tone of verbs in the participial mood?

157

5. The subjunctive mood

OBJECTIVES

On completion of this section you should be able to:
1. describe the structure and use of the "subjunctive mood positive";
2. explain the semantic application of the subjunctive mood positive;
3. identify predicates expressing the subjunctive mood positive when occurring in a passage.

5.1 The subjunctive as a mood expressing dependent actions

Would you agree that the bold italicised verbs in the following examples express **interdependent** or **interrelated** actions?

(i) Tsaya dijo tse *o di isetse* rraago.

....

(ii) Ke batla gore *o nthuse.*

....

(iii) Legodu la sia, mme *ra le tshwara.*

....

(iv) O ne *a kile a tsoma, a bolaya* tholo.

....

(v) Batla dipholo, *o di golege, o leme* tshimo e.

....

(vi) *Ke di golege, ke leme* ke le nosi?

....

Verbs expressing **interdependent** or **interrelated** or **consecutive** actions are said to be in the **subjunctive mood**.

The subjunctive mood has two tense forms, viz.

(a) the present
(b) the past.

Each of these tenses is known by a particular structure and circumstances under which they are used.

158

5.2 The subjunctive mood positive

5.2.1 Present tense

1. STRUCTURE OF THE PRESENT TENSE

Structurally the present tense of the subjunctive mood can be divided into the positive and the negative. The negative structure is dealt with in section 5.3. The positive structure is characterised by the following:

(i) all the *subjectival concords* are **high toned**, e.g.

Indicative mood: Basimane *ba* tsamaya jaanong.

....

Subjunctive mood: Basimane *bá tsamaye* jaanong.

....

Exercise 11.34

Can you give your own examples that will illustrate the use of this high toned subjectival concord?

(ii) the *subjectival concord* of the **mo- ba-** classes singular becomes *a* instead of *o*, e.g.

Mosimane *a tsamaye* jaanong.

....

Exercise 11.35

You should now be able to give more examples that will illustrate the use of the subjectival concord of the **mo- ba-** *classes in the subjunctive mood.*

(iii) the *ending for the verb stem* in the subjunctive mood is *-ê* instead of *-a*, e.g.

Tla kwano o nthusê!

....

Exercise 11.36

Can you give more examples that will illustrate the use of the ending -ê in the subjunctive mood?

159

2. USE OF THE PRESENT TENSE

Generally speaking this tense of the subjunctive mood is **used** to express present **interdependent** or **interrelated** or **consecutive** actions. We will now take a closer look at the use of the subjunctive mood in the present tense. The subjunctive mood is used:

● *After the conjunctive* **gore**
This is perhaps the most easily recognisable application of the subjunctive mood, e.g.

  (i) Ke ba laetse **gore** *ba fetse* ka bonako.

  ....

  (ii) Re kopile ntate madi **gore** *re duele* dibuka.

  ....

  (iii) Thiboga **gore** *ke fete.*

  ....

  (iv) Ke tla mo rapela **gore** *a nthuse.*

  ....

Exercise 11.37

You should now be able to add to these examples of the use of the subjunctive mood after the conjunctive **gore.**

● *When appearing as part of a series of commands*
The first command in the series is in the imperative mood and it is followed by predicates expressing the **interrelated** actions associated with the subjunctive mood, e.g.

  (i) Tsoga ngwanaka, **o apare, o je, o tsamaye.**

  ....

  (ii) Tsamaya, **o iketle, o fitlhe.**

  ....

These interrelated actions should not be confused with a series of separate commands, e.g.

    Tsoga! Apara! Ja! Tsamaya!

  ....

160

Exercise 11.38

Can you add to these examples in which the subjunctive mood is expressed as part of a series of commands?

- **After certain auxiliary verbs**
The subjunctive mood occurs after the auxiliary verbs printed in bold italicised letters in the following examples, e.g.

(i) Ke batla gore le nose ditlhare tsena *go fitlhela ke tswalele* metsi.

....

(ii) Ntate *o jafile a goroge* mogala o lela.

....

(iii) A batho ba bogolo! Ga ba ise *ba ke ba ye* kwa Gauteng.

....

(iv) Phokojwe *a tlhole a tsome* motshegare.

....

(v) Leta fa, *go tsamaya* malomaago *a boe*.

....

Exercise 11.39

Can you give your own examples illustrating the use of the subjunctive after the abovementioned auxiliaries?

- **In the expression of polite commands and requests**
(a) The hortative prefix *a*
In the formulation of polite commands and requests the high toned *hortative prefix* **a** precedes the subjectival concord, e.g.

A ke go thuse!

....

A ba tsene foo.

....

A re mo letlelele go fetsa.

....

This hortative prefix **a** is commonly used together with the *auxiliary verb* **kê**, e.g.

161

A n***ke*** ke mmone.

....

A o ***ke*** o mo intshwarele.

....

A mosimane yoo *a* ***ke*** a didimale.

....

Did you notice the conjunctively written subjectival concord of the first person in the first example?

A ***n***ke ***ke*** mmone.

....

When the polite command or request is directed at more than one person the *suffix* -***ng*** is added to the verb, e.g.

A re sie***ng***, re mo tlogele***ng*** fano!

....

Exercise 11.40

Can you add your own examples to these examples of the use of the high toned hortative prefix?

(b) The hortative use of the auxiliary verb ***mma*** or ***mme***

Mma ke go tseise rra.

....

Banna, ***mmang*** re boeng.

....

Mme ke go thuse mma.

....

O ***mme*** o mo pege fa o mmona.

....

Exercise 11.41

You should now be able to add to these examples of the hortative use of the auxiliary verbs ***mma*** *or* ***mme***.

• *When asking about instructions or asking for orders*
In these instances the use of the interrogative conjunction is not common, e.g.

Ba bolotse dinamane leng?

....

Wa re balemi **ba leme** kae?

....

Ke tshware jang?

....

Exercise 11.42

Can you give more examples of the use of the subjunctive mood when asking about instructions or asking for orders?

5.2.2 Past tense

1. STRUCTURE OF THE PAST TENSE

Like the present tense, the past tense can also be divided into a positive and a negative form. In this section only the structure of the positive will be discussed while the negative is reserved for section 5.3.
The positive structure is characterised by the following:

(i) the past tense of the subjunctive mood uses a *special subjectival concord* which is formed by adding a morpheme **-a** to the regular set of subjectival concords, e.g.

Subjectival concords of the subjunctive mood	
SINGULAR	PLURAL
1st P. sing: ke + -a > ka	re + -a > ra
2nd P. sing: o + -a > wa	lo + -a > lwa
3rd P. sing: o + -a > a	ba + -a > ba
o + -a > wa	e + -a > ya
le + -a > la	a + -a > a
se + -a > sa	di + -a > tsa
e + -a > ya	di + -a > tsa
lo + -a > lwa	di + -a > tsa
bo + -a > jwa	a + -a > a
go + -a > ga	
go + -a > ga	

163

These subjectival concords are used as the prefixes of predicates appearing in the subjunctive mood, e.g.

Maloba pula *e ne ya na* sentle. Ka jalo **ra** *kgona* go lema. *Re ne*

....

ra *lema* ke bonako, **ra** *fetsa*. *Morago ga moo,* **ra** *rema* dikala

....

mme ntate **a** *kgwasetsa* legora.

....

Exercise 11.43

You should now be able to give examples of your own that will illustrate the use of the subjectival concords of the subjunctive mood.

(ii) Unlike the present tense of the subjunctive mood the past tense *verb ends in* **-a**, e.g.

Nna *ke ne* **ka** *etela* tsala ya me.

....

Re ne **ra** *tsamaya* mmogo go ya go jela nala kwa toropong.

....

2. USE OF THE PAST TENSE

The past tense of the subjunctive mood expresses **interdependent** or **interrelated** or **consecutive** actions taking place in the past. The past tense of the subjunctive mood is also known as the **narrative tense** because it expresses a sequence of past events. It has been observed in the following instances:

● *In the expression of a series of past events*
In examples of this application of the subjunctive mood the first verb in the sentence **may** belong to the indicative mood, e.g.

Ntate o rekile mmotorokara, **a** *ithuta* go o kgweetsa,

....

a *re* pega, **a** *re isa* sekolong.

....

164

Exercise 11.44

Can you give additional examples to illustrate the use of the sub-junctive mood in the expression of a series of past events?

● *After certain auxiliary verbs*
The subjunctive mood occurs after the auxiliary verbs printed in bold italicised letters in the following examples, e.g.

(i) Pule *o ne* a *simolola* go ithuta bongaka *a bo* a *falola* ka dinaledi.

....

(ii) Ntate *o jafile* a *goroga* legodu le tswa mo tlong ka diaparo tsa

....

ga mme.

....

(iii) Batswana *ba kile* ba *tshela* ka go tsoma le go lema.

....

(iv) Ngame *o namile* a *mpha* dimonamone tse dintsi.

....

(v) Ka letsatsi leo, modisa *a nna* a *tlhokomela* motlhape ka gore

....

bophokojwe *ba ne* ba *boitshega.*

....

Exercise 11.45

Can you give your own examples illustrating the use of the subjunc-tive mood after certain auxiliary verbs?

● *After the potential prefix ka*
In examples of this kind the initial verb can be in the participial mood, e.g.

Fa a *ka* lemoga mosola wa kitso, *a boela* sekolong, *a falola*

....

le balekane ba gagwe, *ba ipatlele* tiro, tsotlhe di tla bo di siame.

....

Exercise 11.46

You should now be able to give further examples illustrating the use of the subjunctive mood after the potential aspect?

SELF-ASSESSMENT

1. Which of the following sentences are examples of the subjunctive mood:
   (a) present tense;
   (b) past tense.
   (i) Ke batla gore o re thuse.
   (ii) Batsomi ba bona tau, ba e ratela mme ya ba bona.
   (iii) Tsaya fa, o ye kwa gae, o fe mmaago.
   (iv) Ga twe ditau di kile tsa bonala fano.
   (v) Ntate a boe a re tlele dimonamone.
   (vi) Fa a ka itshwaya phoso, re ka mo thusa.
   (vii) A ke rute bana ba gago go opela?
   (viii) Mma ke le thuse go golega dipholo tseo.
   (ix) Ba ka nna ba re thusa.
   (x) Ba ye go tlhagola kwa kae?
2. In what kind of sentences is the subjunctive mood used?
3. Mention the tense forms in which the subjunctive mood can appear.
4. "The verbs of the subjunctive mood present tense are characterised by the following three characteristics." Name them.
5. "The verbs of the subjunctive mood past tense are characterised by the following two characteristics." Name them.
6. Five instances of the use of the subjunctive mood present tense were illustrated. Can you name these and give one example of each?
7. Three instances of the use of the subjunctive mood past tense were illustrated. Can you name these and give an example of each?

5.3 The subjunctive mood negative

OBJECTIVES

On completion of this section you should be able to:
1. describe the structure and the use of the "subjunctive mood negative";
2. explain the semantic application of the subjunctive mood negative;
3. identify predicates expressing the subjunctive mood negative when occurring in a passage.

In a previous section it was shown that the subjunctive mood is used to express **interdependent** or **interrelated** or **consecutive** actions, e.g.

Bitsa bana **ba tle** go ja.

....

Tau **ya rora**, batsomi **ba re, kgo!**

....

The subjunctive mood was discussed in terms of:

(a) the present tense featuring:
(i) high toned subjectival concords;
(ii) the subjectival concord **a** instead of **o** in the case of the **mo-ba-** classes singular;
(iii) a verb stem ending in **-ê** instead of **-a**, e.g.

Ke batla gore mosimane **á dire**.

....

(b) the past tense featuring:
(i) a special set of subjectival concords of the subjunctive mood;
(ii) a verb stem ending in **-a**, e.g.

Re ne **ra** tsamaya, **ra** kopana le banna ba babedi, **ba** re kopa

....

madi, **ra** gana go **ba** fa.

....

Various examples illustrating the use of the subjunctive mood were discussed.

In this section the structure and the use of the negative of the subjunctive mood in the present and past tense will receive attention.

5.3.1 Present tense

1. STRUCTURE OF THE PRESENT TENSE

Two forms of the negative structure of the subjunctive mood occur. One of the two can be called the **simple negative** structure and is formed by simply adding the *negative prefix* **se** to the positive structure of the subjunctive mood, e.g.

167

Positive	Negative
(i) Re batla gore ena **a fetse**.	(i) Re batla gore ena *a **se** fetse.*
(ii) A **ba tswe** ka kgoro eo.	(ii) A *ba **se** tswe* ka kgoro eo.
(iii) **Le boe** ka bonako.	(iii) *Le **se** boe* ka bonako.
(iv) Mosimane, **o game** kgomo eo.	(iv) Mosimane, *o **se** game* kgomo eo.

Would you agree that the structural characteristics of the present tense positive remained unchanged in the negative sentences? The only addition to the structure of the present tense structure is the *negative prefix* **se** which occurs between the subjectival concord and the verb stem.

The **compound negative** of the subjunctive mood present tense is formed by means of:

(i) the *negative prefix* **se**,
(ii) the *auxiliary verb* **ka** and
(iii) the *main verb* in the structure of the *subjunctive mood past tense*, e.g.

Positive	Negative
(i) Re batla gore ena **a fetse**.	(i) Re batla gore ena **a se ka a fetsa.**
(ii) A **ba tswe** ka kgoro eo.	(ii) A **ba se ka ba tswa** ka kgoro eo.

168

Positive	Negative
(iii) **Le boe** ka bonako.	(iii) **Le se ka la boa** ka bonako.
(iv) Mosimane, **o game**	(iv) Mosimane, **o se ka wa gama**
kgomo eo.	kgomo eo.

Of these two forms of the negative structure of the subjunctive mood present tense you will find that **the compound form is more commonly used.**

2. THE USE OF THE PRESENT TENSE

The various instances illustrating the use of the subjunctive mood in **interdependent** or **interrelated** or **consecutive** actions were exemplified in section 5.2.1. For the purposes of the negative structure only one example from each of these five groups will be illustrated, e.g.

1. Ke ba laetse gore **ba se ka ba fetsa** ka bonako.

2. Tsoga ngwanaka, **o se ka wa apara, o se ka wa ja, o se ka wa tsamaya.**

3. Ntate o jafile **a se ka a goroga** mogala o lela.

4. A **re se ka ra mo letlelela** go fetsa.

5. Wa re balemi **ba se ka ba lema** kae?

Exercise 11.47

Can you give more examples that will illustrate the use of the subjunctive mood present tense negative?

169

5.3.2 Past tense

1. STRUCTURE OF THE PAST TENSE

The past tense also takes a negative form. The structure of the negative is compound and is formed by means of:

(i) the *negative prefix* **se**,
(ii) the *auxiliary verb* **ka** and
(iii) the *main verb* in the positive form of the verb in the *past tense of the subjunctive mood*, e.g.

Positive	Negative
(i) Maloba pula *e ne ya na* .... sentle.	(i) Maloba pula *e ne ya se* .... *ka ya na* sentle.
(ii) Ka jalo *ra kgona* go .... lema.	(ii) Ka jalo *ra se ka ra* .... *kgona* go lema.
(iii) *Re ne ra lema* ka bonako .... *ra fetsa.*	(iii) *Re ne ra se ka ra lema* ka .... bonako *ra se ka ra fetsa.*

2. USE OF THE PAST TENSE

The following examples of the use of the past tense correspond with those appearing in section 5.2.2, e.g.

1. Ntate o rekile mmotorokara, *a se ka a ithuta* go o kgweetsa, ...

   a se ka a re pega, a se ka a re isa sekolong.
   ....

2. Pule o ne *a se ka a simolola* go ithuta bongaka a bo *a se ka*
   ....

170

a falola ka dinaledi.

....

3. Fa a **ka** se **ka** a lemoga mosola wa kitso, **a se ka a boela**

....

sekolong, **a se ka a falola** le balekane ba gagwe, **ba se ka ba**

....

ipatlela tiro, tsotlhe di tla bo di sa siama.

....

Exercise 11.48
Can you give more examples that will illustrate the use of the subjunctive mood past tense negative?

SELF-ASSESSMENT
1. (a) Which of the following sentences are examples of:
   – the positive and
   – the negative form of the verb
   in the subjunctive mood?
   (i) Lo se ka lwa re sia.
   (ii) Ka mo kopa thuso, a gana.
   (iii) Dikgaka tsa tla tsa fula fa.
   (iv) Mo thuse go rwala thoto eo.
   (b) State the tense of the subjunctive in the preceding sentences.
2. Name the types of actions that are expressed by the subjunctive mood.
3. Give an example of your own of each of the following in the subjunctive mood:
   (a) present tense positive
   (b) present tense negative
   (c) past tense positive
   (d) past tense negative
4. Identify and name the structural elements in each of the examples that you have supplied in 2 above.
5. The subjunctive mood present tense can be **used** in **five** different situations as was illustrated in the previous unit. Can you give examples in the negative that will illustrate the use of this mood?
6. The subjunctive mood past tense can be **used** in **three** different situations as was illustrated in the previous section. Can you give examples in the negative that will illustrate the use of this mood?

---

6. The habitual mood

6.1 The habitual as a mood expressing usual or habitual actions

Would you agree that the bold italicised verbs in the following examples express sequences of habitual, customary or repeated actions or processes:

(i) Pula *e a tle e ne* mariga.

(ii) Tlhware *e a tle e tshware* phala.

(iii) Fa gare ga beke *re a ne re ye* gae.

(iv) Diphoko tse *di a ne di thulane* fa di tlhakanela lesaka.

(v) Badisa ba motlhape o, *ba o game, ba o ise* mafulong, *ba o gorose.*

(vi) Kwa gae mmalapa o tlhokomela lelapa, *a apaye, a feele, a bope* dinkgwana, *a roke* diaparo.

(vii) *Ba a nne ba itulele, ba tlotle.*

(viii) Pele o goroga fa gae, *o tshele* molapo *o bone* diruiwa tsa rona.

Verbs like these expressing **a sequence** of **habitual, customary, usual** or **repeated** actions are said to be in the **habitual mood.**

6.2 The habitual mood positive

1. From the preceding examples it is clear that the habitual mood is characterised by the change of the *verbal ending* from *-a* to *-e*. The semantic implication of this change is illustrated by the following sentences:

(i) Mosadimogolo *o a* goro*ga*, *o* bul*a* lebati, *o a* tsen*a*.

....

(ii) Mosadimogolo *a* goro*ga*, *a* bul*a* lebati, *a* tsen*a*.

....

(iii) Mosadimogolo *a* goro*ge*, *a* bul*e* lebati, *a* tsen*e*.

....

The first sentence is an example of the present tense of the **indicative mood**. The second sentence is an example of the past tense of the **subjunctive mood**. The third sentence is an example of the **habitual mood** with the verbal ending *-e*.

2. From the previous three examples it is clear that the *subjectival concord* of the *mo- ba-* class singular changes from *o* in the indicative mood present tense to *a* in the habitual mood. It is common to have a sentence in which the first predicate appears in the indicative mood followed by predicates in the habitual mood, e.g.

Mosimane *o* *tlhokomela* tshingwana ya me, *a* e *tlhogole, a* e

....

nos*e, a* *lete* dithaga, *a* *kotule a* *lebogelwe* matsapa a gagwe.

....

3. The habitual mood frequently occurs as a complement of *auxiliary verbs tle, ne* and *nne*, e.g.

Mebutla *e* **tle** *e* *bonale* motshegare fa o tsamaya mo nageng.

....

Ka jalo *re a **ne** re e batle*, re e tsome ka dintšwa. *Re a **nne***

....

re boele gae re sikere.

....

Can you still distinguish between the structural elements of the preceding compound predicates? If you have a problem you should revise the chapter on the auxiliary verb.

SELF-ASSESSMENT

1. Name the individual bold italicised elements occurring in predicates expressing the habitual mood in the following:
   Pele letsatsi le tlhaba, *o **utlwe*** dinonyane di tsoga, *di **letse*** molodi, *di **fofe*** go ya go sela. *Di a tle di boe* motshegare, mme ka metlha *di **goroge*** fa le kolomela.
2. For what purpose are sentences of the habitual mood used?
3. Name the structural elements occurring in an example of a compound predicate in the habitual mood.
4. Mention three auxiliary verb stems that may precede a verb in the habitual mood.

6.3 The habitual mood negative

OBJECTIVES

On completion of this section you should be able to:
1. describe the structure and use of the "habitual mood negative";
2. explain the semantic application of the habitual mood negative;
3. identify predicates expressing the habitual mood negative when appearing in a passage.

In the previous section it was shown that the habitual mood is used to express **a sequence of habitual, customary, usual or repeated actions.**

Regarding the structure of the predicate in the habitual mood, it was shown that the verb ends in *-e* instead of *-a*, e.g.

174

Fa gare ga beke *re a ne re ye* gae.

....

Bagolo *ba tle ba tshwaragane* le mathata.

....

Pitse *ena e a nne e gane* go palangwa.

....

The subjectival concord of the **mo- ba-** class singular is *a* instead of the regular *o*, e.g.

Modulasetulo o epa pitso, *a simolole* ka thapelo *a feleletse*

....

ka go leboga kopano.

....

The complement of the auxiliary verbs **tle, ne** and **nne** are in the habitual mood, e.g.

Re a tle **re tsoge** phakela.

....

In this section attention will be given to the structure of the habitual mood negative.

The negative of the habitual mood is formed by means of the *negative prefix se* the *auxiliary stem* **ke** which is followed by the complement in the structure of the *habitual mood positive*, e.g.

Positive	*Negative*
(i) Monna *a tsoge a apare* .... *a tswe.*	(i) Monna *a* **se ke** *a tsoge a* .... **se ke** *a apare a* **se ke** *a tswe.* ....
(ii) Ba tle **ba goroge** .... ka nako.	(ii) Ba tle *ba* **se ke** *ba goroge* .... ka nako. ....

Positive	Negative
(iii) Ntate *o a ne a lwale.*	(iii) Ntate *o a ne a se ke* .... *a lwale.* ....

In the negative examples of (ii) and (iii) above you will notice that the compound predicates consist of two auxiliary verbs followed by a complement. In the following examples the subjectival concords of the two auxiliaries and the complement appear in bold italicised type:

Basimane **ba** tle **ba** se ke **ba** goroge ka nako.

....

Ntate **o** a ne **a** se ke **a** lwale.

....

Exercise 11.49

You should now attempt to give examples of your own of verbs in the negative form of the habitual mood.

SELF-ASSESSMENT

1. Name each of the bold italicised structural elements appearing in the following sentences:
   (i) Bogologolo tau le ramošwe di ne di phela mmogo, mme **di thusanye** go tsoma, **di** lale mmogo **di** tlhakanele dijo.
   (ii) Di ne di se ka di lwa, **di se ke di** ganetsanye, di se ke **di timane**, di se ke di kgaogane ka nako epe.
2. What kind of actions or processes are expressed by means of the habitual mood?
3. Describe the structure of the habitual mood positive and negative.
4. Name the auxiliary verbs that can occur in a compound predicate of the habitual mood.

CHAPTER 12

Adverbs

OBJECTIVES

On completion of this chapter you should be able to:
1. explain the meaning of the term "adverb";
2. describe the structure and use of adverbs;
3. identify the different kinds of adverbs in a paragraph.

---

1. The meaning of the term *adverb*

The following examples clearly illustrate that the bold italicised words describe the process or action of the verb in terms of:

(a) **where** it takes place
(b) **when** it takes place
(c) **how** it takes place.

  (i) Banna ba setse ba ile **kwa tirong**.

  (ii) **Maitseboa** bana ba robala **kwa gae**.

  (iii) Tla **ka bonako!** Re **mo bothateng**.

Adverbs like these are divided into:

(a) adverbs of place, e.g. **kwa tirong, teng, Huhudi.**

(b) adverbs of time, e.g. **maitseboa, kgale, monongwaga.**

(c) adverbs of manner, e.g. **ka bonako, sentle, gantsi.**

Let us now devote more attention to the adverbs of **place**. The adverbs of **time** and **manner** will receive more attention later on.

2. Adverbs of place

In the following examples you will notice that the bold italicised parts refer to **localities** where the process or action takes place:

(i) Barutwana ba ile *sekolong.*

....

(ii) *Mo sekolong* ba ithuta go kwala.

....

(iii) *Kwa sekolong* ga ba senye nako.

....

(iv) Bese e ba folosa *fa sekolong.*

....

Would you agree that in the case of the adverb *sekolong* only **a general notion** of locality is conveyed while the addition of the *disjunctively written prefixes mo, kwa* and *fa* give these adverbs the ability to describe the process or action more precisely?

2.1 Primary adverbs of place

Those adverbs, that are used **without** the disjunctively written prefixes *mo, fa* and *kwa* and only convey a **general notion** of locality, are called **primary adverbs of place**. Different types of primary adverbs of place can be distinguished:

1. *Original adverbs of place* which are not related to any other kind of word, e.g.

Ga ke itse gore ba ile *kae.*

....

Malomaagwe o tswa *kae*?

....

2. *Adverbs of place derived from nouns*

(i) This is achieved by *suffixing -ng*, e.g.

Banna ba dira *tshimong.*

....

Re ya *toropong* phakela.

....

178

(ii) Nouns already ending in **-ng** change and use the locative suffixes **-nnye** or **-nnyeng**, e.g.

Basadi ba tswa *bojannye*, mme basetsana ba sa ntse ba ile

....

kgonnyeng.

....

(iii) Place names may also be used as primary adverbs of place and they may require the *suffix -ng* or they may be used without it, e.g.

Lesotho .... Tlhaping ....

Bophuthatswana .... Mafikeng ....

Sefatlhane .... Mangaung ....

(iv) The names or personal names by which people are known can be adopted by using the *disjunctively written prefix* **go**, e.g.

Mariga a tlhabile **go** *rrangwane*.

....

A re ye **go** *bôPule* ka moso!

....

(v) Proper names of rulers are used as primary adverbs of place by means of the conjunctively written *prefixes* **-ga** and **goo-**, e.g.

Goo*Tawana* mafulo a mantle.

....

Banna ba, ke baeng ba **gammaNgwato**.

....

(vi) A number of locative class nouns are used as primary adverbs of place, e.g.

Golo fa ga re go kgone. ....

Ga ba a ya **kgakala**. ....

3. Adverbs of place derived from pronouns. This is achieved by means of the *disjunctively written prefix* **go**, e.g.

179

Tla **go** nna ngwanaka.

....

Tabogela **go** sele o palame.

....

4. Adverbs of place are derived from qualificative structures
by means of the *disjunctively written prefix* **go**, e.g.

O ye **go** yo moleele.

....

Ke tswa **go** yo o dirang yole.

....

Re ka kopa thuso **go** bafe?

....

Tlhatlhelela tsa gago **go** tsa me.

....

Exercise 12.1

*Can you, in the case of each of the four groups of primary adverbs
of place mentioned above, give additional examples of your own?*

2.2 Secondary adverbs of place

Those adverbs that are used *with the disjunctively written prefixes*
mo, fa and **kwa** and convey a more **precise notion** of locality are
called **secondary adverbs of place. Many of the primary adverbs
of place**, discussed in 2.1. above, may use one of the prefixes **mo,
fa** or **kwa to form secondary adverbs of place**, e.g.

Ga ke itse gore ba ile **kwa** kae?

....

Malomaagwe o tswa **fa** kae.

....

Banna ba dira **mo** tshimong.

....

180

Re ya **kwa** *toropong* phakela.

....

Basadi ba tswa **kwa** *bojannye.*

....

Basetsana ba sa ntse ba ile **fa** *kgonnyeng.*

....

Basotho ba nna **kwa** *Lesotho.*

....

Rona re nna **mo** *Bophuthatswana.*

....

Mariga a tlhabile **kwa** *go rrangwane.*

....

A re ye **kwa** *go bôPule* ka moso!

....

Kwa *gooTawana* mafulo a mantle.

....

Banna ba, ke baeng ba **kwa** *gammaNgwato.*

....

Ga ba a ya **kwa** *kgakala.*

....

Tla **kwa** *go nna* ngwanaka.

....

Tabogela **kwa** *go sele* o palame.

....

O ye **fa** *go yo moleele.*

....

Ke tswa **kwa** *go yo o dirang* yole.

....

Re ka kopa thuso *mo* go bafe.

....

Tlhatlhelela tsa gago *mo* go tsa me.

....

The exactness of the locality, as denoted by the prefixes *mo, fa* and *kwa*, can be seen in the following examples:

Ke robala *fa* molapong.

....

Ke robala *mo* molapong.

....

Ke robala *kwa* molapong.

....

Exercise 12.2

You should now be able to give your own examples to illustrate the use and formation of the secondary adverbs of place.

3. Adverbs of time

In the following examples you will notice that the bold italicised parts refer to the **time** when the process or action takes place:

(i) ***Bogologolo*** batho ba ne ba tshela ka go tsoma.

....

(ii) ***Motshegare*** rona ga re na nako ya go ikhutsa.

....

(iii) A lona le lwala ***ka nako*** yotlhe?

....

(iv) ***Ka metlha*** rona re tsoga phakela.

....

Would you agree that we are dealing with **two kinds of adverbs** here? In sentences (i) and (ii) we have examples of original adverbs of time as well as nouns and nominal compounds functioning as adverbs of time. These adverbs are called the **primary adverbs of time**.

In sentence (iii) and (iv) the adverbs are formed by means of a *prefix ka* and they are called the **secondary adverbs of time**.

3.1 Primary adverbs of time

These adverbs are divided into:

(a) original adverbs of time, e.g.

jaanong	kgale	gwetla
....	....	....
isago	jale	leng
....	....	....

(b) unchanged nouns used as adverbs of time, e.g.

maabane	mariga	dikgakologo
....	....	....
letlhafula	selemo	bogologolo
....	....	....

(c) compounds used as adverbs of time, e.g.

motshegare	jaanong-jaana	pelepele
....	....	....
ngwagatlola	motlhamongwe	bosigogare
....	....	....

Exercise 12.3

You should now look up other examples like these and use them in sentences, e.g.

    Basimane ba tlile **pele**.

....

    Selemo *ga go a lemiwa mono.*

....

    Bosigogare *go a tshabega mo sekgweng seno.*

....

3.2 Secondary adverbs of time

(i) These adverbs are formed by means of the *disjunctively written adverbial prefix* **ka** + a noun, e.g.

ka metlha ....

ka Laboraro ....

ka makuku ....

ka Mopitlwe ....

(ii) A next kind of secondary adverb of time is formed by means of the *disjunctively written adverbial prefix* **mô** and a *noun ending* in the conjunctively written *locative suffix* **-ng**, e.g.

mo nako**ng** ....

mo kgwedi**ng** ....

mo maabanyane**ng** ....

mo moso**ng** ....

Exercise 12.4

You should now look up other examples like these and use them in sentences, e.g.

Mo mosong wa letsatsi la bobedi re ne ra khutla ka nako.

....

4. Adverbs of manner

In the following examples you will notice that the italicised parts refer to the **manner** in which the process or action takes place:

(i) **Ruri** ke mo rata **thata.**

....

(ii) Ke tla dira **jang** gore a nthate?

....

(iii) Ke tla patelesega go bua **le moratiwa.**

....

184

(iv) E kete a ka nthata **ka pelo** yotlhe.

....

(v) E kete nka ratiwa **ke ena.**

....

In these sentences you are introduced to two kinds of adverbs of manner. In sentences (i) and (ii) we have examples of **original adverbs of manner**. This group of adverbs is called **primary adverbs of manner.**

In sentences (iii), (iv) and (v) the adverbs are formed by means of the *prefixes* **le, ka** and **ke** and they are called the **secondary adverbs of manner.**

4.1 Primary adverbs of manner

These adverbs are divided into:

(a) original adverbs of manner, e.g.

pila	jang	thata
....	....	....
fela	tota	ruri
....	....	....

A ba bua **pila?**

....

Ruri ga re mo itse!

....

(b) nouns used as adverbs of manner, e.g.

Batlhabani ba lwa **selau.**

....

Bômmangwane ba kgabisa **Sengwaketse.**

....

Mosadi yo o itshotse **sesimane.**

....

Exercise 12.5

By using the dictionary, you should now try to find more examples of these two kinds of primary adverbs of manner.

4.2 Secondary adverbs of manner

(i) These adverbs are formed by means of the *disjunctively written connective prefix le* which gives nouns, pronouns, adjectives and relative constructions an adverbial application, e.g.

Mme o bua *le mosetsana* yo montle le nna ke batla go bua *le ena*.

....

Jaanong ke bua *le yo montle* yole.

....

A wena o mpona ke bua *le yo o bonolo* yole?

....

(ii) Secondary adverbs of manner are also formed by means of the *conjunctively written connective prefix na-*, e.g.

Re tla kopana le bona > Re tla kopana *nabo*.

....

Ba tsamaile le tsona   > Ba tsamaile *natso*.

....

These adverbs are formed by *na-* + the first syllable of the absolute pronoun, e.g.

na- + *bo*na > nabo   ....

na- + *e*na > nae   ....

(iii) Secondary adverbs are also formed by means of the *disjunctively written instrumental prefix ka* which gives nouns, pronouns, adjectives and relative constructions an adverbial application, e.g.

Ntate o betla sepora *ka petlwana*.

....

Ntate o betla sepora *ka yona*.

....

Ntate o betla sepora **ka** *e ntšhwa.*

....

Ntate o betla sepora **ka** *e e bogale.*

....

Ntate o betla sepora **ka** *e a e looditseng.*

....

(iv) The *disjunctively written copulative prefix* **ke** together with nouns, pronouns, adjectives and relative constructions acquire an adverbial sense, e.g.

Rona re kgethilwe **ke** *morafe.*

....

Rona re kgethilwe **ke** *ona.*

....

Rona re kgethilwe **ke** *o motona.*

....

Rona re kgethilwe **ke** *o o kgethang* badiri.

....

(v) A last type of secondary adverb is formed by means of the *disjunctively written prefix* **jaaka** which gives nouns, pronouns, adjectives and relative constructions an adverbial application, e.g.

Wena o aga **jaaka** *setswerere.*

....

Wena o aga **jaaka** *sona.*

....

Wena o aga **jaaka** *se setona.*

....

Wena o aga **jaaka** *se se matlhagatlhaga.*

....

Exercise 12.6

By consulting your dictionary you should be able to give more examples of these secondary adverbs of manner.

1. (a) What is the function of the bold italicised parts of the following examples?
   (i) Ba ile **leng**?
   (ii) Ba tsamaile **maabane**.
   (iii) Morwaake o tla kgona **jang**?
   (iv) Morwaago o tla kgona ka go dira **ka thata** yotlhe.
   (b) To what types of adverbs do the abovementioned examples belong?
   (c) Give two more examples of each of the types mentioned in (b) above.
2. What is the function of the bold italicised parts of the following examples?
   (i) Lenong le timetse **mo lefaufaung.**
   (ii) **Ka mahube-a-naka-tsa-kgomo** balemi ba tsoga go golega dipholo.
   (iii) Go tlile **jang** gore a robege leoto?
3. (a) Describe the structure of the adverbs occurring in the following examples:
   (i) Ditau di utlwala mo sekgweng.
   (ii) Mo tshiping eno re tla fetsa tiro.
   (iii) Tsamaya le ena a go supetse!
   (b) To what types of adverbs do the abovementioned examples belong?
   (c) Give two more examples of each of the types mentioned in (b) above.
4. What does the term "adverb" signify?
5. (a) Name the main kinds of adverbs and state their functions in sentences.
   (b) Give an example of each of the main kinds of adverbs.
6. Can the adverb **kae** be used:
   (a) as an interrogative?
   (b) as a statement?
7. Name two other kinds of words from which primary adverbs of place may be derived and in each case give two examples of your own.
8. (a) Describe the structure of the adverbs of place featuring in the following examples:
   (i) Basetsana ba ile nokeng.
   (ii) Dipodi di fula fa nokeng.
   (iii) Ditshwene di siela ntsweng.
   (iv) Dipela di nna mo ntsweng.

188

      (v) Rangwane o ya Huhudi.

      (vi) Rona re agile mo Huhudi.

  (b) Name the two types of adverbs represented by these examples.

9. When are the suffixes **-nnye** or **-nnyeng** used?

10. When is the disjunctively written prefix *go* used?

11. Explain the concept "adverb" in your own words.

12. Besides the original adverbs of time the primary adverbs of time also accommodate two other kinds of adverbs. Name them and give two examples of each.

13. The secondary adverbs of time are made up of two types of adverbs. Give two examples of each type.

14. The primary adverbs of manner are made up of two types of adverbs. Give two examples of each type.

15. Four prefixes are used in the derivation of the secondary adverbs of manner. Describe the structure of adverbs formed by means of them.

CHAPTER 13

Ideophones

OBJECTIVES

On completion of this chapter you should be able to:
1. explain the meaning of the term "ideophone";
2. describe the derivation and use of ideophones;
3. identify ideophones in a passage.

---

1. The meaning of the term *ideophone*

Read the following sentences attentively and try to establish the function of the words appearing in bold italics:

(i) Basimanyana ba tshameka ba re ***thuu, thuu*** ka ditlhobolonyana

....

tsa bona.

....

(ii) Legodu leo le atlhotswe, ba bo ba mo re ***twatla*** mo kgolegelong.

....

(iii) Leuba la 1983 le ne la re naga ***setlhee.***

....

The bold italicised parts are called **ideophones** and are in many respects similar in function to adverbs. **Ideophones are descriptive of sound, colour, smell, manner or appearance or state of the action or process.**

Ideophones are therefore words describing actions that one experiences with all the organs of sense. They are very commonly used in narratives and are usually accompanied by gestures and grimaces.

Let's illustrate some of these aspects of ideophones.

1.1 Ideophones that are descriptive of sound

In this case the ideophone imitates the sound usually associated with a particular action or process, e.g.

(i) E rile ba goroga pula e bo e re **gwaa**.

....

(ii) Batsomi ba ne ba ratela tholo, losogo **phurr**, tholo **sutlha.**

....

(iii) Mohumi o fetile fano a ntse a re madi, **tsiri** mo kgetsing.

....

(iv) Pule o ne a thulametse, mme balekane ba mo re **phatšha** ka

....

metsi a a tsididi.

....

The following is a list of ideophones that qualify predicates in terms of sound:

pho	swaa	goro	thipo
....	....	....	....
tu/tuu	thuu	ruthu	kgothu
....	....	....	....
porr	tirr	thabu/tobu	thwaa
....	....	....	....
tidididi			
....			

Exercise 13.1

By using your dictionary as a point of departure you should now attempt to use these ideophones in meaningful sentences of your own.

1.2 Ideophones that are descriptive of colour

Some of the ideophones of this group can be linked without difficulty to **adjectival roots** while others only show relationship to the *deideophonic verb stems* that are derived from them, e.g.

(i) Dipone tsa mmotorokara di ne tsa tima go bo go re **tsho.**

....

(ii) Letsatsi la tlhaba le re **hubee**.

....

(iii) Mo leseding thipa ya mmolai, **phatsi**.

....

(iv) Fa legadima le re **lai**, o sa utlwe modumo, o itse gore le kgakala.

....

The following ideophones qualify predicates in terms of colour:

fii..	twaa ....
lai	talaa ....
nyedi	setlhee ....

Exercise 13.2

You should use your dictionary as a point of departure in an attempt to use these ideophones in meaningful sentences of your own.

1.3 Ideophones that are descriptive of smell

A small number of ideophones are used in the description of odours, e.g.

(i) Morago ga renepese lefatshe lotlhe le ne le tletse ditotwanato-twana di re **hesoo**.

....

(ii) Leuba la ba pataletsa go ja dibodu **phuu**.

....

Exercise 13.3

Can you supply more examples of ideophones that describe the predicate in terms of smell? You should be able to use these ideophones in sentences of your own.

1.4 Ideophones that are descriptive of manner or appearance or state of the action or process

Ideophones are especially suited to describe the manner, appearance or state of an action or process, e.g.

(i) Legodu lona, *time*, motlha mapodisa a goroga.

....

(ii) E rile ke tsena mo kamoreng kake e bo e re **lelelele** ka fa

....

tlase ga kobotlo.

....

(iii) Batsomi ba sala tau eo morago mo sekgweng. Ya bo e re **sutlha**.

....

Batsomi **phatla.**

....

(iv) Dintšwa tsa leleka phokojwe a bo a re mosima **golwe.**

....

The following ideophones will also describe predicates in terms of the manner, appearance or state of an action:

kge	tshe	tserr	meno
kgo	tlho	bilo	rago
nwe	ngwee	khuru	rose
seto	tshekge	rowee	pharagatlha

Exercise 13.4

You should use your dictionary as a point of departure in an attempt to use these ideophones in sentences of your own.

2. The derivation of ideophones

1. From the examples quoted above you have noticed that there are a few ideophones that are derived from adjectival roots, e.g.

Ideophone	Adjectival roots
setlhee	< setlha ....
hubee	< hubedu (colour) ....
hibi	< hibidu (heat) ....
talaa	< tala ....
sweuu	< sweu ....

Exercise 13.5

You should now attempt to find more ideophones derived from adjectival roots. The adjectival roots appearing in the dictionary can be used as a point of departure.

2. A small number of ideophones are derived from verbs, e.g.

kgo	< kgonya ....
ne	< na ....

This process should not be confused with the formation of the deideophonic verbs commonly formed by adding the suffixes (i) *-la*, (ii) *-ga*, (iii) *-ma*, (iv) *-sêla*, (v) *-mêla* and (vi) *-mêtsa* to ideophones, e.g.

Ideophone	> Deideophinc verb stem
(i) dike	> dike*la*
....	....
nwe	> nwe*la*
....	....
time	> time*la*
....	....
(ii) rago	> rago*ga*
....	....
seto	> seto*ga*
....	....
kgothu	> kgothu*ga*
....	....

(iii)	tsiri	>	tsiri*ma*
	phapha	>	phapha*ma*
	nyedi	>	nyedi*ma*
(iv)	tete	>	tete*sêla*
	photho	>	photho*sêla*
	nene	>	nene*sêla*
(v)	golwe	>	golo*mêla*
	kotlwe	>	kotlo*mêla*
	khuru	>	khuru*mêla*
(vi)	golwe	>	golo*mêtsa*
	kotlwe	>	kotlo*mêtsa*
	khuru	>	khuru*mêtsa*

3. The use of ideophones

1. In the case of ideophones that have produced deideophonic derivative verb stems the ideophone alone can be used to imply a predicate. The predicate is therefore understood, e.g.

195

(i) Dintšwa tsa mo leleka. Phokojwe **golwe**, mo mosimeng.

....

(ii) Kake ena a lemoga kotsi. **Nene**, ka fa tlase ga letlapa.

....

(iii) Bana ba ne ba palame setlhare. Kala, **kgothu**. Pule **tirr**.

....

(iv) Tlhobolo **thuu**. Madi **goro**. Kolobe **pirigi**.

....

Ideophones descriptive of colour can also be used in this way but it should be borne in mind that they also have a verbal link through the deadjectival verb stems, e.g.

tala   > talafala   > talaa ....

setlha   > setlhafala   > setlhee ....

hibidu   > hibifala   > hibi ....

(v) Mafulo, **talaa** morago ga pula.

....

(vi) Letsatsi la phirima. Loapi, **hibi**.

....

You will have noticed that when the ideophones are used to imply predicates **no use** is made of **subjectival concords.**

When ideophones are used to imply predicates these *ideophones* can be described by means of **adverbs**, e.g.

(vii) Pula, **maabane** *gwaa*, **gompieno** *gwaa*.

....

(viii) Dijalo, **kwa tshimong** *talaa*.

....

(ix) Senokwane, *pote* **ka lebotana**.

....

(x) Mosimane, *ngwee* **le moratiwa**.

....

2. *Ideophones* are usually preceded by the different *tense forms of the verb* **re**, e.g.

PRESENT: Pitse **ya re** *kgo*, mopalami **a re** *pirigi*

....

PERFECT: Nama eo, Dimo **o e rile**, *kuditi*.

....

FUTURE: Mo tlogele **ke tla mo re** *rose* ka lemao.

....

3. When the expression of emphasis is desired the *ideophone* is used together with its **deideophonic verb stem** or with its **deadjectival verb stem**, e.g.

(i) Ka leuba la 1983 naga e ne e **setlhafetse** *setlhee*, go se na mafulo.

....

(ii) Ngwaga ona, dijwalo tsa rona di **talafetse** di ntse di re *talaa*.

....

(iii) Basadi ba ne ba tshogile ba **tetesela** *tete* ba sa itse go dira eng.

....

(iv) Dintšwa tsa kobela ditholo mo nokeng, kwena ya **nwela**,

....

morago ga sebakanyana ntšwa e bo e re *nwe*.

....

SELF-ASSESSMENT

1. What does the term "ideophone" signify?
2. What descriptive function do the following words have?

porr	tididi
phatsi	tsho
phuu	tlho
bilo	hesoo

3. Explain the derivation of the following ideophones: talaa, hubee, kgo, ne, setlhee.
4. Explain the formation of deideophonic verbs and mention the suffixes that are involved.
5. Can ideophones be used to imply a predicate? Give examples.

6. Ideophones usually follow a certain verb. Mention the tenses involved and give examples.
7. How can ideophones be used to emphasise a verb? Give examples.
8. Select ideophones descriptive of (a) sound, (b) colour, (c) smell and (d) manner from the following list and use them in meaningful sentences:

    ruthu, kgwatlha, twaa phuu.

CHAPTER 14

Copulatives

OBJECTIVES

On completion of this chapter you should be able to:

1. explain the meaning of the term "copulative" in respect of the *identifying, descriptive* and *associative copulatives*;
2. describe the structure and use of these copulatives in the *indicative* and *participial moods*;
3. explain the significance of the term "complement" in these copulative structures;
4. enumerate the words and structures that may function as copular complements;
5. describe the structure and use of the copular verb **nna** in these copulatives;
6. identify these copulatives as well as their complements within the context of a passage.

1. The identifying copulative

The term **copulative** is applied to three kinds of structures, viz.

(i) identifying copulatives,
(ii) descriptive copulatives (see page 221),
(iii) associative copulatives (see page 237).

In this chapter the three copulative structures are discussed separately. However, before proceeding to the discussion of the identifying copulative it is advisable to give a brief survey of each of the three copulative structures.

(i) The first copulative structure expresses the **existing identifying relationship** or **equalising relationship** between a subject and a complement, e.g.

Ntate **ke** morutabana. ....

Tau **ke** sebata. ....

Mokgalo **ke** setlhare. ....

199

In these sentences:
Father is identified as being **a teacher.**
The lion is identified as being **a predator.**
The buffalo-thorn is identified as being **a tree.**

The identifying relationship is expressed by means of the copulative **ke.**

The *subjects* of our sentences are:

Ntate,
Tau and
Mokgalo.

The *objects* of the copular predicate are called *complements*, viz.

morutabana,
sebata and
setlhare.

The *copular predicate* consists of the copulative plus the complement, e.g.

Ntate **ke morutabana.** ....

(ii) The second copular structure expresses an existing **descriptive relationship** between a subject and a complement, e.g.

Ntate **o** bonolo. ....

Tau **e** bogale. ....

Mokgalo **o** monate. ....

In these sentences:
Father is described as being **kind.**
The lion is described as being **fierce.**
The buffalo-thorn is described as being **delicious.**

Different bold italicised copulatives are used to express the descriptive relationship.
Can you identify the complements and the predicates of these examples?

(iii) The third copular structure expresses an existing **associative relationship** between a subject and a complement, e.g.

Ntate **o na** le madi. ....

Tau **e na** le seriri. ....

Mokgalo **o na** le moriti. ....

In these sentences it is stated that:

Father is associated with **money.**
The lion is associated with a **mane.**
The buffalo-thorn is associated with **shade.**

The three kinds of non-verbal elements used to express **an existing** *identifying, descriptive* or *associative relationship* between subjects and complements are called **copulatives.**

The term copulative also includes the copulative formed by means of the **copulative verb -nna.** This verb expresses **the entering into a state** and appears in all three the abovementioned kinds of copular structures, e.g.

(i) identifying or equalising copulative

Ntate *o nna* morutabana. ....

Tau *e nna* seruiwa. ....

Mokgalo *o nna* mokalabata. ....

(ii) descriptive copulative

Ntate *o nna* bonolo. ....

Tau *e nna* bosilo. ....

Mokgalo *o nna* botlhoko. ....

(iii) associative copulative

Ntate *o nna* le maitemogelo. ....

Tau *e nna* le letlhoo. ....

Mokgalo *o nna* le diboko. ....

We shall now proceed to a more detailed discussion of the **identifying copulative** while the **two** other copulatives will receive attention on pages 221 and 237.

1.1 The meaning of the term *identifying copulative*

This copulative, as was shown above, expresses an **identifying** or **equalising relationship** between a subject and a complement, e.g.

Ntate **ke** morutabana. ....

1.2 The structure of the identifying copulative

1.2.1 The copular prefixes

You have been introduced to the non-verbal identifying copulative prefix **ke**[1] in:

Ntate **ke** morutabana. ....

This, however, is not the only form of the non-verbal identifying copulative, e.g.

Nna **kè** morutabana. ....

Wena **o** morutabana. ....

Rona **re** barutabana. ....

Lona **le** barutabana. ....

Would you agree that the **existing** identifying relationship, i.e. "is" and "are", in these examples is expressed by means of the **subjectival concords** of the **first** and **second person singular** and **plural** prefixed to the complement?

Did you notice the low toned **kè**, which is the subjectival concord of the first person? in e.g.

Nna **kè** morutabana. ....

Nna **kè** Motswana. ....

Nna **kè** ngaka. ....

If you compare these **kè** sentences with the following, you will notice a **difference in tone** in the case of **ke**, e.g.

Ntate **ké** morutabana. ....

Ntate **ké** Motswana. ....

Ntate **ké** ngaka. ....

In the case of the **third person** the invariable high toned **ké** is prefixed to the complement irrespective of the noun class or singularity or plurality of the subject, e.g.

Ntate **ké** morutabana. ....

Bontate **ké** barutabana. ....

Kgomo **ké** seruiwa. ....

1) Cf. dictionary p. 58.

Dikgomo **ké** diruiwa. ....

Ena **ké** Moagi. ....

Bona **ké** Basotho. ....

The negative of the abovementioned is formed as follows:

	· SINGULAR	PLURAL
1st person:	Nna *ga ké* morutabana.	Rona *ga re* barutabana. ....
2nd person:	Wena *ga ó* morutabana.	Lona *ga lo* barutabana. ....
3rd person:	Ena *ga sé* morutabana.	Bona *ga se* barutabana. ....

As you can see:

(i) a negative prefix *ga* was prefixed to the positive structure, e.g.

Nna *kè* Motswana > Nna *ga* ké Motswana.

In the negative the tone of the identifying copulative prefix changes from *low* to *high*.

(ii) the high toned **ké** is replaced by the negative prefix *se*, e.g.

Ena ké Mosotho > Ena *ga se* Mosotho.

1.2.2 *The copular predicate*

The copular verb *-nna*, i.e. "becomes", expresses **the entering of a state** and it forms its negative by means of the negative prefix *ga* and the verb stem ending in *-e*, e.g.

Ntate *o nna* moagi   > Ntate *ga a nne* moagi.

....

Tau *e nna* seruiwa.   > Tau *ga e nne* seruiwa.

....

Mokgalo *o nna* mokalabata. > Mokgalo *ga o nne* mokalabata.

....

Exercise 14.1

Can you give more examples of your own illustrating the identifying or equalising copulative expressing:
  (i) existing relationships
 (ii) the entering into a relationship.

1.2.3 The complements of the non-verbal identifying copulatives

1. NOUNS AS COPULAR COMPLEMENTS

In all the copular structures quoted here, the complements or "objects" were nouns. The nouns are however not the only word category or structure that may be used as a complement. This will be illustrated in the rest of this section.

It has been shown that the 1st and 2nd persons, as the subjects of the copular construction, use the subjectival concords as non-verbal copulatives, e.g.

Nna **ke** mohumi.   > Rona **re** bahumi.

....

Wena **o** modiidi.   > Lona **le** badiidi.

....

The 3rd person uses the invariable high toned **ké** as the copulative, e.g.

Ena **ké** mohumi.   > Bona **ké** bahumi.

....

The non-verbal copulatives were followed by nouns as complements. This manner of presentation will be used to introduce the rest of the copular complements.

2. ABSOLUTE PRONOUNS AS COPULAR COMPLEMENTS

1st and 2nd person as subject:

Nna **kè nna**, wena **o wena.**

....

Re rona. Lona **lo bomang**?

....

Wena *o ena* yo re mmoneng maabane.

....

3rd person as subject:

Bona! **Ké tsona** ditholo tsa maabane.

....

Ké nna Sello, yo o buang.

....

A **ké ena** yo o tsamayang fale?

....

Exercise 14.2

Can you add to these examples using absolute pronouns as complements?

3. DEMONSTRATIVES AS COPULAR COMPLEMENTS

1st and 2nd person as subject:

Lebelela ditshwantsho tse! Nna **ke yo**, wena *o yole*. **Rona re**

....

bale mo mmotorokareng. Lona *le ba*, ba ba sa kgabang.

....

3rd person as subject:

Basimane **ke bao**! Ba romele kwano!

....

Dinku **ke tsele**, di senya mmidi.

....

Ngwanake **ke yo**, o gorogile.

....

Exercise 14.3

Will you be able to add to these examples using demonstratives as complements?

205

4. ADJECTIVES AS COPULAR COMPLEMENTS

1st and 2nd person as subjects:

Nna *kè yo moleele* mo go bona.

....

Wena *o yo mmotlana* mo go rona.

....

Lona *le ba bakimanyana.*

....

3rd person as subject:

Bona *ké ba basesane* thata.

....

Dikota tse *ké tse dithata* go feta.

....

Selepe se, *ké se sennye* mo go maswe.

....

Exercise 14.4

Can you add to these examples using adjectives as complements?

5. ENUMERATIVES AS COPULAR COMPLEMENTS

1st and 2nd person as subject:

Nna *kè mongwe* wa bone bao.

....

Rona *re basele.*

....

Wena *o ofe*?

....

3rd person as subject:

Podi *ké nngwe* ya tse di suleng.

....

Noga eo, **ké esele.**

....

Morafe oo, **ké osele.**

....

The enumerative root **-pe** can only occur in negative constructions, e.g.

Ga **go epe** fano.

....

Exercise 14.5

Can you give your own examples using enumerative roots as complements?

6. POSSESSIVES AS COPULAR COMPLEMENTS

1st and 2nd person as subjects:

Wena **o wa me**! Ke go nyetse!

....

Nna **ke wa gago**, mma.

....

Banake, **lo ba rona.**

....

3rd person as subject:

Kgomo eo, **ké ya gaetsho**, mme tonki ena, **ké ya gaeno.**

....

Selepe sona, **ké sa gagwe.**

....

Exercise 14.6

Will you be able to add to these examples using possessives as complements?

7. QUANTITATIVES AS COPULAR COMPLEMENTS

The quantitative root *-otlhe* is semantically restricted to be used with plural subjects, e.g.

Dibuka tse, *ké tsotlhe* tse re di dirisang.

Bana ba, *ké botlhe* ba ba gorogileng.

Bojalwa boo, *ké botlhe* ba gompieno.

The full list of the exclusive quantitative *-osi* combined with 1st, 2nd and 3rd person is seldom used. Many people use *nosi*, which is the exclusive quantitative of the first person singular, for all persons and classes, e.g.

Nna *ke nosi.*

Rona *re nosi.*

Tau *e nosi.*

Exercise 14.7

Can you add to these examples using the different quantitatives as complements?

8. ADVERBS AS COPULAR COMPLEMENTS

1st and 2nd persons as subjects:

Nna *ke gaufi.*

Lona *lo kgakala.*

Bona *ba teng.*

3rd person as subject:

Ké ka mokgwa wa Barolong.

208

Go gaufi go ya teng.

....

Ké kwa molapong kwa ba leng teng.

....

Exercise 14.8

Can you add your own examples to these using adverbs of place as complements?

9. RELATIVE CONSTRUCTIONS AS COPULAR COMPLEMENTS

1st and 2nd persons as subjects:

Nna ***ke yo o ganneng.***

....

Wena ***o makgakga.***

....

Lona ***le ba ba thubileng*** fa.

....

3rd person as subject:

Thipa ya me ***ke e e looditsweng.***

....

Hempe eo, ***ga se e e rekilweng.***

....

Selepe seo, ***ke se se boi.***

....

Exercise 14.9

You should now attempt to add your own examples to these using relative constructions as complements.

1.2.4 The complements of the verbal identifying copulative

The copular verb **-nna**, as was stated earlier, expresses **the entering into a state**. Apart from the quantitative and the adverb, mentioned in 1.2.3 above, the copular verb **-nna** may readily assume any of the other word categories as a complement, e.g.

(i) Mmaagwe *o nna* **mooki.**

....

(ii) Rona re tla fetoga re bo *re nna* **lona.**

....

(iii) Dinamune tsa gago *e nna* **tseo.**

....

(iv) Nna *ke nna* **yo moleele** mo go bona.

....

(v) Wena *o tla nna* (moanelwa) **ofe?**

....

(vi) Motabogi, moratiwa, *o tla nna* **wa me.**

....

(vii) Mosimane yo, *o nna* **tlhogoethata.**

....

Did you notice that the examples mentioned above correspond with those of 1.2.3 above?

Exercise 14.10

Can you add more examples to illustrate the use of the copular verb
-nna?

1.3 The use of the identifying copulative

1.3.1 The non-verbal identifying copulatives in the indicative mood

The non-verbal identifying copulatives express **the existing state** in which the subject finds itself and **they only appear in the indicative mood.**

In section 1.2.3 it was shown that the non-verbal copulatives can take any of **nine** possible complements. In this section all **nine** kinds of complements will not feature, but you will be expected to work out your own examples illustrating the use of these different complements.

The following examples will illustrate the basic structure of the non-verbal copulatives in the indicative mood positive and negative:

POSITIVE	
SINGULAR	PLURAL
1st person: Nna **kè morutwana**.	Rona **rè barutwana**.
2nd person: Wena **ò morutwana**.	Lona **lò barutwana**.
3rd person: Ena **ké morutwana**.	Bona **ké barutwana**.

NEGATIVE	
SINGULAR	PLURAL
1st person: Nna **ga ké morutwana**.	Rona **ga ré barutwana**.
2nd person: Wena **ga ó morutwana**.	Lona **ga ló barutwana**.
3rd person: Ena **ga sé morutwana**.	Bona **ga sé barutwana**.

Can you still identify each of the structural elements as described in the previous sections? Have you taken note of the tonal changes of the non-verbal identifying copulatives?

You can now proceed to write your own examples illustrating the use of the rest of the possible complements. The following examples may be of use to you:

Nna **ke fa**, wena **o foo**.

Monna **ke yo o tiileng**.

Banna bao, **ke basele**.

Thipa eo, **ke ya ga ntate**.

1.3.2 *The verbal copulative* **le** *in the participial mood*

The copular verb **le** expresses an existing state in which the subject occurs simultaneously with the main action.

The predicates in the participial mood commonly commence in the conjunctives **fa, le fa** and **ka**. The copulative **le** appears in the present, past and future tenses.

1. THE PRESENT TENSE OF THE PARTICIPIAL MOOD

POSITIVE	
SINGULAR	PLURAL
1st person: Fa **ke le nosi**, mpege!	Fa **re le babedi**, re pege!
2nd person: Fa **o le mosadi**, feta!	Fa **lo le basadi**, feta!
3rd person: Fa **a le gaufi**, mmitse!	Fa **ba le gaufi**, ba bitse!
Fa **e le ngwana**, mo thuse!	Fa **e le bana**, ba thuse!
NEGATIVE	
SINGULAR	PLURAL
1st person: Fa **ke se nosi**, mpege!	Fa **re se babedi**, re pege!
2nd person: Fa **o se mosadi**, feta!	Fa **lo se basadi**, feta!
3rd person: Fa **a se gaufi**, mmitse!	Fa **ba se gaufi**, ba bitse!
Fa **e se ngwana**, mo thuse!	Fa **e se bana**, ba thuse!

In these examples you will have noticed that the structure is made up of:

(i) the conjunctive *fa.*

(ii) the usual subjectival concords of the 1st and 2nd persons, i.e. *ke, re, o* and *lo*.

(iii) the subjectival concords of the 3rd person are the invariable *e* for all classes which may be replaced by *a* and *ba* for the *mo-ba-* classes and classes 1(a) and 2(a).

(iv) the copular verb stems *le* (positive) and *se* (negative)

(v) the complement which may be one of **nine** possibilities as was illustrated in section 1.2.3.

Exercise 14.11

Can you now give your own examples of the verbal copulative **le** *in the present tense of the participial mood?*

The following sentences may be of use to you as examples with nouns as copular complements:

(i) Le fa *o le ngwanake*, ga ke batle maitsholo ao.

....

(ii) Ka ena *a se motsadi*, ga a ke a re tlhaloganya.

....

(iii) Fa *e le selepe* sa me, o tle naso.

....

(iv) Fa nna *ke le morutabana*, nka se bue jalo.

....

2. PAST TENSE OF THE PARTICIPIAL MOOD

POSITIVE	
SINGULAR	PLURAL
1st person: Ka *ke ne ke le rraago*, ke ne ka gana.	Ka **re ne re le borraa-lona**, re ne ra gana.
2nd person: Fa *o ne o le Mpho*, ke ne ke ka go thusa.	Fa *lo ne lo le boMpho*, ke ne ke ka lo thusa.

213

	SINGULAR	PLURAL
3rd person:	Le fa *e ne e le ena*, o ya go duela!	Le fa *e ne e le bona*, ba ya go duela!
	Ka *a ne a le kgosi*, o ne a feta.	Ka *ba ne ba le dikgosi*, ba ne ba feta.

<table>
<tr><td colspan="3" align="center">NEGATIVE</td></tr>
<tr><td></td><td>SINGULAR</td><td>PLURAL</td></tr>
<tr><td>1st person:</td><td>Ka ke ne ke se rraago, ke ne ka gana.</td><td>Ka re ne re se borraalona, re ne ra gana.</td></tr>
<tr><td>2nd person:</td><td>Fa o ne o se Mpho, ke ne ke ka go thusa.</td><td>Fa lo ne lo se boMpho, ke ne ke ka lo thusa.</td></tr>
<tr><td>3rd person:</td><td>Le fa e ne e se ena, o ya go duela!</td><td>Le fa e ne e se bona, ba ya go duela!</td></tr>
<tr><td></td><td>Ka a ne a se kgosi, o ne a feta.</td><td>Ka ba ne ba se dikgosi, ba ne ba feta.</td></tr>
</table>

In these examples you will have noticed the auxiliary verb **ne** which forms a compound copular verb with the copular verbal stems **le** and **se**. Characteristically both the auxiliary and the copular verbs have their own subjectival concords, e.g.

ke ne **ke** le . . .   >   **ke** ne **ke** se . . .

o ne **o** le . . .   >   **o** ne **o** se . . .

e ne **e** le . . .   >   **e** ne **e** se . . .

214

Exercise 14.12

*Will you now be able to form your own examples of the verbal copulative **le** in the past tense of the participial mood?*

The following sentences may be of use to you as examples with adverbs as copular complements:

(i) Le fa **go ne go le kgakala**, re ne ra fitlha.

....

(ii) Ka wena **o ne o le teng** mo gae, o ne o sa tlhoke thuso.

....

(iii) Ka **ba ne ba le gona**, ba ne ba re thusa.

....

(iv) Le fa noga **e ne e se mo kamoreng**, o ne a tshaba.

....

3. FUTURE TENSE OF THE PARTICIPIAL MOOD

POSITIVE	
SINGULAR	PLURAL
1st person: Ka **ke tla bo ke le ngaka**, ke tla go alafa.	Ka **re tla bo re le dingaka**, re tla go alafa.
....	....
2nd person: Le fa **o tla bo o le montle**, ga ke ye go go nyala.	Le fa **lo tla bo lo le bantle**, ga re ye go lo nyala.
....	....
3rd person: Ka **a tla bo a le teng**, a re etele.	Ka **ba tla bo ba le teng**, ba re etele.
....	....
Ka selepe **se tla bo se le boi**, a ka se reme.	Ke dilepe **di tla bo di le boi**, ba ka se reme.
....	....

215

NEGATIVE	
SINGULAR	PLURAL
1st person: Ka *ke tla bo ke se ngaka*, nka se go alafe.	Ka *re tla bo re se dinga-ka*, re ka se go alafe.
2nd person: Le fa *o tla bo o se montle*, ga ke ye go go nyala.	Le fa *lo tla bo lo se ba-ntle*, ga re ye go lo nyala.
3rd person: Ka *a tla bo a se teng*, ga re ye go lo etela.	Ka *ba tla bo ba se teng*, ga re ye go lo etela.
Ka selepe *se tla bo se se boi*, a ka se reme.	Ka dilepe *di tla bo di se boi*, ba ka se reme.

Can you, with the aid of previous sections, still identify the structural elements incorporated in the previous examples?

One of the important observations to make is that in these examples we are dealing with compound verbs because of the presence of the auxiliary verb **bo**. This then would be the reason for the double subjectival concords, i.e. one for the auxiliary verb **bo** and one for the copular verb **le** or **se**, e.g.

Ke tla bo *ke* le ngaka.   > *Ke* tla bo *ke* se ngaka.

O tla bo *o* le montle.   > *O* tla bo *o* se montle.

The **tla** is of course the future tense prefix, e.g.

Ka selepe se **tla** bo se se boi, a ka se reine.

The **o** of the third person changes to **a** in the participial mood, e.g.

Ka **a** tla bo **a** le teng, **a** re etele.

216

Exercise 14.13

*Will you now be able to give your own examples of the verbal copulative **le** in the future tense of the participial mood?*

The following sentences may be of use to you as examples illustrating the use of the possessives as complements:

(i) Le fa *e tla bo e le ya me*, nku eo ga ke e itse.

....

(ii) Ka pitse ena *e tla bo e le ya gaeno*, lo tla re lefa fa e senya.

....

(iii) Fa *ba tla bo ba le bagaetsho*, re tla ba amogela.

....

(iv) Fa e tshwailwe mogatla wa peolwane, *e tla bo e le ya ga malome.*

....

To conclude with it should be mentioned that:

(i) the aspectual prefix *ka* + the auxiliary verb *bo* and
(ii) the aspectual prefix *sa* + the auxiliary verb *ntse* may respectively appear in the present and past tenses discussed above, e.g.

Fa ke *ka bo* ke le nosi, mpege!

....

Fa ke *sa ntse* ke le nosi, mpege!

....

Ka *ke* ne *ke ka bo ke* le rraago, ke ne ke ka gana.

....

Ka *ke* ne *ke sa ntse ke* le rraago, ke ne ke ka gana.

....

In the last two examples, do you recognise the two subjectival concords of the auxiliary verbs and the last one of the copular verb **le**?

1.3.3 The copulative predicate **nna** in the different moods

In a previous section it was mentioned that the copular verb **nna** expresses the state which the subject enters. It was also stated that this copular verb may take **seven** of the **nine** complements that have been mentioned.

217

In this section we will take a closer look at the copular verb **nna**, which some people know as **ba** or **baa**. As you will notice the conjugation of this copular verb follows that of the non-verbal conjugation discussed in section 1.3.

1. THE INFINITIVE MOOD

This mood expresses a present and a past processing to the state specified by the complement, e.g.

POSITIVE	NEGATIVE
go nnile maswabi.	**ga go a nna** maswabi.
go nna ena, mooki.	**go se nne ena**, mooki.
go nna wa me.	**go se nne** wa me.

Can you still name the positive and negative structural features of the verb in these examples? Which form of the verb denotes the present and which the past?

Exercise 14.14

Can you now add to these examples by making use of the other complements from our list appearing in section 1.2.3?

2. THE IMPERATIVE MOOD

This mood expresses commands, requests, admonitions and encouragement to the subject to enter the state specified by the complements, e.g.

POSITIVE	NEGATIVE
nna moeteledipele wa rona!	**se nne** moeteledipele wa rona!
nnang bangwe ba bona!	**se nneng** bangwe ba bona!
nna wa me, moratiwa!	**se nne** wa me, moratiwa!

It will not be easy to find complements from all **seven** kinds but you should try to find as many as you can.

3. THE INDICATIVE MOOD

This mood expresses statements and facts and can appear in the present, perfect and future tenses. In the following examples one sentence from each of these tenses is quoted, e.g.

POSITIVE	NEGATIVE
Ke nna mogakolodi wa gago.	*Ga ke nne* mogakolodi wa gago.
Ke nnile mogakolodi wa gago.	*Ga ke a nna* mogakolodi wa gago.
Ke tla nna mogakolodi wa gago.	*Ga ke kitla ke nna* mogakolodi wa gago.

Can you still name and recognise the structural features of the different tenses? Besides the abovementioned tenses you should also take note of some of the compound copular predicates formed by means of verbal prefixes like the potential *ka*, the progressive *sa* and auxiliary verbs like *nê* and *ntse*, e.g.

(i) *Ke ka (nka) nna* mogakolodi wa gago.

(ii) *Ke sa ntse ke nna* mogakolodi wa gago.

(iii) *Ke ne ke ntse* mogakolodi wa gago.

You should not confuse the auxiliary verb stem *ntse* in example (ii) with the perfect form of *nna* in example (iii).

Exercise 14.15

*You should now try to form your own examples of the use of the copular verb **nna** in the indicative mood.*

219

4. THE SUBJUNCTIVE MOOD

This mood expresses interdependent or interrelated actions and it therefore only occurs in subordinate clauses and after some auxiliary verbs and conjunctions. The subjunctive mood has two tense forms, viz. the present and the past tenses, e.g.

POSITIVE	NEGATIVE
Ke batla gore *o nne* moratiwa wa me.	Ke batla gore *o se nne* moratiwa wa me.
Morago ga moo *ra nna* baagi.	Morago ga moo *ra se ka ra nna* baagi.

Can you still recognise and name the structural features of the different tenses? You should now form your own examples of the use of the copular verb *nna* in the two tenses of the subjunctive mood.

SELF-ASSESSMENT

1. Name the different kinds of copulatives.
2. In what way does the non-verbal copulative *ké* differ from the verbal copulative *nna*?
3. Are the non-verbal copulatives prefixed or suffixed to their complements?
4. Explain the formation of the negatives of the following sentences:

    Mme ke mooki.
    Mme o nna mooki.

5. Name nine possible complements for the identifying copulatives and give one example for each.
6. Rewrite the following sentences and underline the non-verbal copular predicates:
    (i) Sejo seo ga se monate.
    (ii) Bojalwa bo, bo botlha.
    (iii) Mosetsana yo, ke yo o ratang go apaya.
    (iv) Nna ke Mongwato. Ke tlhaga kwa Botswana.
    (v) Motse oo, o kgakala thata.
7. Write nine sentences of your own expressing an existing relationship between the subject and the complement. The complements must correspond with those discussed in these sections.

8. Write nine sentences of your own expressing the change that the subject undergoes. The complements must vary like in par. 1.2.3 of this section.

9. In what moods can the copular verb **nna** appear in the identifying copulative?

10. What state is expressed by means of the copular verb **nna**?

11. Identify the structural elements of the copular predicate in the following sentences:
    (i) Re ka nna baagisani fa re fuduga.
    (ii) Ena o batla go nna yo o bonwang.
    (iii) Se nne ka maitsholo a a maswe!
    (iv) Go nnile motlhofo go falola.
    (v) Le nneng le itekanetse!
    (vi) Re tla nna pinagare ya gaetsho.
    (vii) Rre o kopile gore re se ka ra nna bangwe ba ba fetlhang ntwa.
    (viii) Moruti o batla gore re nne ba ba itseng tshiamo ya bodumedi.

12. What are the differences in structure between the copular predicates of the following sentences?
    (a) Bona ke bagaetsho.
    (b) Fa bona ba le bagaetsho ba amogele!

13. What states or conditions are expressed by means of the copulatives in 12 above?

14. Name the structural elements of the copular predicates in the following sentences:
    (i) Wena ga o moratiwa.
    (ii) Fa ke le lesego, nka falola.
    (iii) Le fa a se ntate, ke a mo rata.
    (iv) Ka ba ne ba le kgakala, ba ne ba sa utlwe.
    (v) Le fa ke ne ke ka bo ke sa ntse ke le mo gae, ga go tlhokege gore o nkomanye.

15. In what moods does the copular verb **nna** appear in the following sentences?
    (i) Mme o ikaetse go nna mooki fa nna ke fetsa sekolo.
    (ii) Malome o ne a re laela a re: "Nnang kgatlhanong le ditiro tsa basenyi!"
    (iii) Moupathaga o tla nna ena yo a re opedisang.
    (iv) Go nnile monate go palama terena morago ga sebaka.
    (v) Re ne ra ba ruta, ba falola, ba nna baeteledipele ba morafe.

2. The descriptive copulative

OBJECTIVES

On completion of this section you should be able to:
1. identify descriptive copulatives and their complements within the context of a passage;
2. enumerate the words and structures that may function as complements;
3. describe the structure and use of the descriptive copulative in the indicative and participial moods;
4. explain the meaning of copulatives in these moods;
5. state the moods in which the copular verb **nna** occurs;
6. describe the structure and the use of the copular verb **nna** in these moods;
7. identify the copular verb **nna** when used in identifying and descriptive copulatives.

On page 198 it was pointed out that there are three kinds of copulative structures, viz.

  (i) identifying copulatives,
 (ii) descriptive copulatives and
(iii) associative copulatives.

2.1 The meaning of the term *descriptive copulative*

This copulative, as was shown above, expresses a descriptive relationship between a subject and a complement, e.g.

    Ntate **o** bonolo. ....

2.2 The structure of the descriptive copulative

The essential difference between the identifying copulative and the descriptive copulative lies in the fact that the identifying copulatives use the subjectival concords of the 1st and 2nd person singular and plural as non-verbal copulatives while the invariable **ké** is used for **all classes** of the 3rd person, e.g.

	SINGULAR	PLURAL
1st person:	Nna **kè** morutwana.	Rona **rè** barutwana.
2nd person:	Wena **ò** morutwana.	Lona **lò** barutwana.

3rd person: Ena **ké** morutwana.	Bona **ké** barutwana.
Sona **ké** morutwana (segole).	Tsona **ké** barutwana.

The descriptive copulative on the other hand makes use of **subjectival concords in all persons and classes**, e.g.

	SINGULAR	PLURAL
1st person:	Nna **kè** bonolo.	Rona **rè** bonolo.
2nd person:	Wena **ò** bonolo.	Lona **lò** bonolo.
3rd person:	Ena **ó** bonolo.	Bona **bá** bonolo.
	Sona **sé** bonolo (segole).	Tsona **dí** bonolo.

The negative of the abovementioned is formed by prefixing **ga** to the non-verbal copulatives. In the case of class 1 and class 1(a) the subjectival concord **o** changes to **a**, e.g.

	SINGULAR	PLURAL
1st person:	Nna **ga ké** bonolo.	Rona **ga ré** bonolo.
2nd person:	Wena **ga ó** bonolo.	Lona **ga ló** bonolo.
3rd person:	Ena **ga á** bonolo.	Bona **ga bá** bonolo.
	Sona **ga sé** bonolo (segole).	Tsona **ga dí** bonolo.

As can be seen, the two groups of examples made use of the noun **bonolo** as the **complement** and they **express an existing situation**.

In the case of the identifying copulative it was shown that the copular verb **nna** was used to denote the entering of a state. This copular verb also appears in the case of the descriptive copulative and it expresses the acquisition of a quality or characteristic or the subject entering a state, e.g.

	POSITIVE	NEGATIVE
1st person:	Nna **ke nna** botlhale.	Nna **ga ke nne** botlhale.
2nd person:	Wena **o nna** botlhale.	Wena **ga o nne** botlhale.
3rd person:	Ena **o nna** botlhale.	Ena **ga a nne** botlhale.

Can you still explain the structure of the copulative in these examples?

2.3 Complements of the descriptive copulative

1. NOUNS AS COPULAR COMPLEMENTS

In the previous examples it was illustrated that the subjectival concords are used as non-verbal copulatives and that they may be followed by a complement which gives a description of the subject in terms of its quality, attributes or characteristics, e.g.

(i) Thipa ya me **e boi.** (ii) Ya gago **e kae**? Re adime re sege ka

yona. (iii) Wai! A thipa ya gago **e kalo**? (iv) Nna ke ne ke re **e**

kana ka ya me.

The copular complements in these examples cannot be readily classified as nouns but they function exactly like the following complements which are nouns.

224

(v) Thipa ya me *ga e **bogale***, mme *e **thata***. (vi) Bona! *E **motlhofo***

....

e bile *ga e **maswe***, mme go sega e a sega.

....

Exercise 14.16

Can you form your own examples, positive and negative, with nouns as complements of descriptive copulatives?

The following abstract nouns will make your task easier because they can be used to denote or describe the various qualities, attributes or characteristics predicated by the descriptive copular verbs:

bokete	bosula	leswe	monate
bokgwabo	bothito	mabela	setswerere
tlhaga	botlhoko	mafura	bobududu
bonya	lehufa	metsi	bosetlha

You will recognise these nouns as a special group of nouns appearing as qualificative clauses in sentences like:

(i) Ke rekile hamole *e e **bokete**.*

....

(ii) Bana ba rata go palama tonki *e e **bokgwabo**.*

....

(iii) Mme o ntheketse hempe *e e **bothito**.*

....

(iv) Mosadi yoo, *yo o **lehufa***, ga a ratiwe.

....

(v) Seaparo *se se **bosetlha*** ga se rekiwe fa.

....

A number of abstract nouns indicating natural stages of day and night, natural states of light and dark as well as seasonal states make use of the subjectival concord of the locative classes, e.g.

(i) **Go bosigo** jaanong, a re robale.

....

(ii) Mo kgorong ya legaga **go lesedi**, mme kwa teng teng **go lefifi**.

....

(iii) Mo tlung go bothitho, mme kwa ntle **go tsididi** ka gore **go mariga**.

....

(iv) **Ga go maruru** fa letsatsi le fisa. **Go mogote.**

....

Exercise 14.17

Can you add your own examples to these using abstract nouns or qualificative clauses as complements?

2. ADJECTIVES AS COPULAR COMPLEMENTS

In the case of the **descriptive copulative** the demonstrative element of the adjectival concord is omitted from the predicate and the copulative is expressed by means of the subjectival concords. These differences between the identifying and descriptive copulatives are illustrated by the following:

IDENTIFYING COPULATIVE	DESCRIPTIVE COPULATIVE
Nna **kè** yo moleele.	Nna **kè** moleele.
Wena **o** yo mosetlhana.	Wena **o** mosetlhana.
Ena **ké** yo mokima.	Ena **o** mokima.
Sona **ké** se sekima (segole).	Sona **se** sekima.

226

These examples also exemplify the difference in meaning between the two kinds of copulatives. Can you identify the structural elements in these examples?

In the negative of the descriptive copulative the negative *ga* is prefixed to the copular predicate and the subjectival concord *o* of classes 1 and 1(a) changes to *a*, e.g.

(i) Nna *ga* ke moleele.

....

(ii) Wena *ga* o mosetlhana.

....

(iii) Ena *ga a* mokima.

....

(iv) Sona *ga* se sekima.

....

In the plural of classes 8, 10 and 12 the prefixes of adjectival stems are often omitted, especially so in the case of numeral adjectival roots, e.g.

(v) Dilepe tse ba di dirisang *di tharo.*

....

(vi) Dipitse *di kgolo* go feta ditonki.

....

(vii) Dimao *di tlhano.* Di ja R2.

....

Exercise 14.18

Will you now be able to add to these examples using adjectives as complements?

3. ENUMERATIVES AS COPULAR COMPLEMENTS

Descriptive copulatives may only be formed from enumerative roots **-ngwe** *and* **-sele**.

In the case of the stem **-ngwe** you will find that it is commonly compounded with the adverb *fela*, e.g.

(i) Nna **ke mongwe fela**, bona ba bararo.

....

(ii) Wena **o mongwe fela**, o tlhoka thuso.

....

(iii) Mosadi **o mongwe fela**. Mo tseise tlhe!

....

(iv) Kgomo e ba e batlang **e nngwe fela.**

....

Can you identify the structural elements forming the copulative?
In the negative of these copulatives the negative **ga** is prefixed to the copular predicate and the subjectival concord **o** of classes 1 and 1(a) changes to **a**, e.g.

(v) Nna **ga** ke mongwe fela.

....

(vi) Wena **ga** o mongwe fela.

....

(vii) Mosadi **ga a** mongwe fela.

....

(viii) Kgomo **ga** e nngwe fela.

....

Exercise 14.19

Can you add to these examples using the enumerative -ngwe as a complement?

In the case of **-sele** the subjectival concords are not used to express the copulative. The complement expresses the copulative, e.g.

(ix) Monna yo, **osele**, ga o mo itse.

....

(x) Ke lo raya ke re ntšwa e re e batlang **esele**.

....

Exercise 14.20

You should now attempt to add to these examples using the enumerative -sele as a complement.

4. QUANTITATIVES AS COPULAR COMPLEMENTS

The descriptive copulatives are formed by prefixing the subjectival concords to the quantitative roots *-osi* and *-otlhe*.

The exclusive quantitative root *-osi* in combination with subjects of the 1st, 2nd and 3rd person is seldom used, e.g.

Rona **re rosi** mono.

....

Dipotsane **di tsosi**, dikonyana di timetse.

....

The use of **nosi**, which is the exclusive quantitative of the first person singular, is more common and is applied to all persons and classes, e.g.

Rona **re nosi.**

....

Dipotsane **di nosi.**

....

The use of the inclusive quantitative root *-otlhe* is also not very popular, e.g.

Madi a bone **a otlhe** jaanong.

....

Dibuka tse re di dirisang **di tsotlhe.**

....

In the case of both *-osi* and *-otlhe* the negative is formed by prefixing the negative **ga** and changing the subjectival concord, in the case of *-osi*, of classes 1 and 1(a) to **a**, e.g.

Monna **ga a** nosi, o na le mosadi.

....

Batho **ga ba botlhe**, go tlhokega bana.

....

229

Can you add to these examples using quantitatives as complements?

5. ADVERBS AS COPULAR COMPLEMENTS

In this case the descriptive copulatives are formed by prefixing the subjectival concords to the adverbial complement, e.g.

   (i) Motse wa rona *o gaufi.*

   ....

   (ii) Mme *o mo tlung.*

   ....

   (iii) Ntate *o kwa tirong.*

   ....

   (iv) Bana *ba fa molapong.*

   ....

   (v) *O kae? Ke teng.*

   ....

   (vi) Lesea *le ka fa tlase* ga tafole.

   ....

Did you notice that the copular complement can be formed by adverbs of place only? The negative is formed by prefixing the negative *ga* to the predicate while the subjectival concord of classes 1 and 1(a) changes from *o* to *a*, e.g.

   (vii) Motse wa rona *ga* o gaufi.

   ....

   (viii) Mme *ga a* mo tlung.

   ....

   (ix) Ntate *ga a* kwa tirong.

   ....

Exercise 14.22

You should now attempt to add your own examples to these by using adverbs as complements.

The negative of the adverb **teng** in example (v) is formed by the negative prefix **ga**, e.g.

POSITIVE	NEGATIVE
Ntate **o teng.**	Ntate **ga a teng.**

It is however also common to replace **teng** with the enclitic **yo**, e.g.

Ntate ga a **yo.** ....

The enclictic **yo** can, in subordinate clauses, take the relative **-ng**, e.g.

Dinku tse di **se yong** mo sakeng di ya go jewa ke phokojwe.

....

A o raya gore madi a a **se yong** a utswilwe?

....

Note that the negative prefix **se** and the subjectival prefixes are written disjunctively while **-ng** is written conjunctively.

Exercise 14.23

Can you now form your own examples with **yo** *as an adverbial complement?*

2.4 The use of the descriptive copulative

2.4.1 The prefixes of the descriptive copulative in the indicative mood

These non-verbal copulatives appear in the present tense of the indicative mood only, and they express an existing quality, characteristic or state in which the subject finds itself. With an adverbial complement it may also express the situation or locality of the subject, e.g.

POSITIVE	NEGATIVE
Ngwana o mabela.	Ngwana **ga a** mabela.
Kala **e** kima.	Kala **ga e** kima.

Bona **ba** nosi.	Bona **ga ba** nosi.
....	....
Molapo **o** gaufi.	Molapo **ga o** gaufi.
....	....

Can you still identify the structural elements of the predicates in these examples? Can you make sentences exemplifying the complements of the descriptive copulative not included in the previous set of examples? Consult par. 2.3 for the list of complements.

2.4.2 The verbal copulative **le** in the participial mood

The copular verb **le** expresses an existing quality, characteristic or state in which the subject finds itself simultaneously with the main action. The predicates of the participial mood usually commence in the conjunctives **fa, le fa** and **ka**.

The verbal copulative **le** appears in the present, past and future tenses of the participial mood.

1. PRESENT TENSE OF THE PARTICIPIAL MOOD

POSITIVE	NEGATIVE
Ka ntate **a le bosilo**, re a mo tshaba.	Ka ntate **a se bosilo**, re a mo rata.
....	....
Ka khai **e le ntsho**, ga e a siama.	Ka khai **e se ntsho**, ga e a siama.
....	....
Le fa mamepe **a le mafura**, a rafe.	Le fa mamepe **a se mafura**, a rafe.
....	....
Fa **go le gaufi**, re tla phakela.	Fa **go se gaufi**, re tla phakela.
....	....

Can you identify the conjunctives and the structural elements of the predicate?

232

Exercise 14.24

You should now form your own examples of the present tense of the participial mood by means of the 5 kinds of complements discussed in par. 2.3.

2. PAST TENSE OF THE PARTICIPIAL MOOD

POSITIVE	NEGATIVE
Ka setlhare *se ne se le gaufi*, ke ne ka katoga.	Ka setlhare *se ne se se gaufi*, ke ne ka katoga.
Le fa mme *a ne a le moleele*, o ne a tlhaela.	Le fa mme *a ne a se moleele*, o ne a tlhaela.
Fa *ba ne ba le nosi*, re ne re ka ba pega.	Fa *ba ne ba se nosi*, re ne re ka ba pega.

Do you recognise the auxiliary verb *ne* which forms a compound copular verb with the copular verbal stems *le* and *se*? Both the auxiliary verb and the copular verb has its own subjectival concord, e.g.

se ne *se* le . . .	> *se* ne *se* se . . .
o ne *a* le . . .	> *o* ne *a* se . . .
ba ne *ba* le . . .	> *ba* ne *ba* se . . .

What do you notice about the subjectival concord of class 1 and 1(a)?

Exercise 14.25

Can you now give your own examples of the verbal copulative le in the past tense of the participial mood?

Remember to alternate the complements taught in par. 2.3.

3. FUTURE TENSE OF THE PARTICIPIAL MOOD

POSITIVE	NEGATIVE
Le fa **ke tla bo ke le teng**, ga ke ye go go thusa.	Le fa **ke tla bo ke se teng**, ga ke ye go go thusa.
Fa o ja sejo se, **o tla bo o le montle.**	Fa o ja sejo se, **o tla bo o se montle.**
Ka **go tla bo go le lefifi**, ba tla go naya marobalo.	Ka **go tla bo go se lefifi**, ba tla go naya marobalo.

Did you notice that the auxiliary verb **bo** requires its own subjectival concord while the copular verb **le** or **se** also requires its own? e.g.

ke tla bo **ke** le . . .   >   **ke** tla bo **ke** se . . .

o tla bo **o** le . . .   >   **o** tla bo **o** se . . .

go tla bo **go** le . . .   >   **go** tla bo **go** se . . .

Did you notice that the subjectival concord of class 1 remains **o**?

Exercise 14.26

*You should now attempt to give your own examples of the verbal copulative **le** in the future tense of the participial mood.*

2.4.3 The verbal descriptive copulative **nna** in various moods

The subject of a descriptive copulative can acquire a quality or a characteristic or change into a state. These changes are expressed by means of the copular verb **nna.**

As you will notice the conjugation of the copular verb follows the normal verbal conjugation discussed in Chapter 11 where the various moods were discussed.

234

1. THE INFINITIVE MOOD

This mood expresses a present, past and future developing of a quality or a characteristic or a state specified by the complement, e.g.

POSITIVE	NEGATIVE
go tla nna sego	**go ka se nne** sego
go nna go ntsi	**go se nne** go gontsi
go nnile kgakala	**ga go a nna** kgakala
go nnile selemo	**ga go a nna** selemo

Which form of the copular verb represents the present and which the past and future tenses? Can you still identify the structural elements of these tenses, positive and negative?

Exercise 14.27

You should now add to these examples by making use of the other complements of the descriptive copulative as listed in par. 2.3.

2. THE IMPERATIVE MOOD

This mood expresses commands, requests, admonitions and encouragement to the subject to acquire a quality or characteristic or state specified by the complement, e.g.

POSITIVE	NEGATIVE
nna bokgwabo!	**se nne** bokgwabo!
nna maswe!	**se nne** maswe!
nna mongwe wa bona!	**se nne** mongwe wa bona!
nna nosi!	**se nne** nosi

Can you now produce your own examples making use of the other complements mentioned in par. 2.3? You should also be able to name the structural elements of the positive and negative.

3. THE INDICATIVE MOOD

This mood is used to express statements and facts and can appear in the present, perfect and future tenses. Only one example from each of these tenses is quoted in the following:

POSITIVE	NEGATIVE
Mosimane **o nna** moleele.	Mosimane **ga a nne** moleele.
....	....
Di nnile tsotlhe jaanong.	**Ga di a nna** tsotlhe jaanong.
....	....
Ba tla nna nosi.	**Ga ba kitla ba nna** nosi.
....	

Can you still name and recognise the structural features of the different tenses? Besides the abovementioned tenses of the indicative mood you should also take note of some of the compound copular predicates formed by means of verbal prefixes like the potential **ka**, the progressive **sa** and auxiliary verbs like **kitla nê** and **ntse**, e.g.

(i) Wena o **ka** nna mokhutshwane fa o sa je dijo tsa gago.

....

(ii) Mosadi yoo, o **sa ntse** a nna maaka.

....

(iii) Re **ne** re ntse mongwe wa bona sebaka se seleele.

....

Can you differentiate between the stems **ntse** in examples (ii) and (iii)?

Exercise 14.28

*You should now form your own examples using the copular verb **nna** in the indicative mood.*

4. THE SUBJUNCTIVE MOOD

This mood has two tense forms, viz. the present and past tense. It expresses interdependent or interrelated actions and it therefore only occurs in subordinate clauses and after some auxiliary verbs and conjunctives, e.g.

POSITIVE	NEGATIVE
Ke batla gore kofi *e nne* botshe.	Ke batla gore kofi *e se nne* botshe.
Moratiwa a ntemoga, *a nna* lehufa.	Moratiwa a ntemoga, *a se ka a nna* lefufa.

Can you identify the different tenses of the subjunctive mood?

Exercise 14.29

*Attempt to form your own examples of the use of the copular verb **nna** in the two tenses of the subjunctive mood.*

SELF-ASSESSMENT

1. Name the different words or structures that can function as complements and give an example in each instance.
2. What characterises the negatives of the sentences given in 1 above?
3. "The nouns functioning as complements are concrete/abstract." Select the correct word and give a reason for your answer.
4. In what manner does the adjectival copulative of the identifying copulative differ from that of the descriptive copulative?
5. Identify the word or structure representing the complement in the following:
    (i) Tlisa dibuka tsa me! Di mo tafoleng.
    (ii) Ke nosi, ka jalo ke tshwerwe ke bodutu.
    (iii) Diaparo tseo disele. Tse o di batlang ke tse.
    (iv) Fensetere e e thubegileng e nngwe fela.
    (v) Kgomo e e suleng e thamagana.
    (vi) Tlhokomela! Metsi ao, a molelo.
    (vii) Khai e ke a boneng, e bofala.
    (viii) Lebolobolo leo le kana!

6. Give an alternative example for each of those appearing in 5 above.
7. Name the moods in which the descriptive copular verb **nna** may appear.
8. Identify the structural elements of the copular predicates in the following sentences:
   (i) Gore a nne ditemepedi! Nka gana.
   (ii) Go tla nna jang fa o nketela?
   (iii) Masole a nnile pelokgale mo ntweng ele.
   (iv) Pule o kae? Ga a yo. Le maabane o ne a se yo.
   (v) Ntate o nna mogolo jaanong.
   (vi) Ke batla gore o nne nnetlane . . . Go a tweng tlhe?
9. Name the moods in which the copular verb appears in the following sentences:
   (i) Go tla nna bonolo fa ba ka re thusa.
   (ii) Maemo a a kwa godimo ga a go letlelele go nna makgakga.
   (iii) Mariga ao go nnile tsididi go feta.
   (iv) Nna tlhaga fa o dira ngwanaka!
   (v) Go a bonala gore e nna nemeru.
   (vi) Ngwanake o nna botlhale.
   (vii) Dibuka di tla nna tsotlhe fa o busa eo.
   (viii) Ke batla gore mogatsake a nne bonolo.

3. The associative copulative

On page 198 it was pointed out that there are three kinds of copulatives. Thus far you have been introduced to:

(a) the identifying copulatives, e.g.

Nnake **ke** yo moleele.

....

O tla nna morutabana.

....

(b) the descriptive copulatives, e.g.

A malomaago **o bonolo**?

....

A **o teng** gompieno?

....

The last kind of copulative is the:

(c) associative copulative, e.g.

Rona **re na le** madi.

....

Ga re na dijo.

....

3.1 The meaning of the associative copulative

The associative copulative is used:

(i) to express the possessive relationship between the subject and the complement, e.g.

Rona re na **le dipodi.**

....

(ii) to express the association between the subject and the complement, e.g.

Setlhare se na **le matlhare.**

....

In the first example the possessive relationship or the idea of ownership is clear while in the second example the natural association between tree and leaves is obvious.

3.2 The structure of the associative copulative

This copulative is formed by means of the subjectival concord plus the verb **na** followed by a secondary adverb as a complement.

These adverbs are formed by means of the disjunctively written connective prefix **le** which is prefixed to any of a number of words, e.g.

Rakgadi o na **le diaparo** tse dintle. Rona re na **le makgasa**

....

fela.

....

In the negative the disjunctively written negative prefix **ga** is prefixed to the verb and the connective prefix of the secondary prefix **le** falls away. The subjectival concord of classes 1 and 1(a) changes from **o** to **a**, e.g.

239

Rakgadi **ga a** na diaparo tse dintle. Rona **ga** re na makgasa

fela.

The possessive relationship mentioned earlier applies when the subject is a live person or animal, e.g.

Malome o na le **moraka.**

Segodi se na le **bana.**

The associative relationship applies to:

(i) inanimate subjects that naturally go hand in hand with their complements, e.g.

Naga e na le **dimela.**

Setopo se na le **diboko.**

Selepe se na le **mofeng.**

Ntlo e na le **mabotana.**

(ii) animate subjects that are accompanied by their complements, e.g.

Motabogi o na le **basimane.**

Nna ke na le **Segai.**

Exercise 14.29

Can you now form your own examples expressing:

(a) a possessive relationship and

(b) an associative relationship?

240

3.3 The complements of the associative copulative

In the previous section on the associative copulative it was shown that the copular verb is formed by a subjectival concord plus the verb **na** followed by a secondary adverb as a complement, e.g.

Nna ke **na** le bana.

....

These adverbial complements are formed by means of the disjunctively written connective prefix **le** which can be prefixed to a number of words and structures. The following are examples of complements of the associative copulative.

1. NOUNS IN COPULAR COMPLEMENTS

In the previous section examples were given of the noun functioning as a complement in:

(i) possessive relationships, e.g.

Molemirui o na **le metlhape** e mentsi.

....

Moruti o na **le kereke.**

....

(ii) associative relationships, e.g.

Tsela e na **le matlapa.**

....

Wena o na **le mang**?

....

Exercise 14.30

You should now try to form your own examples, positive and negative, with nouns in complements of associative copulatives.

What happened to the **le** in your examples written in the negative?

In the chapter dealing with nouns it was illustrated that the infinitive form of the verb can be used as a noun, e.g.

Go dira go thusa batho.

....

Go lema go bopamisa dipholo.

....

Like ordinary nouns, the nouns of the infinitive class may also function in complements of the associative copulative, e.g.

Mosimane yole, o na **le go utswa.**

....

Lekgarebe le, le na **le go rogana.**

....

The negative of these examples is formed as follows:

Mosimane yole, **ga a** na go utswa.

....

Lekgarebe le, **ga** le na go rogana.

....

What structural changes do you observe in the negatives?

2. ABSOLUTE PRONOUNS IN COPULAR COMPLEMENTS

As in the case of nouns used in copular complements the disjunctively written connective prefix **le** precedes the absolute pronous, e.g.

Barutwana ba na **le tsona** (dibuka).

....

Setlogolo sa me se na **le ona** (madi).

....

Unlike the nouns used in copular complements the connective prefix **le** does not fall away in the negatives of these examples, e.g.

Barutwana *ga ba na* **le** *tsona.*

....

Setlogolo sa me *ga se na* **le** *ona.*

....

Exercise 14.31

Can you form additional examples illustrating the use of absolute pronouns, positive and negative, as complements in associative copulatives?

As was demonstrated, the prefix **na-** which is conjunctively written with the first syllable of the absolute pronoun can also form a complement, e.g.

Barutwana *ba na* **na**tso (dibuka).

Setlogolo sa me *se na* **na**o (madi).

Lefatshe leo, *le na* **na**yo (teemane).

Koloi eo, *e na* **na**bo (bapalami).

The negatives of these sentences are:

Barutwana **ga** *ba na* **natso.**

Setlogolo sa me **ga** *se na* **nao.**

Lefatshe leo, **ga** *le na* **nayo.**

Koloi eo, **ga** *e na* **nabo.**

Alternatively the prefix **na** may be omitted and the first syllable of the pronoun may be joined to the verb stem **na**, e.g.

POSITIVE	NEGATIVE
Barutwana *ba* **natso.**	Barutwana **ga** *ba* **natso.**
Setlogolo sa me *se* **nao.**	Setlogolo sa me **ga** *se* **nao.**
Lefatshe leo, *le* **nayo.**	Lefatshe leo, **ga** *le* **nayo.**
Koloi eo, *e* **nabo.**	Koloi eo, **ga** *e* **nabo.**

Exercise 14.32

Will you now be able to form your own examples of the associative copulative positive and negative making use of the adverbial prefix **na**?

3. DEMONSTRATIVES IN COPULAR COMPLEMENTS

In the positive the disjunctively written connective prefix **le** is prefixed to the demonstratives, e.g.

A dibuka tse dintle! Ke na **le ena.**

....

O batla dikoko? Re na **le tse**, tse di bopameng.

....

The connective prefix **le** falls away in the negative, e.g.

A dibuka tse dintle! **Ga** ke na **ena.**

....

O batla dikoko? **Ga** re na **tse**, tse di bopameng.

....

Exercise 14.33

Can you form your own examples illustrating the use of demonstratives, positive and negative, as complements in associative copulatives?

4. ADJECTIVES IN COPULAR COMPLEMENTS

The disjunctively written **le** is prefixed to the adjectives, e.g.

Setlhare se, se na **le o mokima** (moretologa).

....

Malome o na **le tse dithamaga** (dipholo).

....

What happens to the **le** in the negative?

Exercise 14.34

Consult Chapter 4 and make your own examples, positive and negative, by using the different kinds of adjectival roots as complements in associative copulatives.

5. ENUMERATIVES IN COPULAR COMPLEMENTS

The disjunctively written **le** is prefixed to the enumeratives, e.g.

(i) Le na **le sefe**? (senotlolo)

....

(ii) **Ga** go na **le ope** yo o itseng.

....

(iii) Ba na **le esele** e ba e balang mo sekolong monongwaga.

....

(iv) **Ga** ba na **le esele** e ba e balang.

....

(v) Go na **le mongwe** yo o utswang.

....

Exercise 14.35

You should now be able to make your own examples using the differ-ent enumerative roots as complements of the associative copulative.

6. POSSESSIVES IN COPULAR COMPLEMENTS

The disjunctively written **le** is prefixed to the possessives, e.g.

Ke na **le ya gago** (thipa).

....

Di na **le tsa gaetsho** (dikgomo).

....

Exercise 14.36

Can you make your own examples using different possessives as complements of the associative copulative positive and negative?

What observation have you made in respect of the connective prefix?

7. RELATIVE CONSTRUCTIONS IN COPULAR COMPLEMENTS

Both the nominal and the verbal relative constructions can be preced-ed by the connective prefix **le**, e.g.

Re na *le e e bokwabo* (pitse).

....

Mmemogolo o na *le e e bothitho* (kobo).

....

Re na *le e e katisitsweng* (pitse).

....

Mmemogolo o na *le e e logilweng* (kobo).

....

What happens to the connective prefix in the negatives of these sentences?

Exercise 14.37

Can you now form your own examples illustrating the use of the relative constructions as complements of the associative copulative?

8. THE QUANTITATIVE ROOT -*OTLHE* IN THE COPULAR COMPLEMENT

The disjunctively written *le* is prefixed to the inclusive quantitative, e.g.

Ke na *le tsotlhe* (didiriswa) tsa rona.

....

Lekgotla le na *le yotlhe* tetla e e tlhokegang.

....

Exercise 14.38

Will you now be able to form your own examples illustrating the use of the quantitative root -otlhe as complements of the associative copulative positive and negative?

3.4 The use of the associative copulative

In the two previous sections it was shown that the associative copulative is formed by means of the subjectival concord plus the verb *na* followed by a secondary adverb as a complement. These adverbs are formed by means of the disjunctively written connective prefix *le*, e.g.

Re *na le madi* otlhe jaanong.

....

246

The associative copulative, as will be presently illustrated can appear in the indicative mood and the participial mood.

3.4.1 The copulative predicate **na** in the indicative mood

The majority of the examples that you have encountered up to now were those of the associative copulative in the indicative mood.

In the case of the associative copulative the indicative mood expresses:

(i) an existing possessive relationship between the subject and the complement, e.g.

*Wena **o na** le pene.* ....

(ii) an existing association between the subject and the complement, e.g.

*Loapi **le na** le maru.* ....

POSITIVE	NEGATIVE
Nna **ke na** le batsadi.	Nna **ga ke na** batsadi.
....	....
Wena **o nnile** le kitso.	Wena **ga o a nna** le kitso.
....	....
Moopa **o tla nna** le bana.	Moopa **ga a ne a nna** le bana.
....	....

Can you still identify the structural elements of the predicates in these examples?

Exercise 14.39

You should now be able to make your own sentences exemplifying the different complements of the associative copulative not included in this table.

Consult par. 3.3 for the list of possible complements in order to make your own sentences in the indicative mood.

3.4.2 The copulative predicate *na* in the participial mood

This mood is used to express an existing possessive or associative relationship, between the subject and the complement, which exists simultaneously with the main action. Predicates of the participial mood commonly commence in the conjunctives *fa*, *le fa* and *ka*. The copular verb *na* appears in the present, past and future tenses of the participial mood.

1. PRESENT TENSE OF THE PARTICIPIAL MOOD

POSITIVE	NEGATIVE
Fa *o na le garawe*, o tla re thusa.	Fa *o se na garawe*, o tla re thusa.
Le fa Pita *a na le madi*, o a re dumedisa.	Le fa Pita *a se na madi*, o a re dumedisa.
Ka thaba *e na le majwe* re rwala ditlhako.	Ka thaba *e se na majwe* re rwala ditlhako.

Can you identify the:

(i) conjunctives?
(ii) copular verb positive and negative?
(iii) the subjectival concord of class 1 which is not the usual *o*?
(iv) the copular complements?

Exercise 14.40

You should now form your own examples of the present tense of the participial mood by means of the 8 kinds of complements discussed in par. 3.3.

2. PAST TENSE OF THE PARTICIPIAL MOOD

The negatives of the following sentences have been adapted slightly to keep them meaningful.

248

POSITIVE	NEGATIVE
Ka *re ne re na* le *mogoma* re ne ra o adima batho.	Ka *re ne re se na* mogoma, re ne ra o adima.
Fa ntate *a ne a na* le *thipa*, re ne re ka e dirisa.	Fa ntate *a ne a se na* thipa, re ne re ka dirisa eng?
Le fa monna *a ne a na* le peterolo, re ne re sa ntse re tlhaela.	Le fa monna *a ne a se na* peterolo, re ne ra kgona go o tsamaisa.

Do you recognise:

- (i) the auxiliary verb *ne* in these examples?
- (ii) the subjectival concords of the auxiliary verb *ne* and the copular verb *na*?
- (iii) the negative prefix *se*?
- (iv) the independent main clause or main action?
- (v) the dependent or subordinate clause?
- (vi) the change in the form of the subjectival concord of class 1 and 1(a)?

Exercise 14.41

*Can you now give your own examples of the copular verb **na** used in the past tense of the participial mood? Remember to alternate the complements discussed in par. 3.3.*

3. FUTURE TENSE OF THE PARTICIPIAL MOOD

The negatives of the following sentences have been adapted slightly to keep them meaningful.

POSITIVE	NEGATIVE
Ka *o tla bo o na* le nako, o ka re kwalela.	Ka *o tla bo o se na* nako go tla, o ka re kwalela.
Fa rraabo a ka tlhokafala, *ba tla bo ba na* le motlhoko-medi.	Fa rraabo a ka tlhokafala, *ba tla bo ba se na* motlhoko-medi.
Le fa *ke tla bo ke na* le ena, o re bulele lebati.	Le fa *ke tla bo ke se na* le ena, o mpulele lebati.

Did you notice that:
- (i) the auxiliary verb *bo* has its own subjectival concord?
- (ii) the copular verb *na* has its own subjectival concord?
- (iii) the compound predicate can consist of up to 6 different structural items, e.g. *o tla bo o se na . . .*

Exercise 14.42

*You should now attempt to give your own examples of the verbal copulative **na** in the future tense of the participial mood. Remember to alternate your complements by consulting par. 3.3.*

To conclude it should be mentioned that:
- (i) the aspectual prefix *ka* + the auxiliary verb *bo*; and
- (ii) the aspectual prefix *sa* + the auxiliary verb *ntse* may respectively appear in the present and past tenses discussed above, e.g.

Fa o *ka bo* o *na* le garawe, o ne o ka re thusa.

Ka *re ne re sa ntse re na* le mogoma, re ne re o adima batho.

Can you identify the subjectival concords of the auxiliary verbs and the copular verb in these examples?

3.4.3 The associative copulative **nna** in various moods

The subject of an associative copulative can enter into a possessive relationship or an associative relationship with its complement. This change in relationship is expressed by means of the copular verb **nna**.

250

The conjugation of the copular verb **nna** follows the normal verbal conjugation.

1. THE INFINITIVE MOOD

This mood of the associative copulative expresses the entering into a possessive or an associative relationship in the present tense, e.g.

POSITIVE	NEGATIVE
go nna le balatedi	**go se nne** le balatedi
go nna le matlhare	**go se nne** le matlhare
go nna le dijo	**go se nne** le dijo

What are the structural characteristics of these tenses in the positive and negative?

Exercise 14.43

You should now add to these examples making use of the list of alternative complements of the associative copulative as listed in par. 3.3.

2. THE IMPERATIVE MOOD

This mood expresses commands, requests, admonitions and encouragement to the subject to acquire something or to enter into an association with the complement, e.g.

POSITIVE	NEGATIVE
Nna le pelotlhomogi tlhe!	**Se nne** le pelotlhomogi!
Nna le mosola mo botshelong!	**Se nne** le mosola mo botshelong!
Mosimane! **Nna** le boikarabelo!	Mosimane! **Se nne** le boikarabelo!

In these examples you should be on the alert because of the tendency to confuse the verb **nna** with the copulative **nna**[1], e.g.

Re **nna** le mme kwa gae.

....

Re **nna** le maitsholo fa re laelwa.

....

Exercise 14.44

Can you now form your examples of the imperative mood?

3. THE INDICATIVE MOOD

This mood of the associative copulative factually states the subject's present, past or future entering or its being in a possessive or associative relationship with a complement. Only one example from each of these tenses is quoted in the following:

POSITIVE	NEGATIVE
Ke a dira. Ka jalo **ke nna** le madi.	Ga ke dire. Ka jalo **ga ke nne** le madi.
Re lemile. Jaanong **re nnile** le dijo.	Ga re a lema. Jaanong **ga re a nna** le dijo.
Naga **e tla nna** le bojang.	Naga **ga e ne e nna** le bojang.

Do you recognise the structural features of the different tenses? The potential prefix **ka** and the progressive prefix **sa** may also appear in sentences of the indicative mood, e.g.

Setlhare seo, *se **ka** nna* le dikungwa.

....

Barutwana *ba **ka** nna* le kitso eo.

....

Setlhare seo, *se **sa** ntse* se nna le dikungwa.

....

1) *Cf. dictionary p. 108.*

Barutwana *ba **sa ntse** ba nna* le kitso eo.

....

In the last two sentences, as you have seen, **sa** + the auxiliary verb **ntse** form a compound copular predicate with the copular verb **nna**.

Exercise 14.45

*You should now be able to form your own sentences in the indicative mood by means of the copular verb **nna**.*

4. THE SUBJUNCTIVE MOOD

This mood has two tense forms, viz. the present and past tense. It expresses interdependent or interrelated actions and therefore only occurs in subordinate clauses and after some auxiliary verbs and conjuctives, e.g.

POSITIVE	NEGATIVE
Mme o batla gore **ke nne** le kitso.	Mme o batla gore **ke se nne** le kitso.
Dinokwane di ne di mmatla, *a* **nna** le letshogo.	Dinokwane di ne di mmatla, *a* **se ka a nna** le letshogo

Do you recognise the interdependent or interrelated actions of the subjunctive mood? You should also be able to recognise the two main tenses in the examples cited above.

Exercise 14.46

*You should now attempt to form your own examples making use of the copular verb **nna**. Remember to make sentences in both tenses.*

SELF-ASSESSMENT

1. Enumerate the different words and structures that can function as complements and give an example in each instance.
2. Name the bold italicised structural and syntactical elements in the following sentences:

(i) Malome *o na le dinku.*
Malome *ga a na dinku.*
(ii) Katse *e na le go ratela.*
Katse *ga e na go ratela.*
(iii) *Ke na natso, ditempe* tse o di batlang.
Ga ke na natso, ditempe tse o di batlang.
3. In the case of which complement is the connective prefix retained in the negative?
4. Identify the complements in the following sentences:
(i) Mosimane yoo, ga a na maitseo a mantle.
(ii) Tshimo eo, e na le mofero o o maswe.
(iii) Ga ba na nabo (boikarabelo).
(iv) Mmotorokara o nalo, leotwana le lešwa.
(v) Mohumi o na le dithoto tse dintsi.
(vi) Dikgole, ba ne ba na le disele.
(vii) Ba ne ba na le wa gago, mmotorokara.
(viii) Ngwanaka! O na le go ntshwenya bobe.
(ix) Ga go na ope yo o fetang fa.
(x) Batshameki bao, ba na le yo o tabogang thata.
5. Give an alternative example for each of the complements, appearing in 4 above.
6. (a) Name the moods in which the associative copular verb *nna* appears.
(b) Give your own examples illustrating each of these moods as well as the tenses of these moods.
7. Identify the following types of copular predicates:
(i) Nna ke tla nna morutabana.
(ii) Ke tla nna botlhale, ke ruta bana.
(iii) Ke nnile le maikemisetso a, ke sa le mosimane.
8. Name the moods in which the copular verb appears in the following sentences:
(i) Go nna le kitso ya pharakano go a batlega mo Gauteng.
(ii) Re tla nna le didiriswa tse di tlhokegang.
(iii) Morafe o, o nnile le dikgosi tse di nnang le botho.
(iv) "Mosimane! O simolola o nna le go senya mo malatsing ano."
(v) "Ngwanaka! Nna le ditlhokego tsa botshelo."
(vi) Ke a bala gore ke se nne le poifo ya go kwala ditlhatlhobo.
(vii) Rona ga re a nna nayo kitso eo.
(viii) Go se nne le tsamaiso ya semmuso go senya dilo.
(ix) Magodu a sa ntse a nna le go thuba.
(x) Barutwana ba ka nna le maitseo a mantle.

254

9. Identify the kinds of copulatives in the following examples:
   (i) Nnake o tla nna mongwe wa mokgatlho wa basupatse-la.
   (ii) Morebodi ga se Mopedi.
   (iii) Seatla sa me se botlhoko fa.
   (iv) Fa ke le wena, nka didimala.
   (v) Selemo se gaufi. Ke nnete.
10. Identify the structural differences between the following copulatives:
   (i) Morebodi **ke** Mopedi, **ga a** Motswana.
   (ii) Morebodi **o** bonolo, **ga a** setlhogo.
   (iii) Morebodi o **nna** botlhale, ga a **nne** boatla.
11. In what way does (iii) differ from (i) and (ii)?
12. Identify the predicate in 10 above.
13. What are the differences in structure between the copular predicates of the following sentences?
   (a) Moratiwa o pelonamagadi.
   (b) Fa moratiwa a le pelonamagadi ba tla mo tsietsa.
14. What quality or characteristic or state of the subject is expressed by each of the copulatives in 13 above?
15. In what words do the predicates of the participial mood usually commence? Give your own example of each.
16. In what tenses does the copulative *le* appear?
17. Name the structural elements of the copular predicates in the following sentences:
   (i) Ka go tla bo go le mariga, re tla tlhoka dikgong go besa.
   (ii) Fa a le moleele, a ka re thusa.
   (iii) Le fa re ne re le bahumi, re ka se kgone go duela madi a a kana.
   (iv) Kgomo eo, e mokodue, ga ke e batle.
18. All three kinds of copulatives appear in the following examples. Can you identify and name them?
   (i) Monna yo, o bonolo go gaisa yole.
   (ii) Monna yo o bonolo ke malome.
   (iii) Ntšwa e na le dikgofa tse ditona.
   (iv) Nna ke morutabana, ke na le tetla go ruta mo sekolong se.
   (v) Re nna bangwe ba setlhopha seo.
19. Give the negatives of the sentences in 18 above.
20. Name the elements forming the following sentences:
   (i) Ditau di na le ditawana.
   (ii) Loapi ga lo na dinaledi.
21. What kind of word is **le ditawana** in 20 above?

22. What change does the subjectival concord of classes 1 and 1(a) undergo in the associative copulative? Give an example in the positive and the negative to illustrate your point.

23. Name the two relationships between the subjects and the complements of the following sentences:

    Rangwane o na le koloi.

    Noka e na le metsi.

24. In what ways do the subjects of the sentences in 23 above differ?

25. Write down the mood as well as the tense of the following copular verbs:

    (i) Go a bonala gore o na le maitseo.

    (ii) Ke thweetse ditlhako. Ke na le tse le tseo.

    (iii) Mono ga go na ope yo o re itseng.

    (iv) Mosimane yo, Shole, o na le go ngongorega.

    (v) Basimane bao ga ba na le bona, boikarabelo.

    (vi) Ke a itse gore ntšwa eo e nao, matsetse.

    (vii) A ga go na bangwe ba ba itseng mono?

    (viii) Dibuka di na le mebala e mentsi. Go na le tse ditala le tse dikhibidu.

    (ix) Dikgomo tsa gaetsho di na le tsa gaeno.

    (x) Fa o na le yo o gananang mo romele kwa go nna.

    (xi) Ke ne ke tla bo ke se na mothusi.

    (xii) Ba ne ba na le ditamati le boupe.

    (xiii) Fa o ka bo o na le bathusi, o ka bo o feditse ka nako.

    (xiv) Le fa ba ne ba sa ntse ba lema, ba ne ba se na dipholo.

    (xv) Ka re tla bo re na le dithoto, go tla re tsaya sebaka.

26. What is the difference in the relationship between subject and complement as expressed by (i) the non-verbal copulative and (ii) the copulative verb **nna**?

27. Explain the relationship expressed between the subject and the complement in the case of:

    (a) the identifying copulative

    (b) the descriptive copulative

    (c) the associative copulative.

28. Rewrite the following sentences and underline the complements of each copular structure:

    Mosadimogolo ke mmangwane.

    Mmangwane o bosilo thata.

    Bosilo bo na le mowa o o seng monate.

29. Rewrite the following sentences and underline the copular predicate in each:

Nna ke na le thipa.
Wena o na le ntšwa.
Thipa ke sediriswa se se tlhokegang.
Ntšwa ke seruiwa se se re direlang.
Thipa e bogale go na le selepe.
Ntšwa e bosilo go gaisa katse.
30. Write down the complements of the copulatives used in 29 above.
31. Name the bold italicised elements of the following sentences:
   (i) **Ke na le madi**, mme wena **ga o na sepe**.
   (ii) Fa **a na le madi**, mme wena **o se na sepe**, re tla dirang?
32. Explain the terms copulative and complement by referring to the following examples:
   Monna ke modiri.
   Mosadi o bonolo.
   Mosimane o na le maitsholo.
33. Describe the relationship expressed by the:
   (i) associative copulative in the indicative mood
   (ii) associative copulative in the participial mood.
34. How are the aspectual morphemes used in copular verbs?

257

CHAPTER 15

Interjectives

> **OBJECTIVES**
>
> On completion of this chapter you should be able to:
> 1. explain the meaning of the term "interjective";
> 2. describe the derivation and use of interjectives;
> 3. identify interjectives when appearing in a passage.

1. The meaning of the term *interjective*

Interjectives are words of an exclamatory nature. They are usually used in one-word sentences and they are used to express some emotion or to express assent or dissent. In addition they can be used vocatively or imperatively, e.g.

> ***Utshi!***[1] Ke eng o mpolaya? ....
>
> ***Ee!*** Ba gana go re thusa. ....
>
> ***Nnyaa!*** Ena ga ke mo itse. ....
>
> ***Mosimane!*** Thiboga foo! ....
>
> ***Thiboga!*** O mo tseleng! ....

From these examples it is clear that some of the interjectives are original interjectives that do not reveal any connection with other word categories, e.g.

> ***utshi, ee*** and ***nnyaa.***

We also have interjectives derived from other word categories, e.g.

> ***mosimane*** and ***thiboga.***

2. The derivation and use of interjectives

As far as the origin or derivation of interjectives is concerned, we distinguish between:

1) *Cf. dictionary p. 206.*

(i) original interjectives
(ii) vocative interjectives
(iii) imperative interjectives
(iv) idiomatic interjectives.

2.1 Original interjectives

These interjectives are characterised by the fact that they cannot be analysed into smaller structural elements. Some of the original interjectives, for example, consist of sounds or sound sequences that do not occur in normal words, e.g.

X![2] O a bo o dirile eng?

....

Pc! A le bone gore o nkarabile jang?

....

1. The original interjectives are used to express assent or dissent, e.g.

    Ee! Jaanong o nepile. ....

    Ehee! Mo kabole ditsebe, a tle a bake.

    ....

    Nnyaya! Wena ga o tlhaloganye.

    ....

    M-m! Se bue jaalo! ....

Exercise 15.1

You should now attempt to use the following examples of original interjectives in sentences of your own:
   e-e! *(dissent),* **mm!** *(assent).*

2. The original interjectives are used to express a wide range of emotions or fear or physical pain, e.g.

    Ao! Mosimane ke wena. A o a nkitse?

    ....

    Ija! A tiragalo e e maswe.

    ....

_____

2) *Cf. dictionary p. 207.*

Tshikhi! E kete re ka gotsa molelo.

....

Wai! Wena o tla a bona kae madi go reka ntlo.

....

Exercise 15.2

You should now attempt to use the following examples of original interjectives used to express emotions or fear or pain in sentences of your own:

ijo!	....	***ijoo!***	....
c-c-c-c!	....	***xx!***	....
tshutshu!	....	***mmalo!***	....
pc!	....	***utšhh!***	....

3. The original interjectives are used to call for attention or to express a request, e.g.

Heelang! Le ya kae le ise le fetse?

....

Koko! A go na le mongwe?

....

Tsweetswee! Bagaetsho, ke batla tsela.

....

Hee? A o ne o mpatla?

....

Exercise 15.3

You should now be able to use the following examples of original interjectives in sentences expressing a request or calling for attention.

s!	....	***mme!***	....	***tlhao!***	....
nxae!	....	***biuu!***	....	***q-q-q-q!***	....
x-x-x-x!	....	***aya!***	....	***pcw!***	....

2.2 Vocative interjectives

1. Nouns, quantitatives and pronouns of the second person are used vocatively to call or to address people, e.g.

Monna! Thiboga foo!

....

Ngwanaka! A ga o a bona hamole ya me?

....

Wena! O dira eng foo?

....

E seng wena fela! *Lotlhe!*

....

Bagaetsho! Gompieno go gorogile moeng ona.

....

Exercise 15.4

You should now be able to find additional examples of vocative interjectives used when calling or addressing people.

2. Another important group of vocative interjectives is associated with the nouns occurring in the sub-classes of the **mo- ba-** classes. In the following examples of relationship terms you will notice that the nouns end in *-ê* while the vocative interjectives, singular and plural end in *-a*, e.g.

Nouns	*Vocative interjective*
rrê	rra! ....
borrê	borra! ....
mmê	mma! ....
bommê	bomma! ....
nnakê	nnaka! ....
bonnakê	bonnaka! ....

Exercise 15.5

You should now be able to give more examples of the vocative interjectives that are associated with relationship terms ending in -a.

261

By now you will have realised that relationship terms like the following are the same in their nominal and their interjective forms, e.g.

Noun		Vocative interjective	
malome	....	malome!	....
rakgadi	....	rakgadi!	....
nkgonne	....	nkgonne!	....
rangwane	....	rangwane!	....

Exercise 15.6

You should now be able to give more examples of the vocative interjective used as relationship terms that do not differ from their nominal forms.

3. Other kinds of vocative interjectives are the names of tribal totems which are commonly used as courteous or honorific forms of address, e.g.

Kgabo! Le tlhotse jang?

....

Kwena! Re a go dumedisa.

....

Motshweneng! Le tsogile jang?

....

Exercise 15.7

Can you give more examples of interjectives used as courteous or honorific forms of address?

2.3 Imperative interjectives

1. Imperatives are used interjectively, e.g.

Tsamaya! ....

Tsamayang! ....

Se tsamaeng! ....

2. These imperative interjectives may take objects or adverbial descriptions, e.g.

Fetsa **tiro** eo! ....

Dira **ka bonako**! ....

E fetse! ....

Boa **ka moso!** ....

Ema **foo!** ....

Exercise 15.8

Can you give your own examples of these two kinds of imperative interjectives?

2.4 Idiomatic interjectives

A number of interjectives, miscellaneous in nature, are used interjectively in a number of idiomatic expressions, e.g.

Ka Modimo! Ga re itse sepe.

....

Ruri! Nna ga ke ye go ba thusa.

....

Gore ke go adime madi! **Le go ka!**

....

Bakwena ba kae! A setlhare se sekima!

....

Sala sentle! ....

Tsamayang sentle! ....

3. The use of the enclitics *tlhe* and *wee* with interjectives

Some of the interjectives that have been illustrated in the course of this chapter may be used together with the enclitics **tlhe** and **wee**. **Enclitics** are disjunctively written suffixal morphemes added to some words.

1. In the case of **tlhe** the addition of the enclitic expresses impatience or annoyance, e.g.

Ngwanaka! *Itlhaganele* **tlhe!**

Ruri *tlhe!* Re go neetse karabo!

Dumelang **tlhe** basimane!

Utšhh **tlhe**! O dirang?

Exercise 15.9

Can you give more examples from the four abovementioned groups of interjectives that function in conjunction with **tlhe**?

2. In the case of *wee* the enclitic can be used when calling someone at a distance, e.g.

Mokwatatsie a bitsa a re: *"Phokojwe* **wee!**"

Malome **wee!** Re kwano!

Heela **wee!**

Exercise 15.10

Can you give your own examples illustrating the vocative use of **wee**?

3. The enclitic *wee* can be used as a form of addressing an associate, e.g.

Pholo **wee!** O ya go ipolaya ka selo seo.

Dikeledi **wee!** Tla o bone fa!

Exercise 15.11

Will you now be able to give more examples illustrating the use of ***wee*** *when addressing an associate?*

4. The enclitic ***wee*** is used in idiomatic expressions, e.g.

Mma ***wee!*** Ngwana o ya kwa seterateng.

....

Ijo ***wee!*** Go diragetseng?

....

Exercise 15.12

Can you give more examples of ***wee*** *used in idiomatic expressions of fear, pain or distress?*

SELF-ASSESSMENT

1. Explain the term "interjective" in your own words.
2. Name the four different kinds of interjectives giving an example of each kind.
3. Can you give an example of an interjective used to express:
   (i) assent or dissent?
   (ii) fear or pain?
4. Use two original interjectives used to express a request in sentences.
5. Explain the term "vocative interjective" and give three examples to illustrate the term.
6. Explain the term "imperative interjective" and give an example.
7. Identify and name the different kinds of interjectives in the following sentences:
     (i) Morwa! Tlisa molamu ke tsamaye.
    (ii) Mosimane wee! Kganelela foo.
   (iii) Nxae! Ke ne ke sa go bone ntate.
    (iv) Lona! Le fitlha eng foo!
     (v) Rangwane! Ke go tlisetse sengwe.
    (vi) Di kganele foo! Tlhao!
   (vii) Ga ke dumele. E-e!
  (viii) Tlhobogang! Ga le itse!
    (ix) C-c-c-c! A motho wa Modimo!
     (x) Ee tlhe! Re a go rata.

CHAPTER 16

Conjunctives

OBJECTIVES

On completion of this chapter you should be able to:
1. explain the meaning of the term "conjunctive";
2. describe the use of conjunctives;
3. identify conjunctives in a passage.

---

1. The meaning of the term *conjunctive*

The term conjunctive refers to a group of words which are used **to join** sentences or **to introduce** sentences.

2. The use of conjunctives

Conjunctives may be used to:

(a) introduce sentences
(b) join sentences.

2.1 Conjunctives introducing sentences

The following conjunctives are used to introduce sentences and interjective phrases:

(i) The low toned interrogative *a*, e.g.
   A o itse mosimane yole?

....

(ii) The high toned *a* introducing interjective phrases, e.g.
   A legodu!

....

(iii) *aitse*, e.g.
   Aitse ga ke ngwana! Se bue jaana le nna.

....

(iv) **_ntsiaana_**, e.g.
A **_ntsiaana_** o ne o ntse o lwala?

....

(v) **_e kete_**, e.g.
E kete mmotorokara ona o senyegile.

....

(vi) **_gongwe_**, e.g.
Gongwe ba tloga ba goroga.

....

(vii) **_jaanong he_** is mainly used in narratives, e.g.
Jaanong he, ba tsaya thoto ya bona ba wela mo tseleng.

....

(viii) **_jalo he_** is mainly used in narratives, e.g.
Jalo he ka mo utlwela botlhoko, mme ka mo thusa.

....

(ix) **_kana_**, e.g.
Kana wena o mang?

....

(x) **_kooteng_**, e.g.
Kooteng ba tlhagetswe ke mathata.

....

(xi) **_motlhamongwe_**, e.g.
Motlhamongwe ga ba go itse.

....

(xii) **_naa_**, e.g.
Naa o utlwang?

....

(xiii) **_ntekane_**, e.g.
Ntekane e ne e le wena maabane!

....

(xiv) **_ntlha_**, e.g.
Ntlha o ntidimaletse!

....

(xv) **tota**, e.g.
Tota ke la ntlha ke bona selo se.

....

(xvi) **kgotsa**, e.g.
Kgotsa ba tla goroga pele ga nako.

....

(xvii) **abo**, e.g.
Abo o le montle, moratiwa!

....

Exercise 16.1

Can you give your own examples of sentences introduced by the abovementioned conjunctives?

Although the abovementioned conjunctives have been classified as those introducing sentences, some of them can also be used to join sentences.

Exercise 16.2

In order to get a clear picture of the abovementioned use of the conjunctives, it is advised that you write down two of your own examples for each of the 17 conjunctives mentioned above.

2.2 Conjunctives joining sentences

Conjunctives are commonly used to join sentences and the result is usually a complex or a co-ordinate sentence. Conjunctives that are used in this way are the following:

(i) **boo** which is usually used with a negative implication,e .g.
Ao! A nka go adima madi **boo** ke le mohumi.

....

(ii) **e kete**, e.g.
Mosadi yole, **e kete** o utlwa tsotlhe tse di buiwang.

....

(iii) **e seng**, e.g.
Tswelela o fetse, **e seng** jalo re tla bonana gape.

....

(iv) **fela**, e.g.
Ntate o ile toropong, **fela** ga ke itse gore o tla goroga leng teng.

....

(v) **gape**, e.g.
Monna ole o nthogile **gape** o gatile ntšwa ya me ka mmotorokara.

....

(vi) **gongwe**, e.g.
A ke go thuse ka dithuto tsa gago, **gongwe** o tla falola.

....

(vii) **gore**, e.g.
Mme o batla **gore** ke fetse tiro ena ka bonako.

....

(viii) The following conjunctives are similar in meaning:
ka gonne, ka gobo, ka gobane, ka gore, gobo, gonne, e.g.
Ba batla tiro, **ka gore** difalana di lolea.

....

(ix) **le gone**, e.g.
Ba kgetlile dinamune kwa ntle ga tetla, **le gone** ba latlhetse matlape mo tlung.

....

(x) **le gale**, e.g.
Ngwanaka, o lekile ka thata yotlhe, **le gale** ga a kgone tiro ele.

....

(xi) **mme**, e.g.
Nkile ka mo adima madi, **mme** morago ga moo a gana go a busa.

....

(xii) **motlhamongwe**, e.g.
Tla kwano ke go thuse, **motlhamongwe** nka go sedimosetsa.

....

(xiii) The following conjunctives are similar in meaning:
kgotsa, kana, kampo, ampo, ana, e.g.
O tlile go adima eng, šaga **ampo** petlwana?

....

(xiv) **e tswa**, e.g.
Ba gana go nthusa **e tswa** ke ba kopile thuso.

....

(xv) **fa**, e.g.
Fa o rata, o ka ya gae jaanong.

....

(xvi) **ka**, e.g.
Ke ya go go tlalea **ka** o ntshenyeditse.

....

(xvii) **le fa**, e.g.
Le fa pula e ka na jaanong ga re ye go roba sepe.

....

(xviii) **le mororo**, e.g.
Ga a ka ke a go adima madi **le mororo** a jele boswa jwa mohumi.

....

Exercise 16.3

You should now be able to give your own examples of sentences joined by the abovementioned conjunctives.

SELF-ASSESSMENT

1. Explain the term "conjunctive" in your own words.
2. What kinds of sentences are formed when they are joined by conjunctives?
3. Give an example of a conjunctive that:
   (a) introduces a sentence
   (b) joins sentences.
4. What is the function of the bold parts of the following sentences?
   (i) Basimane ba ya toropong **le mororo** rraabo a gana.
   (ii) **Le fa** a ka re o batla go ntuela, ga ke tlhole ke a batla.
   (iii) A o rekile mmidi **kampo** dinawa?
   (iv) **Ntlha** ke fitlhetse rraagwe kwa gae, **mme** ena o supile gore ga a yo.
   (v) A re yeng, **le gale** re tla kopana gape mo bekeng e e tlang.
   (vi) **Kana** ga ke go itse rra.
   (vii) **Aitse** ke bone dilo tseo di diragala.
   (viii) Ke batla mosadi **e seng** motlhokomedi.
   (ix) **A** makgakga!
   (x) **Naa** ke sejo se?

CHAPTER 17

The different types of sentences and clauses

OBJECTIVES

On completion of this chapter you should be able to:
1. describe the structure of the different sentence types and clauses;
2. explain the semantic application of the different sentence types and clauses;
3. identify the different sentence types and clauses when occurring in a passage.

1. What is implied by the term *sentence*

A sentence expressing a complete thought can consist of a single word as is illustrated by means of a dialogue consisting of the following eight single word sentences, e.g.

A : Taboga! ....

B : Mang? ....

A : Wena! ....

B : Nna? ....

A : Ee! ....

B : Goreng? ....

A : Fela! ....

B : Ao! ....

This type of exchange is not uncommon in our daily communication. However, a related group of words can also express a complete thought, e.g.

Ngwanake taboga ka bonako!

....

271

In this case the sentence consists of three words, viz. a noun *ngwanake*, a verb *taboga* and an adverb *ka bonako*.

2. For what purposes are sentences used?

Sentences are used to express complete thoughts dealing with:

(i) **statements of facts**, e.g.

Pula e a na. ....

Ntate o tla jwala mabele. ....

Such sentences are called **declarative sentences**.

(ii) **questions**, e.g.

Pula e na kae? ....

A ntate o tla jwala mabele? ....

Such sentences are called **interrogative sentences**.

(iii) **commands**, e.g.

Lema tshimo eo! ....

A o ke a leme tshimo eo. ....

Such sentences are called **imperative sentences**.

(iv) **exclamations**, e.g.

Bona! ....

Sia! ....

Such sentences are formed by means of interjectives and they are called **exclamatory sentences**.

The preceding division of sentences is based on the **basic meaning or thought** conveyed by each of the types of sentences.

3. Can sentences be grouped according to their individual structure?

Sentences can indeed be grouped according to the syntactic elements contained in them. The sentences that are distinguished along structural lines are:

(i) **the simple sentence;**
(ii) **the co-ordinate sentence;**
(iii) **the complex sentence.**

3.1 The simple sentence

The simple sentence is formed by a single independent **predicate** which may be;

(i) **simple**, i.e. consisting of one verb stem, e.g.

O a *bona*. ....

(ii) **compound**, i.e. consisting of one verb stem and one or more auxiliary stems forming a single semantic unit, e.g.

Ba *ne* ba se *kitla* ba **bona**.

....

The simple sentence may have an **object** which may be:

(i) **simple**, i.e. consisting of one noun or pronoun, e.g.

O ne a se kitla a bona *tau*.

....

(ii) **compound**, i.e. consisting of two or more nouns or pronouns, e.g.

O ne a se kitla a bona *tau le noga*.

....

The object forms part of the predicate — a fact which is proved by the fact that the objectival concord can enter the structure of the verb, e.g.

O ne a se kitla a *di* bona, tau le noga.

....

The simple sentence may have a **subject** which may be:

(i) **simple**, i.e. consisting of one noun or pronoun, e.g.

Mosimane o ne a se kitla a bona tau le noga.

....

(ii) **compound**, i.e. consisting of two or more nouns or pronouns, e.g.

Mosimane le mosetsana ba ne ba se kitla ba bona tau le noga.

....

The subject and the object may be **qualified**, i.e.

Basimane le basetsana *ba bantsi* ba ne ba se kitla ba bona tau

le noga *tse dinnye.*

The verb may be described by **adverbs**, e.g.

Basimane le basetsana ba bantsi ba ne ba se kitla ba bona

tau le noga tse dinnye *sentle.*

From this it is clear that the term *a simple sentence* covers a fairly wide structural field.

3.2 The co-ordinate sentence

In brief one could say that the co-ordinate sentence consists of two or more simple sentences joined together by **co-ordinating conjunctives**. The co-ordinate sentence will therefore contain two or more independent predicates, e.g.

Ba a bona.

Ke a ba di bontsha.

These independent predicates may be combined by a co-ordinating conjunction *mme* (also see Chapter 16), e.g.

Ba a bona, *mme* ke a ba di bontsha.

In a wider scope this co-ordinate sentence may then read as follows:

Basimane le basetsana ba bantsi ba ne ba se kitla ba bona

tau le noga tse dinnye sentle, *mme* ke a ba di bontsha.

Through the co-ordinating conjunction the two or more independent predicates express a compound action.

3.3 The complex sentence

The complex sentence consists of **one independent predicate** and **one or more dependent predicates**. To put it in another way — the complex sentence consists of a simple sentence plus one or more predicates that depend on the simple sentence to make them meaningful, e.g.

Re tla tsamaya = independent predicate

(Fa letsatsi) le phirima = dependent predicate

These two predicates combine to form a **complex sentence**, e.g.

Re tla tsamaya fa letsatsi le phirima.

The independent predicate is also known as a **main clause** while the dependent predicate is also known as a **subordinate clause**.

4. What is a clause?

A clause is a group of words containing a subject and a predicate, but forming a part of a complex sentence. A main clause will therefore consist of a subject plus an **independent predicate**, e.g.

Re tla thusana.

A subordinate clause will therefore consist of a subject plus a **dependent predicate**, e.g.

gonne re a ratana

In the following examples the *main clause* appears in bold italicised type while the *subordinate clause* appears in medium italics:

Batho *ba ba itirelang* ***ba tla godisa maemo a bona.***

Ga ba itse *gore o tla boa leng.*

Ke dirisitse garawe *kwa o mponeng teng.*

Ntate o ne a itse fa re sa ya sekolong.

....

Mariga a a fetileng **re ne ra lwala thata.**

....

Re a tle re rakane le bona kwa re ragelang kgwele teng.

....

SELF-ASSESSMENT

1. Give an example of each of the following types of sentences:
   (i) interrogative sentences
   (ii) imperative sentences
   (iii) exclamatory sentences
   (iv) declarative sentences
   (v) simple sentences
   (vi) co-ordinate sentences
   (vii) complex sentences.
2. What are the structural characteristics of the following sentence types?
   (i) simple sentences
   (ii) co-ordinate sentences
   (iii) complex sentences.
3. Explain the following terms and give an example of each:
   (i) simple subject
   (ii) compound object
   (iii) simple predicate
   (iv) compound predicate.
4. Is the object connected to the predicate? Give a reason.
5. On the basis of their **meaning** sentences may be divided into:
   declarative sentences
   interrogative sentences
   imperative sentences
   exclamatory sentences
   Classify the following sentences according to these semantic groups:
   A : Itlhaganele! Re tla siiwa ke bese ya rona.
   B : Ao! O tabogetse kae? Go sa ntse go na le nako e ntsi.
   A : A tota? Sesupanako sa me sa re bese e tloga e goroga.
   B : Mma wee! O bua nnete! A re tla e fitlhela?

6. Classify the following sentences according to structure:
    (i) Nna le wena re tla thusana.
    (ii) A o rata kofi ampo a o rata tee?
    (iii) Mosadi yo a neng a feta fa, ke mmaagwe.
    (iv) A wena o itse monna yo o buang yole?
    (v) Ke rata Motabogi, fela ga a nthate.
    (vi) Monna yo mokima le mosadi yo monnye ba palame karaki e ntšhwa.

Clauses, as we have seen above, are syntactic structures found in complex sentences. A clause is characterised by the following:

 (i) it is a group of words containing a subject and a predicate;
 (ii) it is part of a complex or a compound sentence;
 (iii) its predicate can be **dependent**, in which case we are dealing with a **subordinate clause**;
 (iv) its predicate can be **independent**, in which case we are dealing with a **main clause.**

Let us test these characteristics against the following sentences where the **main clause** appears in **bold italics** while the *subordinate clause* appears in *medium italics:*

 (i) ***Ke ne ke kopa*** *gore o re tlhomogele pelo.*

 ....

 (ii) ***Nna ke a dumela*** *fa ntšwa eo e loma.*

 ....

 (iii) *Gore o montle,* ***wena o a itse.***

 ....

Would you agree that the main clauses can function independently? Read the following:

 (i) Ke ne ke kopa. ....

 (ii) Nna ke a dumela. ....

 (iii) Wena o a itse. ....

Would you agree that the subordinate clauses cannot function independently?

 (i) . . . gore o re tlhomogele pelo. ....

 (ii) . . . fa ntšwa eo e loma. ....

 (iii) Gore o montle . . . .

277

In order to become meaningful these **subordinate clauses** have to be used together with the **main or independent clauses.**

According to their function in a sentence one may classify the subordinate clauses into three types, viz.

(i) nominal clauses;
(ii) qualificative clauses and
(iii) adverbial clauses.

4.1 The nominal clause

OBJECTIVES

At the completion of this section you should be able to:
1. explain the meaning of the term "nominal clause";
2. identify a nominal clause appearing in a sentence or passage;
3. describe the structure and use of the nominal clause.

The meaning of the term nominal clause

The nominal clause, as the name suggests, is a noun-like expression that assumes the same function and position as a noun in a sentence. This implies that a nominal clause should be able to function as an object or a subject of a sentence.

The structure and use of the nominal clause

1. THE NOMINAL CLAUSE AS A SUBJECT

A noun as a subject	A nominal clause as a subject
(a) **Wena** o tla fetsa.	**Fa a ka go thusa** o tla fetsa.
(b) **Go bua** go senya nako.	**Gore o ye go tlhapa** go senya nako.

Would you agree that the absolute pronoun **wena** and the clause **Fa a ka go thusa** . . . both function as the subjects of the same verb, viz. **o tla fetsa**? Once again we have an example of a noun and a clause that are interchangeable. In other words, **Fa a ka go thusa** . . . is a nominal clause.

To what conclusion do you come in the case of **Go bua** . . . and **Gore o ye go tlhapa** . . .?

278

Does the verb stem **bua** in **Go bua** . . . confuse you? This should not be the case because the **go** or infinitive class is one of the noun classes consisting of a disjunctively written prefix **go** and a verb stem. The **go** or infinitive class of nouns has the subjectival concord **go** as you can see in the predicate of our example, viz. **go senya**.

Would you now agree that the noun of the infinitive class **Go bua** . . . and the clause **Gore o ye go tlhapa** . . . both function as subjects?

Once again you should test the nominal clauses occurring in the subjectival position against the following criteria:

(i) Do the clauses contain subjects?
    Yes: The omitted subject **ena** in:
           Fa **(ena)** a ka go thusa . . .
    The omitted subject **wena** in:
    Gore **(wena)** o ye go tlhapa . . .

(ii) Do the clauses contain predicates?
    Yes: Fa a ka **go thusa** . . .
    Gore **o ye** go tlhapa . . .

(iii) Are the predicates of the clauses dependent or independent?
    Both predicates are dependent and they depend on the main clauses for their full meaning.

The main or independent clauses of our complex sentences appear in bold italics:

Fa a ka go thusa **o tla fetsa.**

....

Gore o ye go tlhapa **go senya nako.**

....

Nominal clauses are commonly introduced by the conjunctives **gore** and **fa**, e.g.

(i) Kabelo, ke batla **gore o nkepele mosima fa.**

....

(ii) **Fa ba ka go tshwenya**, o tle kwano.

....

(iii) Ke itse **gore Motabogi o a nthata.**

....

(iv) Malome o begela kgosi *fa a kopane le baeng.*

....

(v) **Gore** *re falotse mo ditlhatlhobong,* go itsiwe ke botlhe.

....

(vi) **Fa** *o ka tla jaanong* ke tla go thusa.

....

Which of these nominal clauses are used subjectivally and which are used objectivally?

2. THE NOMINAL CLAUSE AS AN OBJECT

A noun as an object	*A nominal clause as an object*
(a) Ke utlwa **bana.**	Ke utlwa *fa ba bua.*
....	....
(b) Re itse **dikarabo** tsotlhe.	Re itse *gore lo arabile* tsotlhe.
....	....

Would you agree that the noun **bana** and the clause *fa ba bua* in (a) both function as objects of the same verb, viz. **Ke utlwa** . . .?

The fact that a noun and a clause are syntactically interchangeable explains why such a clause is called a nominal clause. Test the applicability of this statement in the case of sentence (b) above. Did you conclude that . . . **gore lo arabile** . . . is a nominal clause?

At this stage it is essential that you test the abovementioned two nominal clauses against the criteria stipulated for a clause earlier in this section:

(i) Do our clauses contain subjects?
    Yes: The omitted subject **bana in:**
        . . . *fa (bana)* ba bua.
    The ommitted subject **lona** in:
        . . . gore *(lona)* lo arabile . . .

(ii) Do our clauses contain predicates?
    Yes: . . . fa **ba bua.**
        . . . gore **lo arabile** tsotlhe

(iii) Are these predicates of the clauses dependent or independent?
    The predicates are **dependent** because they cannot stand alone

and they depend on the main clause for their full meaning. The main or independent clauses of our complex sentences appear in bold italics:

Ke utlwa fa ba bua. ....

Re itse gore lo arabile tsotlhe. ....

Exercise 17.1

You should now be able to form complex sentences like those above. The following list of verb stems should appear in their main clauses:

dumela	gopola	bona
batla	itse	utlwa
bolelela	rata	gopola
nagana	lora	bolela
tlhomamisa	laya	kopa

To conclude with, you should test your sentences by applying the four criteria applicable to clauses in order to establish whether you have indeed formed complex sentences.

SELF-ASSESSMENT

1. Replace the nominal clauses in the following sentences with suitable subjects and objects:
   (i) Morwaaka, ke batla gore o reetse sentle.
   (ii) Fa le ka ithuta ka tshwanelo le tla falola ka dinaledi.
   (iii) Gore re tlhalefile go a bonala.
   (iv) Ke tla go emela fa o diegile.
2. Are the sentences that you formed in 1 above still complex sentences or are they simple sentences? Give reasons for your answer.
3. Apply the four criteria for a nominal clause to the following sentence:
   Romeo o ne a itse gore Juliet o mo rata ka pelo yotlhe.
4. What part of the sentence in 3 above constitutes the main clause?
5. What characterises a main clause?
6. Name the other two types of clauses that will be discussed later in this chapter.
7. Give an example of a nominal clause functioning as:
   (i) the subject of a sentence and
   (ii) the object of the sentence.
8. What conjunctives commonly introduce a nominal clause?

4.2 The qualificative (relative) clause

The qualificative clause is a clause that qualifies words that can be used as subjects or objects of sentences. Like the adjectives in Chapter 4 they qualify in respect of appearance, nature, size and colour, e.g.

(i) Modiri *yo o tala* ga a kgone.

....

(ii) Thipa *e e boi* e tla loodiwa.

....

(iii) Seno *se se botshe* se monate.

....

(iv) Kgomo *e e bofala* ga e bonale gantsi.

....

(v) Pholo *e e digwetlha* ga e fule gompieno.

....

(vi) Dinamane *tse di lesibi* ke tsa gaetsho.

....

(vii) Mosetsana *yo o tlhogo-ethata* ga a laolege.

....

(viii) Balemirui *ba ba dikgomodintsi* ga ba tlhoke mašwi.

....

Besides these qualificative clauses with a **nominal base** one should also distinguish those with a **verbal base**, e.g.

(ix) Nna, *yo ke balang fa*, ke ithuta Setswana.

....

(x) Motlhatlheledi *yo o nthutang* o dirisa buka *e e bidiwang* "Tswana for beginners".

....

(xi) "Tswana for beginners" ke buka *e e kwadilweng* ke setlho-tswana sa batho.

....

282

(xii) Mosadi *yo o leng bonolo* ke mme.

....

In addition to the qualificative clauses with a verbal base, one should also distinguish those with a **copulative base**, e.g.

(xiii) Monna *yo e leng kgosi* ke ntate.

....

(xiv) Batho *ba ba leng botlhale* ga ba palelwe ke dithuto.

....

(xv) Batho *ba ba nang le kgatlego ya go ikaga* ba a dira gore dithuto di atlege.

....

In section 4.2.1 we will concentrate on the qualificative clauses with a nominal base while those with a verbal and a copulative base will respectively be dealt with in sections 4.2.2 and 4.2.3.

4.2.1 The qualificative (relative) clause with a nominal base

---

OBJECTIVES

At the completion of this section you should be able to:
1. explain the meaning of the term "qualificative (relative) clause" as applied to structures with a nominal base;
2. describe the structure of the qualificative clause with a nominal base;
3. identify examples of this qualificative (relative) clause when used in a paragraph.

The structure of these qualificative clauses is built up around the nominal base and is made up as follows:

 (i) the basic demonstrative of the word qualified by means of the clause;
 (ii) the subjectival concord of the word qualified by means of the clause;
(iii) the qualificative or relative stem and, lastly, if required;
(iv) the diminutive suffixes *-ana* or *-nyana*.

These structural elements appear as similarly numbered items in the following examples:

283

Letlapa **le le bokete** le mo wetse.
   (i) (ii) (iii)

....

Mosetsana **yo o mabelanyana** ga a ratiwe.
   (i) (ii) (iii)   (iv)

....

Metsi **a a bothithwana** a ka diriswa.
  (i) (ii)   (iii)   (iv)

....

The basic demonstrative in the structure of the qualificative clause no longer has a demonstrative function. As a matter of fact **one has to add** a demonstrative if you want to express the position of the subject, e.g.

Letlapa **le**, le le bokete le mo wetse.

....

Mosetsana **yo**, yo o mabelanyana ga a ratiwe.

....

Metsi **a**, a a bothithwana a ka dirisiwa.

....

Likewise the subjectival concord of the word qualified by the clause is not used as a mere verbal prefix. The subjectival concord is in fact used as a non-verbal copulative and is followed by the nominal complement, e.g.

Letlapa le **le** bokete le mo wetse.

....

Mosetsana yo **o** mabelanyana ga a ratiwe.

....

Metsi a **a** bothithwana a ka diriswa.

....

In the structure of the qualificative clause with a nominal base the basic demonstrative and the subjectival concord are known as the **qualificative concords.**

284

Exercise 17.2

Can you supply the full series of qualificative concords? You should now attempt to use these concords in qualificative clauses. (The following list of qualificative concords can serve as a checklist.)

Qualificative concords

SINGULAR		PLURAL
1st person	Nna: yô ke	Rona: ba re
2nd person	Wena: yô o	Lona: ba lo
3rd person	1. mo-: yô o	2. ba-: ba ba
	1.(a) —: yô o	2.(a) ba: ba ba
	3. mo-: o o	4. me-: ê e
	5. le-: lê le	6. ma-: a a
	7. se-: sê se	8. di-: tsê di
	9. N-: ê e	10. diN-: tsê di
	11. lo-: lô lo	10. diN-: tsê di
	14. bo-: bô bo/jô bo	6. ma-: a a
	15. go: gô go	
	16. fa-: fa go	
	17. go-: kwa go	
	18. mo-: mô go	

These qualificative concords together with a large number of nominal stems combine to form clauses that are obviously connected with the descriptive copulatives, e.g.

Descriptive copulative	Complex sentences
Kobo e bothitho.	Ke itheketse kobo *e e bothitho.*
Legong le motlhofo.	O tlile a rwele legong *le le motlhofo.*
Mosimane o sego.	Mosimane *yo o sego* o bone noga ka nako.
Mosetsana o kae?	Ba bua ka ga mosetsana *yo o kae*?
Sefofu se botlhale.	Sefofu *se se botlhale* se itse go opela dipina tsotlhe.

Can you see the connection between the copulatives and the qualificative clauses appearing in the abovementioned complex sentences?

You should of course not confuse the following copulative predicates with qualificative clauses:

Kobo e, *e bothitho.*

....

Legong le, *le motlhofo.*

....

In the sentence:

Ke itheketse kobo e e bothitho

....

we have a main clause conveying the main idea, i.e.

Ke itheketse kobo

and the subordinate clause *e e bothitho* qualifying the object of the main clause. The noun *kobo* has a second function, viz. as subject or antecedent of the qualificative clause, e.g.

kobo e e bothitho.

Can you identify the antecedents of the qualificative clauses in the following sentences?

Letsogo le le maatla le ka tsholetsa tshipi e.

....

Ntate o tlhoka namane ya gagwe e e botuba.

....

Pale e e kana e ka dirisiwa jaaka pinagare.

....

At the beginning of this section it was stated that the qualificative clause qualifies a subject or an object in terms of appearance, nature, size and colour. One can therefore expect that the nominal bases would include a fair number of abstract nouns to account for these qualities, e.g.

Nominal bases of qualificative clauses

bonya	....	maswe	....	kana	....
bonolo	....	mafura	....	kalo	....

botlhale	....	maatla	....	kae?	....
botlhoko	....	maaka	....	molemo	....
botshe	....	makgakga	....	monate	....
bokgwabo	....	mabela	....	sego	....
bogale	....	tlhaga	....	tsididi	....
bosula	....	tala	....	lefufa	....
bokete	....	kgopo	....	setswerere	....
botuba	....	digwetlha	....	sekai	....
bobududu	....	molema	....	setshwakga	....
sebola	....	lesibi	....	mokodue	....
kgaka	....	makekete	....	maswe	....

Exercise 17.3

You should now be able to form your own examples of complex sentences making use of the qualificative concords and the qualificative stems that were supplied above.

The following examples might serve as a guide for Exercise 17.3.

(i) Nna **yo ke mafura** nka se tsamaye ka bonako.

....

(ii) Ke bua le wena **yo o makgakga**!

....

(iii) Rona **ba re maatla** re tla go tseisa.

....

(iv) Lona **ba lo botlhale** lo tla kgona go nepa palo e.

....

(v) O ne a apere mosese **o o kgaka** wa mosego wa kgale.

....

Seeing that one easily confuses examples of **qualificative clauses** with **adjectives** you should first revise the structure of the adjective construction appearing in Chapter 4.

Instead of the **subjectival concord** the adjective makes use of the class prefix, e.g.

*M*osetsana yo *mosesane*nyana
   (i)   (ii)   (iii)   (iv)

and the **adjectival root** in the place of the qualificative stem used by the qualificative clause, e.g.

Letlapa le *le* **boketе**nyana
   (i) (ii)   (iii)   (iv)

In your study of nominal bases that can be used in qualificative clauses you might have noticed that the following examples may be used as adjectives as well as qualificative or relative stems:

> namagadi
> šampa
> tala

These stems may be used as follows:

As adjectives	As qualificative clauses
Morubisi **o monamagadi** o a elama.	Setlhare **se se namagadi** ga se tshabiwe.
....	....
Mokodue **o mošampa** o sule.	Mosimane **yo o šampa** o tswa kae?
....	....
Magapu **a matala** a kae?	Makau **a a tala** a tla tlhabologa.
....	

Besides single nouns used as qualificative stems there are quite a number of compound nouns that can be used as nominal bases. Quite a number of these compounds include nouns for parts of the body and express abstract qualifications not otherwise accounted for, e.g.

ditemepedi	pelonamagadi
matlhomahibidu	pelotshetlha
tlhogo-ethata	pelokgale
tlhogotona	pelo-ethata
ntšwapedi	pelonolo

Did you notice that the hyphen is used to keep vowel ending and vowel initial elements apart while those that commence with consonants are written conjunctively?

All adverbs of place and a few adverbs of manner can be used as the base of qualificative stems. These adverbs were discussed in Chapter 12, e.g.

(i) Mosadimogolo **yo o mo kokelong** ga a tlhole a kgona go tsamaya.

....

(ii) Ke selepe **se se jang** se ntate a se rekileng?

....

(iii) Tiro **e e thata** e ka se kgonwe ke wena.

....

(iv) Bojalwa **jo bo mo nkgwaneng** bo beetswe moletlo.

....

Exercise 17.4

You should now attempt to give your own examples of adverbs used as qualificative bases.

SELF-ASSESSMENT

1. Identify the structural elements of the qualificative clauses in the following sentences:
   (i) Pholo e e molema e robegile dinaka.
   (ii) Fa re lapile re rata go nwa seno se se tsididi.
   (iii) Monna yo o bogale o itsege ka leina la Ntwadumela.
   (iv) Nna ke tla ipatlela batho ba ba pelonamagadi.
2. What is the difference between the following two qualificative structures?
   Matlapa a makana a ka dirisiwa fa.
   Matlapa a a kana a ka dirisiwa fa.
3. What is the function and meaning of the qualificative clause?
4. Why is it easy to confuse the adjectives with qualificative clauses?
5. What kind of qualificative clause will be dealt with in a following section?
6. Give 5 examples of your own qualificative stems consisting of:
   (i) single nouns and
   (ii) compound nouns.
7. Name the elements forming a qualificative clause with a nominal base.
8. What is an antecedent?
9. Is a qualificative clause dependent or independent?
10. Identify the main and subordinate clause in:
    Legodu le le setlhogo, le utswetse mme.

4.2.2 The qualificative (relative) clause with a verbal base

OBJECTIVES

At the completion of this section you should be able to:
1. explain the meaning of the term "qualificative (relative) clause" as applied to structures with a verbal base;
2. describe the structure of the qualificative clause with a verbal base;
3. identify examples of this qualificative (relative) clause when used in a paragraph.

Like the qualificative clause with a nominal base those with a verbal base are also used to qualify subjects and objects of sentences. Unlike the adjectives and the qualificatives with a nominal base those with a verbal base qualify subjects and objects in terms of the actions performed or undergone by the subjects and objects, e.g.

(i) Nna **yo ke balang fa**, ke rutiwa ke motlhatlhedi **yo o dirisang**

....

buka **e e bidiwang "Tswana for beginners"**.

....

(ii) Pele **ke ya sekolong** le morago ga gore **ke tswa kwa unibese-**

....

thing ke ne ke thusa mme ka ditiro tsa lelapa.

....

(iii) Lekgarebe **le le tlholang le kgaba** ke Selebatso.

....

Would you agree that the bold italicised parts of the abovementioned sentences cannot stand alone but that they depend on the main clauses for their full meaning? Would you also agree that the bold italicised parts qualify their antecedents in terms of the actions performed or undergone by the antecedents?

In the case of the quantitative clause with a nominal base as well as the quantitative clause with a verbal base the qualificative concords consist of:

(i) the **basic demonstrative** derived from the antecedent of the clause;

(ii) the **subjectival concord** of the antecedent followed by the
(iii) **verbal base** to which **-ng** is suffixed, e.g.

Kabelo o thusa molemi **yo o golegang** dipholo.
(i) (ii)   (iii)

In this example the bold italicised qualificative clause qualifies the object **molemi** in terms of the action performed by him, i.e. the inspanning of the oxen. The **assistance** given by Kabelo and the **inspanning** of the oxen takes place at the same time. This is why the qualificative clause appears in the participial mood which is the mood used for expressing simultaneous actions or an action that coincides with the main action of the sentence. The easiest way to establish the mood of a qualificative clause is to put the whole sentence in the negative, e.g.

Kabelo **ga a thuse** molemi **yo a sa golegeng dipholo.**

The main clause is in the indicative mood as can be seen from the **ga** negative prefix while the subordinate qualificative clause is in the participial mood as can be derived from the **sa** negative prefix.

The qualificative clause with a verbal base can occur in the following tenses.

1. QUALIFICATIVE CLAUSES IN THE PRESENT TENSE

Positive

(i) Mosadi **yo o kgweetsang mmotorokara** ke mme.

(ii) Ntšwa **e e robalang kwa sakeng** e disa dinku.

Negative

(i) Mosadi *yo o* **sa** *kgweetseng mmotorokara* ke mme.

(ii) Ntšwa *e e* **sa** *robaleng* kwa sakeng e disa dinku.

Do you recognise the negative prefix **sa** and the change in the bold italicised ending of the verb stem?

Exercise 17.4

You should now be able to form your own examples with qualificative clauses in the present tense.

2. QUALIFICATIVE CLAUSES IN THE PERFECT TENSE

Positive

(i) Mosadi *yo o kgwee**ditseng** mmotorkara* ke mme.

....

(ii) Ntšwa *e e robe**tseng** kwa sakeng* e disa dinku.

....

Negative

(i) Mosadi *yo o **sa** kgweetsang* mmotorokara ke mme.

....

(ii) Ntšwa *e e **sa** robalang kwa sakeng* e disa dinku.

....

Compare the structural characteristics of the perfect tense with the present tense.

Exercise 17.5

You should be able to form your own examples with the qualificative clauses in the perfect tense.

3. QUALIFICATIVE CLAUSES IN THE FUTURE TENSE

Positive

(i) Mosadi *yo o **tla** kgweetsang* mmotorokara ke mme.

....

(ii) Ntšwa *e e **tla** robalang* kwa sakeng e disa dinku.

....

Negative

(i) Mosadi *yo o tla **se neng a** kgweetsa* mmotorokara ke mme.

....

(ii) Ntšwa *e e **se neng e** robala kwa sakeng* e disa dinku.

....

Do you recognise the following structural features that also appeared in Chapter 14?

(a) the negative prefix **se** appearing together with the auxiliary verb stem **ne**? (Alternatively the auxiliary verb **kitla** could have been used here.)

(b) the reduplication of the subjectival concord with the auxiliary verb stem as well as with the verb stems **kgweetsa** and **robala**?

(c) the **-ng** ending as being suffixed to the auxiliary verb stem **ne** instead of to the verb stems **kgweetsa** and **robala**?

Exercise 17.6

You should now be able to form your own examples with the qualificative clauses in the future tense.

Passive verbal structures used after the locative nouns **pele** and **morago** form another type of qualificative clause, e.g.

(i) Pele **ga go ka iwa baesekopong**, o fetse dithuto tsa gago.

....

(ii) Morago **ga gore tshimo e lengwe**, re jwala mabele, maraka, lebelebele le ditloo.

....

(iii) Pele **ga go tlhabololwa**, Masarwa a ne a tshela ka go tsoma le

....

go epa digwere.

....

(iv) Morago **ga go rutwa**, bana ba tshwanetse go ya gae.

....

Exercise 17.7

*You should now be able to form your own sentences using passive verbs after the locative nouns **pele** and **morago**.*

SELF-ASSESSMENT

1. Identify the structural elements of the qualificative clauses in the following sentences:
    (i) Pele ga o ka ya go tshameka, o tlhagole tema ya gago mo serapeng, mme morago ga moo o ye nokeng.

(ii) Ngwana yo o thusang batsadi o ithuta ditiro tse di tlhokegang.

(iii) Ke bone basimane ba tshameka mo mogobeng ba katogile dikgomo tse di senyang dijwalo.

2. What is the difference between the qualificative structures of the following sentences?

Mosadi yo o maswe o bua a iketlile.

Mosadi yo o iketlileng o bua maswe.

3. What is the function and meaning of a qualificative clause with a verbal base?

4. Can a qualificative clause stand alone?

5. In terms of what does a qualificative clause qualify its antecedent?

6. Give one example of each of the three kinds of qualificative clauses with a verbal base.

7. (a) In what tenses can the qualificative clause like the following appear?

Morutwana yo o balang polelo e, ke nna.

(b) Use the example in (a) above in two of these tenses.

(c) Give the negative of the sentences formed in (b) above as well as the negative of the example in (a) above.

8. Which negative prefix is used in the main clause and which in the qualificative clauses?

4.2.3 The qualificative (relative) clause with a copulative base

OBJECTIVES

At the completion of this section you should be able to:

1. explain the meaning of the term "qualificative (relative) clause" as applied to structures with a copular base;

2. describe the structure of the qualificative clause with a copular base;

3. identify examples of this qualificative (relative) clause when used in a paragraph.

The copular structures that are involved in this section are those of the descriptive as well as those of the associative copulative. These copulatives, as you will remember, were discussed in Chapter 14.

Descriptive and associative copulatives can also form qualificative clauses. In the case of the **descriptive copulative** such a clause would qualify the antecedent in terms of a quality, characteristic or state in which the antecedent is, e.g.

Motlhabani **yo o leng boi** o tla sia fa a kopana le mmaba.

In the case of the **associative copulative** such a clause would qualify the antecendent in terms of an existing possessive relationship or an association between the antecedent (or subject) of the qualificative and the complement (or object), e.g.

Selepe **se se nang le mofeng** se thudilwe ke ntatemogolo.

The structural characteristics of these copulatives will not be discussed in detail as you were introduced to this data only a number of chapters ago. You are therefore expected to revise these sections and to identify the structures of the different moods and tenses of the qualificative clauses with a copular base from the following examples.

1. DESCRIPTIVE COPULATIVES AS QUALIFICATIVE CLAUSES

Positive

(i) Ngwana *yo o leng tlhaga* o ithuta malatsi otlhe.

(ii) Dijo *tse di neng di le monate* di fedile.

(iii) Kalakune **e e tla bong e le mafura** e tla tlhabiwa.

(iv) Mosimane yo, ke mo itse jaaka mongwe *yo o nnang makgakga.*

(v) Letsogo *le le nnileng botlhoko* le palelwa ke go tshwara.

(vi) Banna ba, ba tshwaragane le tiro ya go aga kago *e e ka nnang kana ka setlhare sa lebolukomo.*

Negative

(i) Ngwana **yo a seng tlhaga** o tshameka malatsi otlhe.

(ii) Dijo **tse di neng di se monate** di fedile.

(iii) Kalakune **e e tla bong e se mafura** e tla tlhabiwa.

(iv) Mosimane yo, ke mo itse jaaka mongwe **yo a sa nneng makga-kga.**

(v) Letsogo **le le sa nnang** botlhoko le palelwa ke go tshwara.

(vi) Banna ba, ba tshwaragane le tiro ya go aga kago **e e ka se nneng**

kana ka setlhare sa lebolukomo.

Do you still recognise the different structural features of the various copular structures in the positive and negative?

Exercise 17.8
You should now be able to form your own examples of the descriptive copulative used in qualificative clauses.

2. ASSOCIATIVE COPULATIVES AS QUALIFICATIVE CLAUSES
Positive

(i) Tau **e e nang le ditawana** e bogale go feta nare **e e nang le**

namane.

(ii) Go tswa letsatsi leo, mosadimogolo **yo o nnileng le pelotelele**

o ne a tshegofadiwa.

(iii) Moeteledipele **yo o tla nnang le kitso ya go agisanya merafe**,

....

o tla itsege jaaka mmoloki wa Aferika Borwa.

....

Negative

(i) Tau **e e se nang ditawana** e bogale go feta nare **e e se nang**

....

namane.

....

(ii) Go tswa letsatsi leo, mosadimogolo **yo o sa nnang le bopelote-**

....

lele o ne a atlafala.

....

(iii) Moeteledipele **yo a tla se neng a nna le kitso ya go agisanya**

....

merafe o tla itsege jaaka mosiamolodi mo Aferika Borwa.

....

Can you still identify the different structural features of the copular predicates in the positive and negative?

Exercise 17.9

You should now attempt to form your own sentences of the associative copulative used in qualificative clauses.

SELF-ASSESSMENT

1. Identify and write down the structural elements of the qualificative clauses in the following sentences:
   (i) Batho ba ba se nang maitseo, ba swabisa ba bangwe.
   (ii) Jaaka ke itse, le tla fiwa teko e e tla bong e le palela gotlhe-lele.
   (iii) Segokgo se se nang le kitso ya go loga bobi, se gaisa segokgo se se tlholang se tsoma.
   (iv) Merafe e e kileng ya nna le kgono ya go rafa gauta e ne e agile mono.

---

2. What types of qualificative clauses are the following?
   (i) Ga ke batle pale e e kana ke tlhoka e e kalo.
   (ii) Leuba le kgoreletsa balemirui ba ba ruileng dikgomo go di rekisa.
   (iii) Kgamelo e e nang le molepo e ka dirisiwa ke basimane fa ba ya nokeng.
   (iv) Monna yo o leng bosilo a ka se kgone go tlhokomela bana ba me.
3. What is the function and meaning of a qualificative clause with a copulative base?
4. In what way does a qualificative clause with a verbal base differ from a qualificative clause with a copular base?
5. (a) Name the two kinds of copulatives that may appear in qualificative clauses.
   (b) Give an example of each in the positive and negative.
   (c) In what tenses can the qualificative clauses, mentioned in (a) above, appear?

4.3 The adverbial clause

OBJECTIVES

At the completion of this section you should be able to:
1. explain the meaning of the term "adverbial clause of place, time and manner";
2. name the structures introducing the adverbial clauses of place, time and manner;
3. identify examples of these clauses when used in a paragraph.

In Chapter 12 it was pointed out that the adverb was a word that describes a process or an action, i.e. the verb, in terms of:

(a) **where** it takes place, e.g.

Ntate o ile **kwa morakeng.**

....

(b) **when** it take place, e.g.

Ka moso re tla fetsa go lema.

....

(c) **how** it take place, e.g.

Ngwanaka o dirile **sentle.**

....

298

The different kinds of adverbs are however not the only means of describing the action of the verb. A similar function can be achieved by means of descriptive or adverbial clauses e.g.

Ntate o ile **kwa a bileditsweng teng.**

....

Fa letsatsi le phirima re tla fetsa go lema.

....

Ngwanaka o dirile **ka ntlha ya gore o tlhaga.**

....

Would you agree that:

(a) the bold italicised parts of the three sentences have a descriptive function?

(b) the bold italicised parts are in actual fact clauses?

If you have a problem in answering the (b) question you should first establish what the characteristics of a clause are. Let us repeat them here to refresh your memory:

(i) a clause is a group of words containing a **subject** and a **predicate**;

(ii) a clause forms **part of a complex or a compound sentence**;

(iii) the predicate in a clause can be **dependent** in which case we are dealing with a **subordinate clause**;

(iv) the predicate in a clause can be **independent** in which case we are dealing with a **main clause.**

Let us now apply these characteristics to the following sentence:

Ntate o ile **kwa a bileditsweng teng.**

....

(i) the bold italicised part has a subject represented in the subjectival concord **a** and it has a predicate, i.e. **a bileditsweng teng;**

(ii) the bold italicised part occurs in a **complex sentence;**

(iii) the bold italicised part is dependent and is therefore a **subordinate clause** depending on the main clause.

Ntate o ile . . .   .

You should now make a similar application of the four criteria characterising a clause to our other two examples, i.e.

Fa letsatsi le phirima re tla fetsa go lema.

....

Ngwanaka o dirile *ka ntlha ya gore o tlhaga.*

....

From our introductory reasoning it is clear that the adverbial clauses have functions similar to the different kinds of adverbs. It therefore follows that there are adverbial clauses of

(a) place,
(b) time and
(c) manner.

4.3.1 The meaning of the adverbial clause of place

From our introduction it is clear that an adverbial clause of place performs **a descriptive function** like an adverb of place and it even occupies **similar syntactic positions** in a sentence, e.g.

Adverbs	*Adverbial clauses of place*
(i) Rona re ya **sekolong.**	(i) Rona re ya **kwa wena o yang teng.**
(ii) **Mo mosimeng** go na le noga.	(ii) **Mo ba tseneng teng** go na le noga.
(iii) A re ikhutseng *fa thoko ga tsela.*	(iii) A re ikhutseng *fa bona ba rapameng teng.*

Would you agree that the bold italicised adverbial clauses of place cannot stand alone but that they depend on the main clauses for their full meaning? Would you also agree that the bold italicised parts describe the actions of the main verb in terms of the place where the actions take place?

The structure and use of the adverbial clause of place

If you compare the following examples of adverbial clauses of place with those in 1 above you will notice certain elements that are recurrent:

(i) Rona re rata go jela nala **kwa** *lona le yang* **teng.**

....

(ii) Ba paletswe ke go feta **fa** *re neng re eme* **teng.**

....

(iii) Re ba fitlhetse mo kamoreng **mo** *re tlholang re kopana* **teng.**

....

The elements that one notices at a glance are:

(a) the demonstratives of the locative classes, viz. **kwa, fa** and **mo**;
(b) the **-ng** ending suffixed to the auxiliary or to the verb contained in the adverbial clause;
(c) the noun of the locative class, viz. **teng.**

Did you also notice that sentence (iii) contained an adverb **mo kamoreng**? This adverb describes the verb **re ba fitlhetse** and is in its turn described by the clause **mo re tlholang re kopana teng**. Like adverbs the adverbial clause can therefore be used to describe verbs and adverbs as well as adverbial clauses, e.g.

(i) Ba dirile *sentle* **jaanong.**

....

(ii) Mosadi yo o bua *bobe* **gompieno.**

....

(iii) Magodu a ne a nna *mo logageng le le sa itsegeng* **kwa thabeng**

....

e re e fetileng maabane.

....

(iv) Mme o ne a sala *kwa gae* **fa a tlholang a itirela tsa gagwe.**

....

Exercise 17.10

You should now be able to form your own complex sentences containing adverbial clauses of place.

4.3.2 The meaning of the adverbial clause of time

We will now illustrate that an adverbial clause of time performs **a**

descriptive function like an adverb of time and it even occupies **similar syntactic** positions in a sentence, e.g.

Adverbs	Adverbial clauses of time
Maitsiboa ba tla goroga ka terena.	**Fa re ile go itisa** ba tla goroga ka terena.
O boele kwa gae **ka nako.**	O boele kwa gae **o sena go fetsa go nosa.**
Rona re tsoga **ka ura ya bosupa.**	Rona re tsoga **letsatsi le ise le tlhabe.**
Ntate o tsamaile **ka thapama.**	Ntate o tsamaile **a sa bolo go go emela.**

Would you say that the individual bold italicised adverbial clauses of time can be used on their own or do they need the main clause to give them their full meaning? Can you see that the adverbial clauses of time describe the verb of the main clause in terms of the time that the action takes place?

The structure and use of the adverbial clause of time

Like the adverbial clause of place, the adverbial clause of time is characterised by a number of recurrent structures. These structures will become obvious when you compare the following examples with those in 3 above.

(i) **Fa** *thete e ralala* o ka se fitlhele motho mo tseleng e e ralalang sekgwa sele.

(ii) Morutabana, *fa a* **sena** *go re ruta* Setswana, o palama

mmotorokara a ye gae.

(iii) Maabane ke fitlhetse badisa *ba **ise** ba tsoge.*

....

(iv) Mosimane ke wena! *Ga ke **bolo** go go laela* go gorosa dikgomo

....

ka maneelo a dikonyana.

....

The following are some of the structural elements that also occur in 3 above:

(a) the conjunctive *fa*
(b) the auxiliary verb stems **ise, bolo** and **sena** often occur in adverbial clauses of time.

Sentence (iii) above, you will have noticed, also contains an adverb of time **maabane** which is, together with the clause, **ba ise ba tsoge**, used to describe the verb **ke fitlhetse**. Adverbs like adverbial clauses, as you know by now, can be either used to describe verbs or adverbs or adverbial clauses, e.g.

(i) Re gorogile *phakela **maabane.***

....

(ii) *Gompieno **ka tshokologo ya letsatsi**,* re tla wela mo tseleng.

....

(iii) Re gorogile kwa gae *maitsiboa **Morebodi a sa ntse a gama.***

....

(iv) *Fa ngwedi a roga* masole a tla tshoganyetsa mmaba *a ise a ipaakanye.*

....

Exercise 17.11
You should now be able to form your own examples of complex sentences containing adverbial clauses of time.

Subordinate clauses in the participial mood, as it appeared in Chapter 11, may also describe the predicate of the main clause as adverbial clauses denoting a simultaneous action or occurrence, e.g.

(i) Kwa gae ke fitlhetse kake *a **ikgarile mo bolaong.***

....

303

(ii) Maabane ke bone legwere *le metsa bana ba thaga.*

....

(iii) Ntatemogolo a re o kile a utlwa phika *e suma mo logageng la dipela.*

....

(iv) Bosigo boo ba ne ba raka tlhware *e leka go kgama lesea le robetse.*

....

Exercise 17.12

Can you now form your own examples of complex sentences with subordinate clauses in the participial mood describing the main clause?

SELF-ASSESSMENT

1. Replace the following adverbial clauses with:
   (a) suitable adverbs
   (b) alternative adverbial clauses
   (i) Diphelefu tsele, di thulana kwa di rakanang teng.
   (ii) Fa le sena go ja, le tleng go pegolola llori.
   (iii) Ke beile buka mo e ka bonalang teng.
   (iv) Gompieno ga re ise re utlwe mo madi ale a tsentsweng teng.
   (v) Bana ba tla bo ba robetse fa re boa kwa moletlong.
2. What is the function and meaning of an adverbial:
   (i) clause of time?
   (ii) clause of place?
3. Can an adverb and an adverbial clause occupy identical syntactic positions? Illustrate by means of examples.
4. Can adverbial clauses be used independently of the main clause?
5. Name three structural items that recur in adverbial clauses of place and give three examples illustrating them.
6. Can an adverbial clause describe an adverb or another adverbial clause? Give an example if it is possible.
7. Name four structural items that recur in adverbial clauses of time and give four examples illustrating them.

4.3.3 The meaning of the adverbial clause of manner

The term adverbial clause of manner is a general term for a number of adverbial clauses that are neither **clauses of place nor time**. These clauses are, up to a certain degree, interchangeable with the **adverbs of manner** which were discussed in Chapter 12. The adverbial clauses of manner can be subdivided into:

(a) adverbial clauses of **condition**, e.g.
   Fa o ka nkadima buka eo, nka itumela.

   ....

(b) adverbial clauses of **reason**, e.g.
   Re tla mo romela kwa gae ***ka gonne ga a batle go ithuta.***

   ....

(c) adverbial clauses of **concession**, e.g.
   Le fa o ka nkgoreletsa, ke tla ya gae.

   ....

(d) adverbial clauses of **comparison**, e.g.
   Re tla dira ***jaaka o re laetse.***

   ....

(e) adverbial clauses of **consequence**, e.g.
   Ga o rate go bala ***jala o tla nna fa, o ithuta dithuto tsa gago.***

   ....

(f) adverbial clauses of **degree**, e.g.
   Ke ne ka mo tlhalosetsa ***go fitlha mo a tlhaloganyang.***

   ....

In this section we will deal with the first three types of adverbial clauses while the last three will be dealt with in the next section.

1. THE ADVERBIAL CLAUSE OF CONDITION

This clause states a condition or a circumstance which is met in the main clause. The adverbial clause of condition occupies syntactic positions similar to the adverb of manner, e.g.

Adverbs	Adverbial clause of condition
Ruri, ke tla go adima madi.	**Fa o ka nkopa**, ke tla go adima madi.
Tota, o ka bo a gorogile ka nako.	**Fa ba ne ba sa mo kgoreletsa**, o ka bo a gorogile ka nako.
Re ka bo re mo felegeditse **fela.**	Re ka bo re mo felegeditse **fa a ka bo a re kopile.**

Would you agree that:

(i) the bold italicised adverbial clauses of condition cannot be used on their own?

(ii) the adverbial clauses of condition express certain conditions or circumstances that are met by the main clause?

The adverbial clauses of condition are introduced by the conjunctive **fa** . . . and they can, like adverbs of manner be used pre-verbally or post-verbally, e.g.

(i) **Fa** *o ka bua jalo* re tla tsaya gore o mongwe wa bona.

(ii) Re ka bo re mo tsholetse dijo **fa** *re ka bo re tshotse sejana.*

(iii) **Fa** *ena a ka nthuta* ke tla tlhaloganya dithuto tse.

(iv) Ba ka bo ba go pegile **fa** *ba ne ba go bone.*

Exercise 17.13

You should now be able to form your own examples of complex sentences containing adverbial clauses of condition.

2. THE ADVERBIAL CLAUSE OF REASON

This clause supplies the reason why the action of the main clause is performed. The adverbial clause of reason, like adverbs of manner, occupies a pre-verbal or a post-verbal position, e.g.

Adverbs	Adverbial clauses of reason
Ruri, o tla nna mosupi wa rona.	**Ka a bone basenyi**, o tla nna mosupi wa rona.
Modisa o tlhatlhela dinku mo sakeng **ka kelotlhoko.**	Modisa o tlhatlhela dinku mo sakeng **ka ntlha ya go na le bophokojwe mono.**

Would you agree that:

(i) the bold italicised adverbial clauses of reason cannot be used on their own?

(ii) the adverbial clauses of reason supply the reason why the action in the main clause is performed?

The adverbial clauses of reason are introduced by the following conjunctives:

ka .... **ka gore** ....

ka ntlha ya gore .... **gonne** ....

ka gonne .... **ka ntlha ya fa** ....

gobo .... **ka gobo** ....

The adverbial clauses of reason introduced by these conjunctives can appear pre-verbally as well as post-verbally, e.g.

(i) Mapodisa a a mmatla **ka gore** o thubile ntlo kwa Gauteng.

....

(ii) **Ka gonne** a sa rate go laolwa, o bogisa batsadi ba gagwe.

....

(iii) Nna ke ya go mo nyala **ka gobane** ke mo rata ka pelo yotlhe.

....

(iv) **Ka gobo** *mosadi a gana*, bana ga ba letlelelwe go tshameka

....

mo tseleng.

....

You should now be able to form your own examples of complex sentences containing adverbial clauses of reason.

3. THE ADVERBIAL CLAUSE OF CONCESSION

This clause concedes that the action of the main clause will take place in spite of the circumstances predicated by the clause. The adverbial clause of concession, like adverbs of manner, occupies a pre-verbal or a post-verbal position, e.g.

Adverbs	Adverbial clause of concession
Nna ke tsamaya **le ditsala tsa me**.	Nna ke tsamaya **le fa ditsala tsa me di sala**.
....	....
Ka nnete Zola o ya go mo sia.	**Le mororo a le lebelo**, Zola o ya go mo sia.
....	....
O a itatola **fela**.	O a itatola **e tswa a ne a sentse le ena**.
....	....

Would you concede that:

(i) the bold italicised adverbial clauses of concession cannot be used on their own?

(ii) the adverbial clauses of concession state the circumstances in spite of which the action of the main clause takes place?

The adverbial clauses of concession are introduced by the following conjunctives:

> *le fa* . . .
> *le mororo* . . .
> *e tswa* . . .

The adverbial clauses of concession introduced by these conjunctives can be used pre-verbally and post-verbally, e.g.

(i) Mosupatsela o botlhale, *le fa a sa ithute* o bona maduo a a kwa

....

godimo mo ditlhatlhobong.

....

(ii) Monna yole o setlhogo, o a ntlhoa *e tswa e le nna yo o mo rutileng*

....

tiro.

....

(iii) *Le mororo ntate a sa rutega*, kitso ya gagwe ya tsa botshelo e

....

ne e gaisa ya bontsi jwa batsadi.

....

(iv) Ga ke tlhole ke ya go mo gakolola *le fa a ka nthapela a eme ka*

....

mangole.

....

Exercise 17.15

You should now be able to form your own complex sentences containing adverbial clauses of concession.

To conclude with, it should be mentioned that **the abovementioned three kinds of adverbial clauses of manner** can also be used in conjunction with adverbs and other adverbial clauses, e.g.

(i) *Le fa o bala fa letsatsi le setse le phirimile*, ga o ye go fetsa

....

buka e, *bosa bo ise bo se.*

....

(**adverbial clause of concession** + *adverbial clause of time*)

(ii) Rona re ya *kwa wena o yang teng* **le fa wena o sa rate** fa re

....

go sala morago.

....

(*adverbial clause of place* + **adverbial clause of concession**
+ nominal clause)

(iii) *Fa re setse re lebile kwa toropong,* **kwa mme a re emetseng**

....

teng, ntate o ne a re biletsa kwa gae e tswa a re romile.

....

(*adverbial clause of time* + **adverbial clause of place** + adverbial clause of concession)

(iv) Maabane, *fa re sena go fitlhola,* ke fitlhetse badisa **ba ba gamang**

....

ba ise ba tsoge **mo dikobong tse di bothitho.**

....

Can you identify the adverbial clauses represented by the divergent
letter types in sentence (iv) above?

Exercise 17.16

*You should now be able to join different types of clauses to form com-
plex sentences of your own.*

4. THE ADVERBIAL CLAUSE OF COMPARISON

In these clauses the action of the main clause is contrasted with the
action expressed in the clause of comparison. These adverbial clauses
of comparison only occur post-verbally and their syntactic distribu-
tion is therefore restricted in comparison with other adverbial clauses,
e.g.

Adverbs	Adverbial clause of comparison
Nnake o rata go kwala **ka kgololosego**.	Nnake o rata go kwala **jaaka nna ke kwala**.
Bana ba me ba rata go tsena sekolo **ka malatsi otlhe**.	Bana ba me ba rata go tsena sekolo **go feta go itisa kwa gae**.
Ke tla tlhalosa **sentle**.	Ke tla tlhalosa **ka mo ke itseng ka teng**.

Would you agree that:

(i) the bold italicised clauses of comparison cannot be used on their own?

(ii) the clause of comparison contrasts the action of the main clause with that of the subordinate clause?

The adverbial clause of comparison can be introduced by:

(a) the adverbial prefix **jaaka** . . .;
(b) the conjunctive **e kete** . . .;
(c) the infinitives **go feta** . . . and **go gaisa** . . .;
(d) the adverbial prefix **ka** + the locative demonstrative **fa** or **mo** + a verb ending in **-ng** + the adverbial prefix **ka** + **teng**.

The adverbial clauses of comparison are used post-verbally only, e.g.

(i) Bapedi ga ba age **jaaka** Batswana ba aga.

(ii) Ntate o rora fela **jaaka** tau e rora.

(iii) O taboga **e kete** o lelekwa ke sengwe.

(iv) Ntšwa ya bogolo e ne ya nteba **e kete** e batla go kopa boitshwarelo.

(v) Ke rata go bala Setswana *go feta* *go bala Sekgoa.*

....

(vi) Rona re rata go nwa kofi *go gaisa* *go nwa tee.*

....

(vii) Bana ba sekolo sa rona ba dira *ka mo* *mogokgo* *a ba laetseng*

....

ka teng.

....

(viii) Morafe wa Batswana o tla tlhabologa *ka fa* *Batswana* *ba*

....

ratang *tswelelopele* *ka teng.*

....

Exercise 17.17

These examples should enable you to form your own complex sentences containing adverbial clauses of comparison.

5. THE ADVERBIAL CLAUSE OF CONSEQUENCE

This clause describes the main clause in terms of the consequences of the action depicted by the main clause. The adverbial clause of concession is used post-verbally only, e.g.

Adverb	Adverbial clause of consequence
Ke ne ke tlhokomologa bana ba me *gantsi*	Ke ne ke tlhokomologa bana ba me, *ka jalo ba senyega.* ....
Moupathaga o rata mogatsagwe *mo go maswe.*	Moupathaga o rata mogatsagwe, *ka lebaka leo ga a ke a mo katoga.* ....

Would you agree that:
(i) the bold italicised adverbial clauses of consequence cannot be used on their own?

312

(ii) the adverbial clauses of consequence describe the main clause in terms of the actions of the main clause?

The adverbial clauses of reason are introduced by:

(a) the conjunctive *jalo* . . .;
(b) the adverb *ka lebaka leo*. . .

The adverbial clauses of consequence are used post-verbally only, e.g.

(i) Ntatemogolo o re rutile go dirisa ngakale, *jalo re tla kgwasetsa*

....

legora.

....

(ii) Rangwane o nthutile go dirisa petlwana **ka lebaka leo** *ga ke ye*

....

go tlhoka go ipetlela.

....

Exercise 17.18

You should now be able to form your own complex sentences containing adverbial clauses of consequence.

6. THE ADVERBIAL CLAUSE OF DEGREE

This clause expresses the degree of intensity or the duration of the main action. This adverbial clause can occur in the same syntactic position as post-verbal adverbs, e.g.

Adverbs	Adverbial clause of degree
Banna ba ne ba kgatha thite **ka bonya**.	Banna ba ne ba kgatha thite **go fitlha ba fetsa tshimo yotlhe**.
Nna ke ya go ithuta Setswana **segolo**.	Nna ke ya go ithuta Setsana **go fitlha ke se bue ka tshwanelo**.

Would you agree that:

(i) the bold italicised adverbial clauses of degree cannot be used on their own;

(ii) the adverbial clauses of degree describe the verb of the main action in terms of the intensity or duration of the main action?

The adverbial clauses of degree are introduced by the infinitive **go fitlha** . . . and is used post-verbally only, e.g.

(i) Mosadi o ne a omanya **go fitlhela** *monna a lapa.*

....

(ii) Phokojwe o kile a laela Phiri go tshegetsa lejwe **go fitlha** Phiri

....

a lape a wele fa fatshe.

....

As in the case of the concluding part of the previous sections, it has to be mentioned that the adverbial clauses introduced in this section can also be used in conjunction with adverbs and other adverbial clauses, e.g.

(i) Ke tla tlhalosa **kwa ba ileng teng** *ka mo ke itseng ka teng.*

....

(adverbial clause of place + adverbial clause of comparison)

(ii) Bana ba sekolo sa rona ba dira *ka mo mogokgo a ba laetseng*

....

ka teng **pele ba ya gae** kwa ba ithulelang teng.

....

(*adverbial clause of comparison* + **adverbial clause of time** + adverbial clause of place)

(iii) Basimane *ga ba bolo go emela terena* **e e ba isang kwa**

....

mmerekong o ba yang go o dira go fitlha ba o fetsa.

....

Can you identify the adverbial clauses represented by the divergent letter types in sentence (iii) above?

Exercise 17.19

You should now be able to join different types of clauses to form complex sentences of your own.

SELF-ASSESSMENT

1. Replace the following adverbs with adverbial clauses of manner:
   - (i) Re bona fela.
   - (ii) Morutabana o re ruta tota.
   - (iii) Rona re tsamaya ka boiketlo.
   - (iv) Bona ba dira ka selepe.
   - (v) Ka nnete wena ga ke ise ke go bone.
2. Form three complex sentences each containing one of the adverbial clauses of manner discussed in this section.
3. What is the function and meaning of an adverbial clause of manner?
4. (a) Name the six subdivisions of the adverbial clause of manner.
   - (b) Which of these were discussed in this section?
   - (c) Give an example of each of the three subdivisions that were discussed in this section.
   - (d) What conjunctives introduce each of these three subdivisions of the adverbial clause of manner?
   - (e) Can these adverbial clauses of manner be used pre-verbally?
5. May an adverbial clause of manner occupy the same syntactic positions as adverbs of manner? Give examples.
6. Can more than one clause be used to describe a verb? Give two sentences as examples and name the clauses that you use.
7. Replace the following adverbs with adverbial clauses of manner:
   - (i) O tshegetse gone jaana.
   - (ii) Tswelelang lo ithuteng sešwa.
   - (iii) Ngwana o lwala mo gonnye.
   - (iv) Rremogolo o bua pila.
8. Form three complex sentences each containing one of the adverbial clauses of manner discussed in this section.
9. What is the function and meaning of an adverbial clause of manner?
10. Can more than one adverbial clause be used to describe a verb? Give two sentences as examples and name the clauses that you used.

315